THE POWER OF CONFUSION: HOW SEVEN SIMPLE TOOLS CAN CLARIFY CONFUSION IN YOUR CAREER AND WORK

THE POWER OF CONFUSION: HOW SEVEN SIMPLE TOOLS CAN CLARIFY CONFUSION IN YOUR CAREER AND WORK

Martin F. Stankard

Includes Bibliographic References
Management Consulting, Management Development, Organizational Development, Leadership, Systems Thinking, Leadership from Mid Organization, and Reflective Practice.

ISBN-13: 9780692754986
ISBN-10: 0692754989

Table of contents

Figures

I n 2005 I began teaching in a graduate program at Penn and my students, who typically were managers in mid-career, liked the stories I told to illustrate teaching points. Students were eager to learn from real experiences. Over the past twenty-five years as time permitted, I wrote informal case studies about memorable consulting assignments. The writing was a labor of love intended to preserve the experiences with no idea of publication. I had accumulated about a hundred of these stories by the time I began teaching and telling a few of them in classes.

My students' enthusiastic responses sparked me to begin editing and reflecting on my case studies. The reflection process included a root cause analysis of each problem or situation (using the Five Whys tool explained in this book.) The next step was to group stories by similar methods of resolving confusion. This process resulted in a second, much shortened draft manuscript with the working title: *Root Causes – Solving Problems with Deep Thinking.*

A few years ago, Herb Addison (whom I had met through Russ Ackoff at Penn) read a sample of the *Root Causes* stories and gave me helpful advice. He also referred me to an editor, Ms. Martha Nichols, who reviewed the *Root Causes* manuscript and suggested improvements. She in turn referred me to Mrs. Karen J. Ohlson for help reorganizing and editing the first draft of *Power of Confusion.*

About thirty students and alumni of the program I teach in volunteered to read the Introduction and first two chapters of that first draft and provide criticism. Also two former students requested, read and commented critically on the entire *Power of Confusion* manuscript (which was half again longer than this final version). All this feedback resulted in a year spent editing and acting on hundreds of suggestions, both large and small. I am profoundly grateful to these helpful voices—not just because they are members of the audience I hope this book will help—but also for their strong encouragement, which was an unexpected and welcome side effect of pilot testing the manuscript with these readers.

Finally, a former client in the publishing business referred me to Ms. Jacqueline Murphy, who put me in touch with Ms. Constance Devanthery-Lewis, who copyedited the present manuscript and Ms. Stephani Finks who designed the cover.

Martin F. Stankard

Introduction

CONFUSION AND ITS POWER

Confusion is a lack of clarity about an important situation, which causes you to feel so uncertain or uncomfortable that you have difficulty making decisions. You may be confused about whether you fit into an organization; or about what work makes you feel great versus what work you are good at; or about the right thing to do when you are frightened or conflicted. The power of confusion is that it forces you to stop and seek clarity in your life and career. This book will show you how to use simple tools to achieve that clarity.

You were not born with any inherited knowledge or wisdom, yet you are certain to face fear and confusion during your lifetime. You *were* born with curiosity and the ability to ask, why? when you face a confusing situation. You were also born with the ability to think for yourself, listen to others and learn from experience. Confusion spurs you to use these abilities to gain the clarity that leads to wisdom. But you need tools to guide your learning.

Confusion should challenge you to organize what you know and test assumptions. Early in a state of confusion, gathering more facts may increase that confusion. Sometimes you learn that you have asked the wrong questions or made the wrong assumptions. This book contains simple questioning and sense-making tools and methods useful for achieving clarity. As the use of these tools expands your understanding, clarity replaces confusion and increases your confidence in the choices and decisions you are making. Facing confusion with the right tools increases your knowledge and empowers you to take the next step based on deeper understanding.

DON'T PANIC: STOMACH BUTTERFLIES ARE NOT A BAD THING

As a manager or professional working in an organization, how do you know that you are progressing? Are you developing new skills and adding knowledge and experience that lead to a more meaningful and satisfying future? As you work, are you leading or following? Check your gut feelings; do you feel "butterflies in your stomach"?

Feeling butterflies in the gut signals that your challenges seem tougher than expected, or that new information does not fit with what you know or have assumed, or that your uncertainties and risks exceed your comfort level. This book is about accepting your butterfly feelings as a sign and a stimulus for professional learning and growth.

Managers, consultants, designers and other professionals feel butterflies in their stomachs while facing new challenges, greater responsibilities or challenging assignments. Such feelings are normal and healthy. If each new situation demanded only the skills and knowledge you have already, you would not be confused. So, no confusion equals no risk and no learning.

Lack of confusion early in a complex undertaking warns that you may not understand the full situation. Confusion halfway through an important effort warns that your situation is more complex than you had assumed. Confusion late in an undertaking warns that you are running out of time to make sense of your confusion and craft a pathway out. You need more time to gather data, to reflect and understand the situation well enough to take risks in line with rewards.

Psychologists have found that people tend to avoid choices framed as losses but tend to prefer identical choices when viewed as gains. Framing a confusing situation as a chance to lose or make mistakes focuses emotion on failure. In contrast, reframing that same confusing choice or situation as an opportunity to explore and learn is empowering. Such a framing replaces anxiety and fear with hopeful feelings of attention, interest, curiosity and accomplishment.

Reframing anxious situations into learning opportunities offers two benefits. First, some of those who watch you face a tough challenge expect you to fail because they recognize the toughness of your challenge. By accepting the challenge, you do risk failure. If you do fail, those who expected your failure feel vindicated but may respect your courage. A second benefit of protective reframing of a challenging situation is that by tackling that situation you gain experience. You can reflect on the situation and learn from it, whether you succeeded or failed. Reframing confusion so that you accept challenges opens your mind to action learning, which powers faster growth and development than playing it safe to avoid the butterflies.

Each story in this book shares management and consulting situations that started with stomach butterflies, but which stimulated inquiry and experimentation that produced many experiences that yielded lifelong benefits.

FAST THINKING BUT SLOW UNDERSTANDING

Much organizational confusion arises because of what psychologist Daniel Kahneman calls Intuitive, "System 1" thinking. Kahneman says System 1 thinking suffers from WYSIATI bias – the initials stand for "**W**hat **Y**ou **S**ee **Is All T**here **Is**." (Kahneman, 2011) Your intuition constructs the best story that fits all known facts by filling in the gaps in what you know with assumptions. Such thinking is automatic, fast and biased because of the hidden assumptions that fill in the gaps. When your actions based on your WYSIATI story turn out badly or fail altogether, you are left with confusion.

To overcome the WYSIATI bias Kahneman recommends using a range of similar situations—each of which Kahneman calls a reference case—to gain a more complete understanding of the issues at work in each type of situation. Every chapter of this book selects five to ten reference cases to describe each type of confusion in organizations.

CHAPTER SUMMARIES—SEVEN TYPES OF CONFUSION IN CAREER AND WORK

Chapter one on where-you-fit confusion, concerns work, career identity, and how to behave pragmatically and ethically when joining or leaving organizations. Its reference cases include navigating a job search; the value of learning at the bottom of an organization before working near the top; how your own satisfying work experiences can help you discover the skills that energize and engage you; how impressing others shuts doors to opportunities that caring about others opens; how the path to your future may not look best at present; and a final story about bittersweet feelings caused by awareness that it is time to leave a place where you once fit in.

Asking, what is my real calling if not the work I'm doing now? can trigger fit confusion. A story in this chapter shows how tolerating such confusion at the start of your career gives you experiences you can use to find the types of work you find most meaningful. Appendix A — Success Motivated Skill Assessment provides a tool you can use to spot the most energizing skills you used during your most fulfilling experiences. Knowing exactly what types of work fire you up helps you pick winning challenges. Other stories show how reducing career confusion can get you on your personal path to learning and distinction.

Chapter two explores confusion from information overload as you try making sense of an organization that you are new to. Each story introduces a tool—flowcharts, open probing and concrete questioning to obtain usable information from the knowledgeable people around you, "spider-web" diagrams to visualize how a tangle of problems interrelate, and even how to drill through layers of confusion to root causes by asking and answering, why? to the point of absurdity. Related appendices provide how-to examples of how each tool helps you make sense of confusing situations.

Chapter three explores confusion about direction and leadership. Stories in the chapter convey leadership lessons from army generals and sea captains, CEOs, managers and staff people who led from mid-organization. All were similar in four ways; they were ambitious, they dealt with facts, they identified opportunities and barriers and coached those they led in making larger, faster changes than those people would ever dare to attempt without the coaching.

Outstanding leaders created successful organizations by engaging people to eliminate bottlenecks blocking success. One leader helped his bank become competitive by achieving ten years of progress in two. Another told how he steers his large organization through waves of change. Some leaders including army generals, bankers and business executives show how thinking, taking action and learning from outcomes create winning track records. Leadership guts develop the same way that strong muscles do: by working out first on smaller challenges, then building up to bigger, more daring ones.

Chapter four looks at confusion about how effort and results relate to pay, in stories about how some organizations answered the question, what's in it for me? The chapter opens with a story about how linking pay to output does not improve productivity; though productivity can be improved by asking those who do the work for suggestions to make it better and easier. You will hear how incentives give people what they pay for, even if the incentives prompt people to fudge their numbers, use tricks and play games. Examples of quick and easy incentives that hurt more than they helped come from insurance, banking, sales and other situations.

Chapter five looks at how blaming problems on people rather than preventing problems by finding and addressing root causes breeds fear and confusion. Blaming behavior arises from psychological drives. Every person has a psychological hunger for a favorable view of his or her actions and self, and desires others to share those views. So, people behave in ways that satisfy their hunger for self-enhancement. Blaming behavior learned in childhood attributes failure to others in order to deflect unfavorable attention elsewhere—onto a scapegoat.

Chapter five's stories give you practical advice on how to replace scapegoating with seeking deeper root causes of problems. The chapter uses a simple cause and effect discovery tool, the Five Whys drill-down, to spark organizational learning. Examples from international and domestic banking, and commercial real estate, show you how to replace blaming with problem solving. Other stories show how running small pilot tests of changes in a blame-free zone puts learning on a fast track.

Chapter six profiles confusion about teams and teamwork. Forming, leading and relying on strong, diverse employee teams offer major learning and professional development opportunities by sharpening the skills you need to lead organizational changes.

Chapter six shares practical experience in forming cross-functional process improvement teams able to make changes, improve processes and create a more efficient, healthier organization. Teams cannot work magic; but managers facing complex challenges achieve high success rates by relying on teams of expert employees to diagnose situations and create workable solutions. If your ambition is to make changes that impact hundreds or thousands of people, learn to form, coach and lead teams. This chapter shows how.

Chapter seven focuses on confusion caused by committing random acts of improvement without the benefit of a view of your organization as a system with a purpose. The economist Joseph Schumpeter identified creative destruction as a long-term cycle in which new and better products and organizations replace earlier, outdated products and organizations. As outmoded organizations are acquired or disbanded, their human and economic resources are freed up and available for employment in the next wave of innovation in technology, product design and customer delight.

The existence and long-term successes of many huge, older organizations such as General Electric, State Street Bank, Toyota Motor Co., JPMorgan-Chase, and others, may be due to chance. But if not, then creative destruction is not destiny for organizations that systematically generate organization-wide improvement and innovation. Most long-term survivors have learned to find new and better things to do to create and satisfy customer appetites, and new and better ways of doing those things.

Understanding your organization as a system lets you diagnosis which parts of your organization's management system bottleneck its long run success. Stories in chapter seven show how all parts of an organization can work as a system for accomplishing its mission. Other stories clear up confusion about how innovations arise and how great managers relate people's work to organizational purpose. Stories from the military to banking show how viewing your organization as a social system yields insights into how it can achieve mission-level performance that multiplies, rather than combines the performances of its parts.

In addition to the seven chapters described above, eight appendices show how to use a few vital tools to face and learn from organizational and career confusion.

"For every complex problem, there is a solution that is simple, neat, and wrong."

H.L. MENCKEN

"There is no limit to what you can accomplish if you don't care who gets the credit."

HARRY S. TRUMAN

"I learned this, at least, by my experiment: that if one advances confidently in the direction of his dreams, and endeavors to live the life which he has imagined, he will meet with a success unexpected in common hours."

HENRY DAVID THOREAU

Section I: On-Boarding Confusion

Starting your career or making a job change to a new organization can create confusion—and learning. You may experience confusion #1 when answering, where do I fit? in a new work environment. So chapter 1 shows how to use skills you are good at not only to fit in, but also how to use peak experiences to add to your list of skills that make you feel fulfilled and energized. Another aspect of fit confusion is that each job starts your voyage toward an unknown future. A job that does not let you learn and grow may look good now, but may not widen your future options. Finally, even where you have fit in well, confusion arises when you sense that your value or your learning are declining.

Once you start a new job, confusion #2 arises as you try to make sense of what's really going on in the organization you've joined. In chapter 2 you'll see that information overload causes some of this confusion. Stories show how simple questioning tools such as open probing and concrete questioning let you gather data from those who know more than you do. However, as you learn, confusion about what is going on (and why) may grow and make you uncomfortable. So chapter 2 also shows how other simple tools let you organize your data, connect issues and problems to understand what is happening and why, and then test your guesses in smart, low risk, fail-fast tests.

1

Confusion About Where You Fit

YOUNG, NOT SO YOUNG AND IN BETWEEN: WHAT'S YOUR BEST SITUATION?

Whether you are young and just starting out, or older and seeking to change jobs or careers, it's always difficult to know how well you will fit into a new work situation before you enter it. You may feel uncomfortable or unprepared, not sure if you have all the skills you will need. Perhaps you fear that you lack the guts to face tougher job challenges—or worse, that you have the guts but will not encounter challenges that enable you to grow and develop as far and as fast as you wish to. These feelings are the butterflies that come with confusion—and they're a good thing.

Stories in this chapter share lessons learned about resolving confusion relating to finding a good fit between a person and the career opportunities within organizations. Here is a summary of the main lessons you will find in this chapter:

1: Decide early in your career if your real ambition is to run things as captain of your own ship. If you aspire to eventually become the boss, take increasing responsibility in work such as sales, program, or project or line management. Develop your skill at running things and build a support network you can rely on.

2: Choose work that offers a wide range of experiences early in your career, rather than specialized positions that promise a faster path to rank and prestige. A wide range of experiences increases your learning opportunities and expands your self-understanding and competence.

3: Assess your peak work experiences to identify the skills you used often during those high points. These skills will be referred to as your *motivating* skills. Find work that makes extensive use of your motivating skills—and that lets you discover new skills to add to your list of work that energizes you.

4: Reevaluate your skills periodically. When you make changes in your life or seek a new course, knowing what skills energize and motivate you will help you recognize opportunities to excel. As Louis Pasteur once said, "Chance favors the prepared mind."

5: When in doubt, do the right thing. If you question what that is, ask yourself if you would feel comfortable seeing your actions published all over the Internet and discussed in social media. When in doubt about the right thing to do, double check with others whose integrity, knowledge and experience you trust.

6: Listen to those you work with, consider their points of view and feelings, and do your part to make working relationships good at both ends. Emotional connections with those you work with and for are important in how you fit into an organization. Experience and empathy trump smarts every time when you ask someone to trust and rely on you. Be trustworthy; but if you violate a trust, apologize to the person you have disappointed, and explain what happened.

7: Reevaluate your "best fit," not just for the present, but also for years to come. Consider your family's needs. Rather than pursuing quick pay-offs, seek work that offers a wider range of possible new and durable opportunities for you and for those you care about.

8: Move on to bigger and tougher challenges when the organization around you no longer needs or values your help. Organizations grow and change, just as you will. Be grateful for what you've learned in the time you have spent there, and for the friends you have made. You may leave an organization behind, but if you care, good relationships you formed by working together can endure for decades.

The rest of this chapter illustrates these lessons from experiences to help you address butterfly feelings about whether you and your job are a good fit.

GET OFF TO THE RIGHT START

When I finished graduate school the course to steer seemed clear and certain: a job in a university as assistant professor. But, after much wasted effort, that scenario gave way to confusion. Would working in an oil company or a corporate research lab or a large bank, or any of a dozen other organizations be a better fit? Each opportunity required my skills and interests, but each interview increased concern, doubt, and confusion about the choices.

Each job offer seemed like a well-paid opportunity to use existing technical skills, rather than an opportunity to learn, develop and grow in new ways. While I was hesitating, a consulting firm in Massachusetts invited me to visit and explore job opportunities in consulting. During the visit I happened upon a former classmate working there, and we met after my interviews.

When we got together, my friend revealed how he really felt about consulting to managers and other clients. In this firm, he said, each consultant worked on several teams for different clients at the same time. Working with senior colleagues on a variety of projects allowed a new consultant to learn about a range of industries, management problems, and approaches. It felt exciting and provided many learning experiences. After a few years' experience, each consultant could expect to lead his or her own project teams; my friend even showed and explained reports used to lead consulting teams and manage client projects. All this inside information and insight was news to me.

This chance meeting cleared up my confusion by showing me what it actually felt like to work in this consulting firm; what a newcomer could learn and do, and where it might lead. This suggested that consulting provided opportunities to learn and expand skills while creating possibilities and challenges across industries. When you can envision yourself and your skills and ambitions fitting with how an organization really works, your confusion over where you fit resolves. Learning how an organization really works, however, is a challenge.

In this chapter, you'll read about where-you-fit confusion, and find lessons and strategies that grow out of confusing experiences. To overcome fit confusion when looking at a new job, find someone who has worked in the job you seek, and ask what they learned from that job, as well as what work they did. Once you fit into the organization you joined, you need to add judgment to ambition in order to maximize learning from opportunities that come your way. The next section shows how ambition to go too far too fast is no substitute for learning and experience.

NOT STARTING AT THE TOP CAN BENEFIT YOU

When you start out, you may not envision your career journey as a bumpy one with twists and turns along the way. You may see a career goal in sight and want to avoid wasting time by heading straight for it. However, a more meandering path that exposes you to a wide range of experiences, while more confusing, offers more growth opportunities. The more you learn about how to handle a wide variety of situations, the better prepared you will be to find where you fit.

At the start of my consulting career, my first supervisor reinforced the need to learn from experience by refusing my request for a high-profile assignment. A Fortune 500 client company invited several consulting firms, including ours, to propose to help them with their strategic planning. Having taken graduate courses on strategic planning, I was enthusiastic about having a spot on the team preparing the proposal. So I asked my supervisor to assign me to the team. His answer burst my bubble:

"Martin, clients want to see if you can lance a boil before they ask you to perform brain surgery."

His answer stung but rang true. Highly educated, but inexperienced professionals such as surgeons and consultants need to learn from experiences and mentors. Successes and failures with initial challenges build capacity to succeed with ever more complex and confusing problems. Instead of granting my request, my supervisor assigned me to a team he was leading that let me gain needed experience under his guidance. Working with him on that project let me learn how to find out what our client really expected, how to pace the project, how to discover the deeper, "real" problem, when to involve specialists, when to review work in progress with our client, and more.

Top professionals add to their knowledge based on learning by doing. Over two-thirds of your ultimate career success comes from what you learn by taking risks and on-the-job experience. Another twenty percent or so of career expertise comes from watching and learning from mentors and role models. Finally, only ten percent of knowledge helpful in professional success is learned in classrooms. (Rabin, 2014) The confusion in this case is between knowledge that was taught so you could learn it, and the other ninety or so percent you learn from others or on your own. So, if you are young and ambitious, seek experienced mentors willing to coach and advise you when you find that you are "in over your head at the deep end."

Early in your career, ask yourself if you really want to manage an organization (or department or business unit) in the future. If your real ambition is to run something such as a company, ask yourself which of the following two candidates you would choose for general manager of their company's large operation:

Alice managed a small restaurant with a staff of ten for two years after graduating from college. Then, she earned an MBA and took a sales job with a food company. After two years in field sales, she became the manager of a small regional sales office supervising thirty salespeople. After three years there, she became the manager of one of the firm's largest sales regions. In another three years, she started managing the night shift at one of the company's plants, a two-shift operation with 300 employees; she was promoted to plant manager shortly thereafter. Having done an excellent job managing the plant for the last three years, she is now is ready to move on to larger management responsibilities.

Bert was highly successful in college and graduated near the top of his MBA class at a prestigious business school. He worked for a boardroom consulting firm for three years and then moved into an internal staff consulting position working for the CEO of the same company that employs Alice. Bert has participated in or led projects that have saved the company over fifty million dollars, and he has thirteen years of experience leading progressively larger internal consulting projects. He wishes to move on because his boss, the CEO, retired.

Most people choose Alice for the job. When asked why, they usually explain that Bert has no management experience and has never run an operation. Alice has a thirteen-year track record of managing progressively larger sales and production operations and learning from her mistakes. Her track record shows ambition as well as thirteen years of experience running things. Asking Bert to manage one of the company's big operations is risky for the company as well as Bert, who would have to learn from mistakes made in a big operation. Denying Alice the promotion forces her to look outside the company for her next career move.

Staying in internal or management consulting for more than five years right out of school can be a serious career mistake. In the early years of your career, choose work situations that present a wide range of learning experiences, as consulting does—but pay attention to what skills you are developing. If you feel ambitious to run the show, then follow Alice's example: steer your career through a variety of experiences managing things. Top performing professionals usually attain their peak performance twenty or more years after their last academic course. Often their success is in fields they never studied academically. Education gets you started, but it's the knowledge gained from mentors and your own successes and failures that yields success later in your career.

If your ambition and stomach butterflies say that running things does not energize you, but you would rather help *other* people improve how they run their operations or organizations, experience gained working in staff or consulting positions may be your chosen pathway to excellence. In any case, be sure to check that your most motivating skills (the next section and an appendix show how) include negotiating, selling, and analyzing—and that honesty and a strong work ethic are among your strongest character traits.

No matter which career starting line your education puts you on, accept challenges and opportunities that your path offers. Reflect on them, learn from them, expand your skills and sharpen your sense of purpose. The broader your range of skills, the greater your chance of excelling at work that engages your vital motivating skills. Here's how.

YOUR MOST MOTIVATING SKILLS MAY SURPRISE YOU

Figuring out where you fit in your organization or on a project seems like it should be a simple matter: just go where your skills are needed. But what if some of your skills point toward one role and others pull you toward a different role? What if something changes in your life so that you must change your work? Or what if your skills overlap with those of people around you—how do you determine who should do what?

A book, *Career Satisfaction and Success*, by Bernard Haldane describes a simple method for avoiding job frustration by identifying what he called "success motivated skills." (Haldane, 1974) Here, we refer to them as energizing or motivating skills because they make you feel great when you use them heavily in your most satisfying work experiences.

Haldane's book explained that each of us has many abilities. As individuals, using some abilities yields greater feelings of personal excellence, meaning and fulfillment than using others. Suppose two people of equal ability tackle the same job, which requires skills A, B, and C. The first person is average in ability, except she or he finds using skills A, B, and C highly energizing, satisfying and meaningful. The second person is gifted but feels little boost when using skills A, B, and C, other than pay. The average person, when using his or her motivating skills in a job that demands those skills, will thrive in that job—energized by deep drives and accumulated experience.

You might think that figuring out your most energizing skills would be a matter of asking, "What do I like doing?" Not so; the real answers are often hidden in plain sight, obscured by confusing what you are good at with what really deeply engages and energizes you. When you think of yourself as being "good at" skills that you use to earn your living, you may overlook other, more important skills that turn up in many or all of your most successful and meaningful work or volunteer experiences. However there is an objective way to identify the skills that have powered your happiest personal performances. By spending a few hours reviewing your experiences and completing a systematic assessment of them, you can see how often you used skills that gave you the most satisfaction, and in what situations.

Even if you have spent years studying academic subjects that interest you, do not confuse your motivating skills with subjects you studied the most or earned the highest grades in. To assess your skills, first brainstorm up to ten of your most satisfying life and work experiences in the last five years. If you have not had a wide variety of work experiences, include volunteer and personal activities. Once you have your list of highly energizing experiences, you are ready to use my version of Haldane's assessment. My assessment emphasizes technical and managerial activities grouped under headings proposed by Butler and Waldroop (1990).

Most Satisfying Experiences →	1	2	3	4	5	6	7	8	9	10	TOTAL
Heavily Used Skills ↓											
Influencing People with Language and Ideas											
Setting Expectations											
Negotiating win-win agreements											
Negotiating budget, schedule, requirements, etc.											
Rehearsing presentations and speeches											
Presenting or speaking in public											
Writing proposals or reports											
Selling projects											
Reframing ideas to make others feel comfortable											
Making complex ideas easy to understand											
Using stories to persuade or influence											
Influencing customers, users or others											

Figure 1 — Sample of Success Motivated Skill Assessment Table

My version of the self-assessment appears in its entirety in Appendix A — Success Motivated Skill Assessment. Figure 1 shows a small portion of this table. Each row in Figure 1 is labeled with a skill such as, "Negotiating win-win agreements, "or "Presenting or speaking in public," or, "Writing proposals or reports." Blank rows at the end of the table are provided so you can write in additional tasks, skills and traits that do not already appear in the table.

As explained in Appendix A, you examine which skill(s) you made heavy use of in each of your seven to ten most satisfying and meaningful work experiences. Early in a career, it may be hard to identify highly satisfying work experiences, so be patient and take time to remember and enter them as labels for the columns in Figure 1. Then follow the instruction in Appendix A.

After completing your analysis, suppose you made seven check marks in the row for "writing proposals or reports" out of your ten most satisfying experiences (columns in Figure 1). Even if you majored in math, engineering, or science, your analysis shows that a writing activity has been heavily used in seven out of ten work experiences that made you feel great. The odds are that writing is one of your energizing activities. The high correlation between writing and your highly satisfying peak experiences provides evidence that writing makes you feel great and is one of your most energizing and motivating skills, and is likely to continue so in the future.

Without this self-assessment, you may confuse skills you are good at with skills that engage your feelings and thinking in ways that energize you and make you feel great. When you do your own objective skill self-assessment you may experience a "BGO," a "blinding glimpse of the obvious." Some skills you may never have considered your strong suits may actually energize you far more strongly than skills you studied, mastered, and exceled at in your academic studies.

When you analyze your own energizing skills in Appendix A, be true to yourself. Once you identify your highly energizing skills, you may want to explore types of work that that provide opportunities to experience using new and different skills. As you broaden your base of experiences in your career, revisit the skill assessment every few years until your list of highly energizing skills stabilizes. If you settle into a career that demands heavy use of your most energizing skills, congratulate yourself. You may have regrets, but you will not regret having done your personal best and most meaningful work.

This type of skills assessment can also help members of a team divide tasks of a large project among themselves. Sorting out everyone's motivating skills before deciding who should do what helps individual team members reduce confusion. (For details, please see "Team leaders as matchmakers" in Chapter 6.) If your motivating skills are not what you expected and are actually used little in your work, it may be time to explore new career directions that make heavier use of the skills that make you feel great.

Fit confusion arises from assuming that the best person for a job is the smartest, the most experienced, or even the most persuasive, instead of the person who loves, cares about and is most energized by that work. Your career is important to you, and you can overcome fit confusion by exploring and relying on your most motivating skills. Also, Appendix H — Navigating Career Confusion describes a career navigation system to help you steer toward your ideal career goals.

As you progress in your career, you will face situations that present moral dilemmas – confusion over the right thing to do. Here's how to decide if the actions that feel right for you are also right for everyone else who finds out about the action you took.

SIMPLE WAYS TO OVERCOME CONFUSION ABOUT THE RIGHT THING TO DO

Sometimes fit confusion has less to do with your skills than with your moral compass—the feeling that you are doing the right things. A work situation may confront you with ethical choices that make you question your organizational fit or career identity. This is especially true when you know of bad behavior in higher levels of your organization.

What should you do? Here again, listening to your stomach butterflies can be your trusty guide. Instead of brushing off your doubts and forging ahead with actions you may regret, take time to systematically decide which of your options are right.

A mentor taught the rule: When in doubt, always do the right things. However, figuring out which choice is "the right things to do" often ends in confusion. Each person interprets the right thing (in the sense of moral, proper or ethical), according to his or her individual values and perspective. So, if a hundred individuals each choose the right thing to do in the same dilemma, they may choose a hundred different right things to do. Imagine the confusion. Each variation fits an individual but may ignore or violate the values and interests of others with legitimate stakes in the situation.

A more explicit test of whether something is really the right thing to do is to do your job as if your work will be presented to a jury of twelve of your peers. Imagine how you would feel if you (and everyone else) saw your work talked about on social media over the Internet. This test defines the right thing to do in a way that anyone can use. The right thing is legal, defensible, and something you may be proud of, whether or not anyone affected by your action knows what you did. Envisioning how others may feel when news about what you did goes viral on social media will help check if your actions are right more rigorously than just what feels right to you in the moment.

Another proven way to replace confusion about the right thing to do with clarity is to seek advice from someone you trust, as the following ethical dilemma over a public relations (PR) strategy will show.

In the early '80's, before the Internet, Ron, the CEO of an international financial-services company was surprised when his number-one competitor suddenly launched a new computer-based network service with great fanfare. The competitor's PR blitz proclaimed that the new service would benefit their whole industry. However, Ron felt strongly that this new service threatened his company's business model.

Ron had previously commissioned his PR agency to study all public statements made over the previous five years by his competitor's CEO. The pages in their nicely bound report listed public statements by the competitor's CEO in a column on the left side of each page, with dates and sources. The text in an adjacent column on the right summarized how events actually turned out later. The document showed that Ron's competitor consistently said one thing publicly but subsequently quietly did another often privately.

Given this evidence, Ron concluded that it would be out of character for his competitor to tell the truth about his firm's real intentions for the new service. Ron's internal alarm bells were ringing, so he authorized me to lead a crash study to evaluate whether the new service posed a competitive threat to his company's business. He wanted an answer in six weeks, to a question that for such a complex project would take six months at a normal work pace.

A small team of senior consultants spent six intense weeks interviewing, investigating and analyzing until they were confident of their answer. The new service was not an immediate threat to Ron's business because the competitor relied on aging network technology. The team could find no evidence that the competitor was planning to deploy packet-switched network technology (which was new at that time), and which would have made the new service a real threat to the survival of a key segment of Ron's business.

The team's conclusion was worrisome because it was not in line with Ron's instincts, which were usually sound. Was Ron's intuition about the threat posed by this new service right? The team leader feared that in its rush, the team might have overlooked some hidden aspect of the new service that would damage Ron and his company—and embarrass our team. Stomach butterflies were multiplying rapidly with anxiety.

What was the right thing to do in this situation? The answer in this case was to relate the whole situation to one of the most thoughtful, experienced, and helpful mentors in our firm and seek his independent advice. This senior VP always advised clients to "take the high road." If our team reported that the new service had anti-competitive capabilities, Ron planned to launch a PR campaign revealing this negative motive. The mentor felt that Ron's planned PR fight did not sound like the high road. So he suggested that we recommend against it. If the competition's new service was no immediate threat, why pick a fight?

Next, the mentor asked a powerful "what if" question: What if Ron's company built a distributed network using up to date technology? Would that network let Ron defend against or even turn the tables on his competitor?

By the end of our meeting, we agreed that that the high road was to recommend that Ron publicly announce his acceptance of the competitor's claims that the new service was for the benefit of their whole industry. However, we also recommended that Ron hedge against being blindsided, by building a state-of-the-art, worldwide network with sufficient capacity and power to perform all the functions and new services that the competitor's network could not perform with outdated communications technology.

Ron jumped on our recommendations. Within three years, his company trumped its larger competitor by deploying a state-of-the-art network and launching new services and better service delivery, taking huge volumes of business away from that same competitor. In this case listening to doubts and talking with a wise mentor with trustworthy instincts—both professionally and morally—was the right thing to do to clear up confusion over what to recommend to Ron and his organization.

You will inevitably face ethical dilemmas in organizations, and not everyone agrees about what's right in any given situation. If you are confused about the right thing to do, even after applying the "social media test," discuss your doubts with a capable and trustworthy senior mentor. By honestly confronting and resolving your moral and ethical confusion, you ensure that career opportunities fit both your skills *and* your values.

One important thing to do right is to value your customer's trust. Those who offer advice and help often confuse selling a service with providing help that customers feel truly understands and cares about what they need. Here's an example of the confusion between selling and creating opportunities for cooperative, respectful collaboration.

A NEW JOB IS ABOUT THEM, NOT ABOUT YOU

When you find a job that seems like a perfect match for your skills and personal values, and seems like the right fit, you may end up confused if you are interviewed but not chosen for the job.

When that happens (notice I say "when," rather than "if" it happens, because it happens to each of us at some point), realize that your confusion is pointing out an important truth: fitting into an organization is not just a matter of connecting your skills to a job; it's also about making emotional connections. Organizations are made up of people, and those people want to know that they can work with you. They aren't just asking themselves, Can this person do the job well? They are also asking, Do I like and trust this person? Do I enjoy working with this person? Does this person treat me with respect? And, is this someone I feel good about working with? Would I want to spend time with this person? Here is a situation that taught this lesson.

Fred, a senior colleague with decades of experience consulting to managers in financial services, asked me to go with him on my first sales call after finishing a selling skills training program. The prospective client was a senior executive of a large insurance company. The executive had called in Fred to help improve the performance of several large administrative and operations groups reporting to him. I had specialized in large service operations, so Fred thought my experience would be a good fit with his experience in financial industries.

In New York the client walked us through several processing operations that she wanted help with. Fred, (who was in charge), let me take the lead in the conversation, and I used this opportunity to try out my new selling skills. Fred asked a few questions, which I vaguely considered intrusions into my sales dialog with the prospective client about her productivity and customer service issues. So, Fred stopped asking questions and listened. Finally, when time ran out, we promised to prepare a proposal and the executive escorted us out of the building.

As we rode away in a cab, Fred asked me what the client's desired outcome was. I answered. Then, he asked the question again but asked me to answer the question in the client's own words. After a few embarrassing attempts to answer that basic question, I realized that I could not restate the client's desired outcome in her exact words. Back in the office, Fred asked me to write the proposal, which he looked over, and sent to the client. We followed up by phone a few days later and found out that the client did not accept the proposal, which I am sure did not surprise Fred.

In this situation the confusion arose from my assuming that lack of technical knowledge in administrative productivity improvement equaled a lack of qualifications to gain a new client's trust. Fred's experience helping clients define and buy the right type and amount of consulting—and his ability to listen to and connect with clients emotionally in the process—were essential. The how-to technical details, which would be important later, were secondary at the start. Without experience, I had confused my ego and the technical details with the real point of the sales call. The client was seeking a helper who understood how the situation felt and could be trusted to improve her situation.

Fred's questioning showed me that I had confused technical experience and eagerness with what that client was looking for in a consultant—confidence that we cared about her situation and could be trusted to help achieve the results she wanted. Without that foundation, there was no need for how-to details.

While the facts of job or selling interviews are important, they are only surface issues in what should be a deeper conversation. The real need is to build emotional bridges linking yourself to those who rely on you; otherwise why should they trust you? Technical knowledge cannot close a trust gap. Only emotional connections build enough trust for knowledge and advice to move from the givers to those who must rely on it and live with the results.

CHOOSE THE PATH THAT EXPAND YOUR PROSPECTS —NOT THE "BEST" PATH

So far, we've looked at confusion that pops up when you try to find the job or organization that fits you best. But we haven't examined a bigger-picture confusion that many of us overlook: confusing today's best fitting job in the short run, with the best fit for next year and ten years from now.

As you start out, your present decisions impact what is or is not attainable in your future. As your experience grows, you may outgrow today's "best fit" and find yourself looking for a better job. So, it's worth looking ahead to long-term opportunities when you choose a job, even if doing so increases confusion in the short term. Here's how this lesson was taught in a seminar on long-range planning.

The late Russell Ackoff discussed the proposed extension of an interstate highway into the heart of Philadelphia in a graduate seminar. Ackoff was helping city politicians address the question of whether it would be worth demolishing historic colonial neighborhoods and displacing their residents in the short term so that in the future more people could work in the city and live in suburbs outside the city. Politicians and planning officials at the time were deciding such questions, and they needed help.

This seminar produced the insight that city politicians had no interest in making truly optimal decisions. Instead, they evaluated how well each alternative created and maintained more future options. They avoided decisions that narrowed future possibilities, opting instead for decisions with built-in flexibility. Their objective was to be able to change course as political, social, and economic conditions in the city unfolded. In modern terms we would say the politicians preferred agile and robust strategies for dealing with long-term issues in an uncertain world.

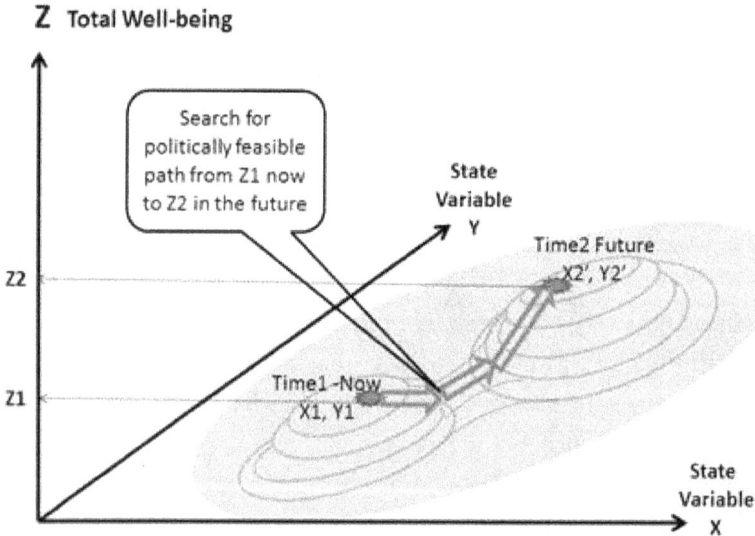

Figure 2 — An Approximation to Russ Ackoff's Planning Map

Ackoff, who was a gifted illustrator, sketched a conceptual diagram—approximated from memory in Figure 2. (Ackoff, 1994; undocumented diagram drawn in a class presentation, 1968) In one panoramic view his map depicted a planner's challenge in searching for a feasible pathway from the present state of affairs to a better future. Standing at the blackboard, Ackoff sketched the present situation as a peak labeled "Time 1 - Now" (See Figure 2.) The well-off stratum of society was at the top of the Now peak in Figure 2 at a wellbeing level of $Z1$ shown on the vertical Z scale. Each level below the peak represented that portion of the city's current population at a lower level of well-being than the $Z1$ peak level.

Next Ackoff sketched a higher and broader peak in the northeastern corner of the map to represent a desired future state of society at a future Time2. For large, city- or region-wide changes, reaching that future peak might take decades. The projected peak level of well-being at future Time2 is much higher than the well-being before the change. Also, a greater proportion of the total future population was better off in terms of well-being in the projected future than they are in the present.

The politician's challenge was to design an achievable pathway from now to the future that minimized and justified the pain during the transition by helping everyone envision how they would be much better off in the future. The planner's challenge was to find a feasible set of political and economic steps from the present (in the lower left) to the broader and better future in the upper right corner of the map. (One such pathway is shown in Figure 2.).

The conclusion was that development explores pathways that minimize temporary distress while leading everyone to a future where they are much better off than where they started.

In making job and career decisions, it's all too easy to confuse the option that seems best today with what will be best for you over the long haul. If you're lucky, the butterflies of confusion will act up and cause you to think before making a shortsighted choice—such as choosing a job offer that pays the highest salary instead of the job that opens up your widest range of appealing futures. Also, if your pathway to the future demands, or better yet, expands your list of energizing skills, your inner satisfaction will help you withstand upsets as your future path unfolds.

Today's "perfect fit" isn't perfect if it limits and restricts your future growth—especially when you're starting a career that will play out over thirty or more years. The finest job opportunities are those that let you experience and learn new skills the most quickly, within an organization that supports and advances you as you learn. No matter how perfect the fit has been however, there comes a time to leave.

SOMETIMES SUCCESS MEANS IT'S TIME FOR YOU TO LEAVE

Some confusing, where-do-I-fit situations arise from finding that you are no longer needed by an organization where you had fit in well, achieved successful results and made friends. This situation may become familiar during a long career, but it can be unsettling at first, as the following experience shows.

Jack, the head of technology for a large manufacturer, was frustrated by previous failures to improve the process for controlling product design changes. Their product designs were produced and sold worldwide, and even small design changes could have large and widespread financial and technical implications. When asked about his desired end results, he instantly replied: "I want more for less," and named two examples of what he wanted more of. After several rounds answering the question, "More of what else?" we listed and agreed upon twelve process outcomes that Jack, customers and the engineering groups he managed all wanted more of.

Then Jack began exploring what he wanted less of. He wanted less delay in changing product designs, less tracking of where changes were in their review and approval process, less investment in expensive information technology, less wasted effort and so on. Jack's list of "mores" and "lesses" became a concrete acid test for analyzing the value added in each step of their process for revising product designs.

After several months of coaching, gathering data and testing how each change in their process gave more for less, Holly, the woman who managed the engineering documentation process, and her team members designed a new lean process and were ready to pilot test it. Our project plan called for Holly's team to brief Jack before testing the new process design. When Holly called, Jack was away on vacation for a month and was busy for a few weeks after his return. So, Holly booked the first available time after Jack's return for the briefing and we agreed to touch base in about six weeks.

Six weeks later, when Holly met with me to prepare our presentation to Jack, she was very excited. During the previous five weeks she and her team had assembled a pilot-processing cell and tested the new process for all product design changes from a medium-sized engineering group. They brought all the necessary staff specialists and equipment into a large room and arranged tables into a U-shaped processing cell. Filing cabinets and a table were positioned behind the workers in the center of the U-shaped cell. On the table fax machines, network terminals and computer equipment were within easy reach of the workers.

Engineers dropped change packages (bundles of forms and design documents) into an in-basket at one end of the U-shape. Then nine staff specialists seated around the inside edge of the U-shaped cell and several trainees (for backup) worked in a continuous flow taking each engineering change from the input-basket through all processing steps until the approved documents reached the output basket at the other end of the U-shaped. This design was influenced by what John Reed had done with service processes at Citibank and what Toyota's Taichi Ohno had done with lean manufacturing.

Holly explained that the first few weeks of pilot operation of the new process produced results beyond everyone's expectations. Nonstop processing cut completion time down from six weeks or longer under the old process to less than two days with a lean process. Also, productivity had risen by more than 40 percent in the first month—and quality and productivity trends were still improving after five weeks of pilot operation as the team tweaked their process during pilot testing. Hearing this good news was great. But Holly and her team had done all of this on their own, which caused mixed feelings about the fact that they had skipped the executive review of the new process design, and started up the pilot without me.

On the day of the presentation to Jack, Holly's team was one of six projects. The audience included Jack and about thirty managers and their project team members. When Holly's turn came, she summarized her team's work and presented slide after slide of actual outcome measurements from the pilot of their new process. As Holly presented each results slide, Jack got more excited and complementary. When Holly finished, he told the audience how pleased he was that the new process was already up and running and generating results.

Holly's design presented spectacular actual results that stood out that day. Her team had hit an improvement home run while the others were still waiting for Jack's approval. They had changed a vital and troublesome process and achieved the goal of doing more for less. The resulting new process performed far better than anyone had expected.

In this situation, the confusion was between plans agreed to months earlier with Jack's objective. When Holly and her team saw they could deliver the "more for less" outcomes he wanted, they cut the plan short and went ahead, without me. They no longer needed my coaching to set up the process I had helped them design.

Organizations, like people, must constantly grow and change—or else. Sometimes this may mean that you outgrow your role in an organization. When you realize that it is time to move on, you too may have mixed feelings. Leaving behind friends you have worked well with is a sad part of any job. But success with each challenge lets you learn and gain experience that leads you to new friends and greater challenges. There is wisdom in the saying that every friend was once a stranger.

So, when considering where you fit, keep in mind that "fit" is not just about you finding a right-sized opening in an organization and plugging yourself into it indefinitely. Both you and your organization will, if you're lucky, continue to grow. Growth in the value you create and your gratification from your work—not your ability to keep your job—is the real measure of success. When your growth and your butterfly feelings stop, it is time to seek new challenges.

CONCLUSION

To help you find where you fit, Appendix H — Navigating Career Confusion outlines the steps to building your personal system for navigating career confusion. Remember to check for butterfly feelings in your gut. If your feelings of confusion or excitement cause you to begin inquiring, not only will you feel less anxious, but your learning will help you stretch and grow. If the butterfly feelings are gone, it's probably time to seek more challenging assignments. Please check out Appendix H when you are pondering a change of course in your career.

When you find yourself in a new organization, surrounded by new faces and new opportunities—you will confront the second major confusion of working in organizations: figuring out what's really going on. Some helpful tools for sorting out this confusion are coming right up in the next chapter.

2

Confusion About What's Really Going On

MAKING SENSE OF YOUR NEW ORGANIZATION

Once you get past the question of fit, your next confusion in a new work environment is to figure out how things work in your new job and organization. That learning goes beyond what your job entails, to understanding what's really going on around you: how does this organization function, and why?

As a newcomer to an organization, you can expect a grace period during which you may be a bit confused as you ask questions and learn the ropes. So, take advantage of your on-boarding grace period. Instead of ignoring your confusion or panicking, *explore it*—and follow its lead to a deeper understanding of how your organization works.

To gain deep insights into what is going on, you need a kit of simple, powerful tools for making sense of confusing information about your new organization. Here is an executive preview of lessons about using tools presented in this chapter's stories (all tools mentioned are detailed in appendices referred to in the chapter).

1: Don't panic when your assumptions clash with your new experiences. Ask the people you respect, "Who should I talk to, about what, and why?" Then, visit with the people they recommend. Use open probing and concrete questioning to gain factual knowledge and learn from those around you.

2: Ask people to explain how things work, listen and draw a flowchart that shows how the parts fit into a flow from start to finish. Creating a flow chart as you learn helps you spot and clear up gaps in your knowledge before they confuse and steer you off course. A story and an appendix show how.

3: While you are learning the ropes, listen to those with lots more experience than you have within your organization. As you learn how your new organization really works, listen also for what's *not* working. Collect problem statements until you no longer hear any new problems. (Be forewarned, there may be hundreds in a large organization.) A story in this chapter shows how a senior manager joined a new organization and involved her direct reports in drawing a spider-web diagram to identify their highest leverage improvement opportunities. A related appendix shows how to create such a spider-web diagram.

4: Several stories show how drilling down by repeatedly asking "why" questions leads you to often absurd root causes of costly problems that recur just because no one prevents the absurdity. Finding root causes gives you deep insights into organizational problems and opportunities —as well as pointing the way to solving previously chronic problems.

5: Avoid rushing into "big bang" changes before trying out new ways of doing things in "fail-fast" pilot tests. These pilots should be small, statistically designed experiments that confirm or refute your guess and pay off fast in added understanding while costing the organization little.

The tools and advice in this chapter will help you get your bearings as you fit into a new organization. They will help you replace initial confusion with a clearer understanding of what's really going on. Used judiciously, your understanding will add further leverage to the motivating skills and abilities you discovered with the skill self-assessment of Chapter 1 and Appendix A — Success Motivated Skill Assessment, to make you a more valuable addition to the organization.

Anyone new to an organization and its challenges has undoubtedly experienced confusion about what's really going on. The following sections show

how key tools can help you turn organizational confusion into understanding quickly and calmly. So, let's start with the simplest confusion-clearing tool of all: the question.

BECOME SMART: ASK STUPID QUESTIONS

No matter how many years of education and experience you have when you join a new organization, learning is more important than knowing. To learn, you must turn to others who know the organization better than you do, and let them teach you—letting go of wrong assumptions in the process. Here is how to gather useful, concrete information from those with knowledge of specific subjects.

First start the flow of information by asking an open probe—a question that cannot be answered simply yes or no. If SUBJECT X is what you want to know about, use the following template to generate an open probe:

"Please tell me about SUBJECT X."

For example, if you want to understand a banker's process for deciding on international loans, (where SUBJECT X = the international loan approval process), you would ask a banker who has several years of experience with that subject:

"Please tell me about the international loan approval process."

Bingo—nine times out of ten such an open probe starts a flow of information.

Second, when you listen to new information, clear your mind. As you listen, try visualizing what you hear based only on concrete images of the words the person uses. One way to do this is to visualize what you hear as a movie playing in your mind.

Third, as you visualize what you have heard, look for gaps in your imaginary movie—places where you can't visualize how the speaker went from scene A to scene B. For example, you would run into trouble when the banker you are talking to says something like the following:

"There are problems in the international loan process between the originating branch and the international credit committee (ICC) in the home office."

You may be able to visualize a bank branch, and a committee meeting in the bank's home office, but not be able to visualize "problems." Any visualization you make would be an assumption from the context—or, more likely, a misunderstanding. The banker has not explained what the word "problems" refers to. It's time to bring in another questioning tool, called "concrete questioning."

Fourth, use concrete questioning to fill blanks in your mental movie with "workable words." To obtain concrete descriptions of *subjects* and *actions*, use the following template to create questions that invite your interviewee help you visualize what he or she has in mind.

"I am not sure I get the picture of SUBJECT. Which SUBJECT specifically? Please give me an example of the SUBJECT."

In this example, the subject is "problems," so you would ask the following concrete question:

"I am not sure that I got the picture when you mentioned problems. Which problems specifically? Please give me an example of the problems that you have in mind between the branch and the ICC."

Fifth, once you have a specific example of the subject (problems) that you can visualize in your mental movie, follow up with a concrete question about the action, using this template:

"Please help me understand. The ACTION how? Specifically, how does the ACTION occur? Please give me an example of the ACTION you are referring to."

In this example, the second concrete question would sound something like this:

"Please help me clarify the picture. How do the problems you've described affect the chain of approvals, specifically? Please give me an example of how the problems between the originating branch and the ICC affect the loan approval process."

You may need several rounds of concrete questions to fill the gaps in your mental movie with concrete details based on your interviewee's concrete descriptions. Staying conscious of what is unclear in your mental movie lets you probe precisely, until you get past points of confusion.

Using the preceding questioning method will help you zero in on areas of confusion and obtain clear details that build understanding. For more general advice about informational interviews—essentials such as preparing a question list, establishing rapport with your interviewee, and how to know whether the "problem" your interviewee is describing is not just a gripe—see Appendix D — Data-Gathering Interviews.

Knowing what to ask and how to listen is the first step in helping overcome confusion about what's going on in your new organizational situation. The second step is to know what to write down—or draw—while you ask and listen. Answers to concrete questions give you the facts you need to draw a flowchart or storyboard.

WHEN THINGS GET BEWILDERING, DITCH THE NOTES AND GO WITH A FLOWCHART

Just as there is an art to asking simple questions in a way that reduces confusion, there is also an art to recording what you learn in a way that increases your clarity and understanding. Words may not be the clearest way to capture the essence of what someone is telling you. Here is a lesson learned about the need to map out what you are being told about complex operations.

A senior consultant invited me to help him solve a problem for a major New York financial institution. The company was experiencing slow delivery of securities needed as collateral on loans. We spent several days following the client's process from point A, where customers ordered security withdrawals, to point Z, where the negotiable stock certificates were delivered to couriers.

On this, my first real assignment, I followed the senior consultant as we walked through the process. The walkthrough was like a relay race, in which we were the baton being passed by a series of supervisors who handed us off from one department to the next. Within each department, we followed the transaction as each worker explained what he or she did. We both occasionally asked questions, while I took detailed notes. In contrast, my senior colleague stood calmly, listened with interest, and jotted occasional notes on his leather-bound note pad.

At the end of our first day of walking through the process, I asked my colleague why he took so few notes. He opened his leather folder and showed me a neatly drawn, detailed flowchart of the parts of the process we had studied that day. The chart fit on a page or two. Each box showed a work activity, each line was labeled, and marginal notes here and there identified bottlenecks and upsets. When I asked him if he always flowcharted an operation he was studying, he answered:

"When I study an operation, I like to understand it before I try to change it. A flowchart is a good way to understand a complicated process like this one."

His flowchart made sense, while many pages of notes left me feeling very confused. So I worked much of that night to construct my own flowchart from my notes. Unfortunately, this after-the-fact flowchart had many loose ends, gaps, and disconnects that my notes could not resolve. Overlooking a tool as appropriate as a flowchart to understand a work flow had confused recording details with really understanding what was happening step by step.

By flowcharting the process as he followed it, my colleague could ask clarifying questions as soon as any detail became unclear. The answer to each of his questions closed some gap in the chart he was drawing, or clarified some confusion about how the parts fitted together. During this walk-through, we moved on to the next department only after my senior colleague saw that his flowchart of the work we had just seen was clear and explainable without any loose ends. By contrast, it was impossible to check if my pages of notes equaled a complete understanding of the process. One flowchart was worth more than a thousand words.

All managers need to understand processes or organizational systems before changing them, or they risk creating greater confusion. Drawing a flowchart as you walk through a process or investigate how an organization works lets you see how each part fits into the overall picture. What's more, disconnects and gaps in the flowchart alert you to confusing points or missing information. Flowcharts not only help you understand how things work in an organization, they also help you see what's *not* working: the real gaps and broken connections that create confusion between parts of that organization as a whole.

For examples of what flowcharts look like and how they work, see Appendix B — Flowcharting Simplified, which flowcharts the process of baking a cake, and Appendix C — Flowchart for Resolving Confusion, which describes a process for appreciating and resolving confusion by using inquiry and sense-making to reduce confusion about some important matter. The flowchart in Appendix C also illustrates how the arrangements of items in the flowchart can be used to imply differences in process work flows. For example, the activity of bounding the area of confusion and its effects moves horizontally, while the sequence of inquiries that replace elements of the confusion with reframing the facts and sense-making are arranged vertically, implying increasing depth of appreciation and understanding.

A careful walk-through observing a complex process usually turns up between 300 and 700 repetitive problems in that process. As you draw a flowchart, note each concrete problem you encounter next to the part of the flowchart where that problem appears. Put a carat symbol (>) in front of each problem statement and number the problems consecutively. When you hear about or spot possible improvements or fixes, note each idea the same way that you document problems, but mark each improvement idea with a delta symbol (Δ) to signify a possible idea for change.

Flowcharts and lists of problems compiled while walking through processes are important tools for clearing up confusion caused by the complexities of service and administrative operations. By reducing confusion, flowcharting lets you focus on the vital few bottlenecks in any organizational flow. Converting lists of problems into a spider-web diagram (as described in the next story) is a valuable addition to flowcharts for taming confusion.

You may be tempted to react to situations in your organization by suggesting how the situation "should be" handled in some better way. It is wise to understand what is, and why it is that way, before you suggest how it could, should or might be better. Otherwise you will be like a physician who prescribes a treatment for a patient before a complete diagnosis of the patient's condition. Such a physician loses credibility with all but a few lucky patients who, by chance, needed just that prescription. Prescribing change before fully diagnosing and understanding why things are the way they currently are confuses prescription with diagnosis.

Flowcharts are not the only tool you can use to get at problems causing confusion in an organization. The next section describes a tool that will help you untangle whole sets of problems to see how they're related. This can help point you toward changes with the greatest impact on outcomes.

A SPIDER WEB CAN BE A GOOD THING FOR CATCHING BIG PROBLEMS

The deeper you get into trying to figure out what's really going on in an organization, the more you will find yourself trying to untangle confusing layers of connected problem causes and effects: "Wait… is the problem really X, or is there an underlying problem Y?" In most cases just a few high-leverage problems drive a whole mess of interrelated incidents, problems and symptoms. Finding the vital few problems can clear up the confusion, and solving them can put a stop to many undesired outcomes at once. My favorite tool for untangling a web of related problems has turned out to be a sort of web: a spider-web diagram.

A spider-web diagram is simply a circle of problem statements with a web of arrows connecting each problem around the edge of the web to any other problem that it causes or aggravates. (Describing the problems and determining their relationships is a group process, which Appendix E — Interrelationship (Spider-web) Diagram) discusses.

In Figure 3 an arrow from a problem A to another problem, C, for example, shows that A drives or worsens C. The process of drawing arrows must be repeated for each problem, A, B, C and so on against all the rest—which may be tedious but pays off by replacing confusion with clear focus.

When the spider-web diagram is completed, the number of out-arrows from a problem B, for example, shows how many other problems Problem B worsens. In the example diagram, Problems B and E, each with four out-arrows, have the highest count of out-arrows in the diagram. This implies that removing Problem B (My current job limits my opportunities for new types of work) will ameliorate four out of the nine other problems, and resolving Problem E (My current job does not teach me new skills that qualify me for a promotion) has a comparable impact. The high out-arrow counts of Problems B and E show that they are the top drivers of confusion in this career dilemma.

The number of in-arrows pointing to each particular problem shows the number of other problems in the spider-web that impact that problem. So, Problem C (I am unsure if this is the time to stay or leave my current organization) is made worse by five other problems. Problem A, The demands of my work conflict with what my family needs from me) has no in-arrows and one out-arrow. So this problem does not play a significant part in the job confusion (although it would have major effects on deciding whether or not to make a change).

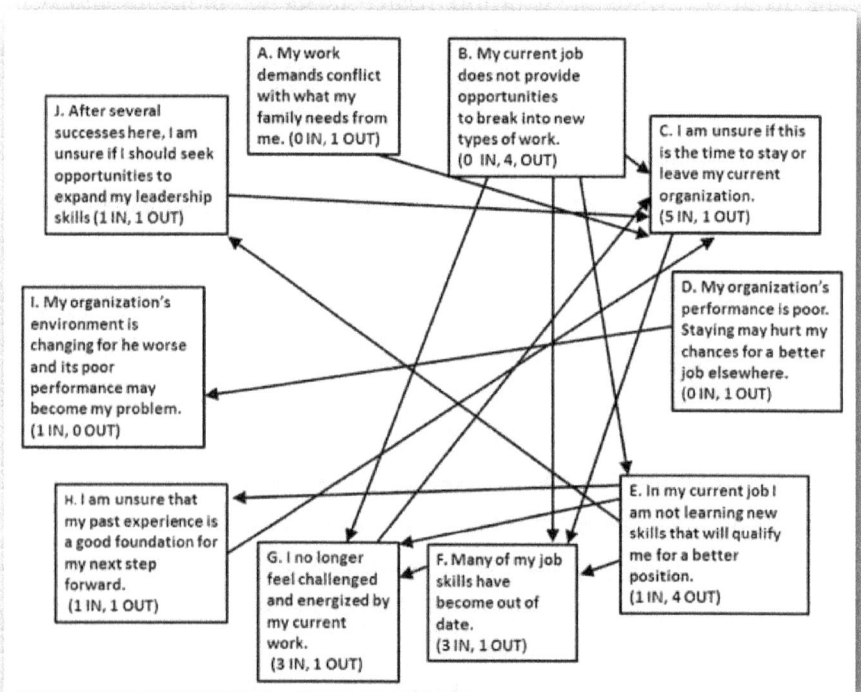

Figure 3 — Interrelationship (Spider-web) Diagram

Spider-web diagrams are helpful when you come on board in a new organization—as Lois's experience shows in the following story.

Lois, a former client of our firm, moved out west to manage the operations of a growing cable network. I had coached Lois's improvement teams working on several processes of a media company in the Boston area. She asked me to train three teams in process improvement, so I flew out to San Jose and ran the training as Lois requested. When the class reached the topic of how to use a spider-web diagram, the whole class began laughing.

A participant explained that when Lois arrived as the new Operations VP, no one knew what to expect. For weeks, she rarely went into her office. Instead, she rode around on trucks, tagged along on service calls and installations, visited all the service depots, talked with service and operating people, listened in on customer calls at the call centers, and met with managers and supervisors throughout the whole area served by the network. After several weeks, she called a daylong meeting with her whole management team.

When the managers arrived at Lois's meeting, there was a large diagram taped up on the wall. Around the edge of the diagram, Lois had placed dozens of sticky notes with a problem statement printed on each. (These were problems Lois had observed firsthand in her travels,) Lois then walked her managers through specific examples of each problem on the diagram and began leading them in analyzing how each problem affected every other problem, drawing arrows from cause to effect. When Lois and her managers completed the analysis, it was clear that three problems (with the highest out-arrow counts) either caused or worsened damage from all the rest of their operational problems. Lois then led her managers in deciding who should be on the improvement teams for each high-leverage (high out-arrow count) problem. The members of those three teams of managers were my training audience in the room that day.

This explanation was so surprising that I forgot to ask again what they had found so funny about the spider-web demonstration. Perhaps it was a feeling of relief that they could use such a simple tool to make sense out of what appeared to be an overwhelming confusion of problems in their operation. However, it might just be that they laughed at my teaching them something that Lois had already turned them into experts at—using a spider-web analysis for catching the vital few problems in a confusing mess.

You can learn the fine points of spider-web diagramming in Appendix E — Interrelationship (Spider-web) Diagram. You'll find the diagramming process to be a powerful way to work through confusing organizational messes, and you can become proficient at it with a little practice.

As you create spider-web diagrams, here are a few points to keep in mind. Be sure to bring together a group of experienced people who know which problems affect which other problems. The combined knowledge and discussions in the room will help you diagnose a situation more fully than any one specialist ever could.

If you're looking at more than forty or fifty problems—which happens when you're trying to figure out what is driving a confusing organizational situation—you'll want to start by grouping types of problem together based on similarities of cause and effect. This is covered in the appendix. Also, do not limit yourself to known, visible problems. Sometimes important problems aren't what you see; but are in fact gaps between the current organization and a complete, "should-be" system for managing that organization. So ask yourself, "What's not going on that should be?" Gaps or missing parts of a management system (such as planning, training, corrective and preventive action, or planned process improvement) often amplify other problems.

After you use the spider-web technique to sift through an organizational mess of problems to make sense of the vital few serious problems and challenges, you will be much closer to understanding what is really going on and why. You may not be free of all confusion; because knowing *what* the key problems are may not tell you *why* they happen. To answer the why question, you can use another simple tool of enormous power: The Five Whys, also known as *root cause analysis*.

TO LEARN, ASK "WHY?" UNTIL THE ANSWER IS ABSURD

The "what you see is all there is" (WYSIATI) thinking bias explains why so many organizational problems reappear after they were supposedly solved.

People tend to leap to common-sense answers based on what they saw, rather than face the fact that what you see is *almost never* all there is. The way out of WYSIATI confusion is to dig deeper to uncover a problem's root causes, which are usually hidden beneath surface symptoms. One embarrassing instance of being suckered by WYSIATI thinking occurred about a dozen years ago:

> After an exceptionally wet spring, my wife and I noticed that our "environmentally conscious" front lawn (no weed killers or fertilizers) had become a carpet of bright yellow dandelions. After seeing looks of dismay on our neighbors' faces, we decided to make the dandelion problem go away. After lowering the blades on our rotary lawnmower and mowing the front yard, our yellow-dotted lawn became a solid area of thin but well-mulched grass. But three days of wet weather later, the lawn sprouted an even denser carpet of dandelions. Determined to strike them down, I mowed the lawn again… only to produce an abundance of short-stemmed dandelions a few days later.
>
> Finally, I faced my confusion and sought help from my local garden center's lawn specialist. She told me about an environmentally sound method of dandelion removal, which was a root-digging tool resembling a large screwdriver with a pronged edge. By pushing the tool into the ground next to a dandelion's stem, you can pop the plant out by its roots—stem, flower, and all. Two weekend sessions of popping dandelions and hauling them away did the trick. Our lawn stayed relatively dandelion-free throughout the summer, because I had finally dealt with the root cause of the dandelion problem.

Of course, problems in organizations are generally more complex than chronic dandelions. Often, they occur in processes involving many people and multiple steps, where a small misstep early on creates a domino effect of worsening outcomes that ripple along the process, impacting later outcomes. Consider the situation in this centuries-old childhood rhyme:

> "For want of a nail, the shoe was lost.
> For want of the shoe, the horse was lost.
> For want of the horse, the rider was lost.

For want of the rider, the order was lost.
For want of the order, the battle was lost.
For want of the battle, the kingdom was lost;
All for the want of a nail."

What you see, a conquered kingdom, would never suggest to you that a thing as trivial as a missing nail could have led to losing a crucial battle. The idea seems absurd. And yet, the root causes of problems in an organization often are just as absurd —and therefore just as likely to be overlooked in favor of more obvious guesses about what caused the problem. Consider what leaving the Challenger space shuttle out overnight in unusually cold Florida weather led to.

Fortunately, a simple technique can get you to that deep, often-absurd root cause: asking "why," and "why," and "why" again in succession. Some call this root-cause investigation technique "drilling down." The technique is also called The Five Whys, and has been popularized by its importance for achieving world-class quality outcomes. The Five Whys often involve asking as many levels of why questions as needed to arrive at the root of a problem (sometimes two or three whys suffice, while more than Five Whys may be needed on occasion).

Here's how the Five Whys work: you start by stating the facts of your problem, and ask, why? After you discover the factual "because" answer, you take your investigation to a deeper level, by asking why that last because occurred. You then repeat this questioning with as many why questions as you need to link a problem to its deepest (and often apparently absurd) root cause. For example, if you were trying to find a root cause for the loss of the kingdom in the childhood rhyme, your questioning might go as follows:

Why 1: Why did the King lose his kingdom to the enemy?
Because 1: The kingdom was lost because the battle was lost.
Note that it's important not to jump to an intuitive assumption here about why the battle was lost, such as "Oh, the King must not have had a big enough army. Next time an enemy threatens, we need to deploy a larger force." Instead, focus on your confusion; you still have why questions, so ask on…

Why 2. Why was the battle lost?

Because 2: The battle was lost because the rider carrying orders was lost.

    Why 3: Why was the rider carrying the orders lost?

    Because 3: The rider was lost because his horse was lost.

        Why 4: Why was the rider's horse lost?

        Because 4: The horse was lost because it tossed its shoe and went lame.

            Why 5: Why did the rider's horse lose its shoe?

            Because 5: The horse lost its shoe for want of a nail.

Aha! An answer so absurd that no one would have expected it—yet the answer is verifiable by checking the facts and then easily prevented. Every drill-down that penetrates layers of confusion to find and remove the root cause of the problem saves you the future expense of fixing that problem over and over again. As a result, the long-term payoff on root-cause investigations that result in preventive action is often huge.

Here is a story about finding the root cause of a product-quality problem from the early days of Japanese competition with GM, Ford and Chrysler.

In the face of austere post-war poverty, Japanese auto firms replaced "high-quality-is-not-free" thinking—copied from U.S. automakers who assumed that improving quality would raise costs and reduce sales—with continuous-investigation and improvement strategies taught by American quality consultants such as Deming, Juran and others. Unlike the US automakers who equated better quality with high cost, Japanese automakers' first step was to seek out first-hand knowledge of quality by listening to the voices of automobile customers.

By listening as new car buyers discussed their likes and dislikes, the Japanese automakers learned that they disliked body squeaks and wind noises when driving their new cars on bumpy roads or in rainy weather. Knowing what potential customers really cared about, these automakers drilled down to root causes by asking why five times.

Why 1: Why do new cars squeak?

Because 1: The car squeaks when driving over a bump because the motion causes friction between rubber seals and the car's steel body panels.

Why 2. Why are there rubber seals between steel body panels?

Because 2: Because gaps between edges of the steel panels must be sealed to prevent wind noise, rain leaks, and metal-on-metal friction.

Why 3: Why are there air gaps, water leaks, and friction points between panels of an auto body?

Because 3: Because the way body panels are stamped in large presses causes panels to vary slightly in size from one to another, creating gaps between panels, which are not air- and water-tight.

Why 4: Why do the exact sizes of the body panels vary from one another?

Because 4: Because the flat metal sheets to be stamped into body panels are clamped at their edges, which lets each sheet move slightly when being stamped, resulting in part-to-part variation.

Why 5: Why do we clamp the sheet metal in a way that lets it move slightly when stamped?

Because 5: Because that is the manufacturing process we adopted from the American auto industry.

Using a method that guarantees defective variations from part to part was absurd in a society facing starvation after World War II. Unless Japanese engineers improved upon this manufacturing method, their body panels would always be of inconsistent quality. So, Japanese production engineers chose to eliminate the need to clamp the edges of sheet metal by punching two small locator holes in each piece of sheet metal while it was flat. Then, the first step in each subsequent stamping operation locked locator pins in the two holes to prevent any motion of the sheet metal. The result was uniformly identical body parts, piece after piece. The last process step trimmed the locator holes from each finished part.

With uniform parts, Japanese manufacturers could weld metal panels together into rigid, frameless, air- and water-tight auto bodies—no rubber needed. Listening to their customers and drilling down through confusion about body squeaks enabled Japanese organizations to prevent the root cause of an unwanted variation. That change eliminated sloppy parts, unnecessary frames, and much waste— and produced stronger, tighter bodies at far lower manufacturing cost. Quality was not just free; it actually saved money and boosted customer appetite for the improved products.

The drill-down questioning technique looks so obvious that you may wonder why it isn't used more widely. Part of the answer is that not everyone knows this technique. But another reason for limited use is that drilling down to root causes is trickier than it first appears. It takes a willingness to admit and tolerate confusion as well as diligence, attention to detail, and an undiplomatic insistence on facts, proven facts, and only facts—instead of excuses, opinions or guesses. When solving problems, do not confuse what you see with all there is. Problem solving takes root cause analysis to peel back layer after layer of causes beneath the surface problem until you see the problem's hidden roots.

Your root cause investigations must go wherever each question leads, across departmental lines if necessary. The answers may embarrass people who confuse finding cause with finding fault. That's why it's important that no drill-down should ever be—or even seem to be—a witch hunt. If those asking the questions blame others, the blaming will generate fear, denial and push back. (In Chapter 5, we'll look deeper into the problems that arise when people confuse problem solving with a search for people to blame.) To calm fears people might have, make sure that your actions show that your why questions are about learning and solving problems, not blaming people. Keeping a sense of humor can also help. As you look for a root cause that may turn out to be on the absurd side, your motto should be: go hard on the process and easy on the people.

Another surprising and memorable root-cause investigation was on a retail chain's bounced-check process about twenty years ago, before debit cards became popular. The improvement team in this investigation included the manager of a collection department, an analyst from the finance department and several others who worked on the debt-collection process. A sub-team was figuring out the root cause of delays in collecting on bounced checks.

Their drill-down went something like this:

Why 1: Why do checks returned to the treasury for insufficient funds take over two days to arrive at the collection department?

Because 1: Because the treasury uses interoffice mail to send bounced checks to the collection department, and interoffice mail takes two days of cycle time.

Why 2. Why do we use interoffice mail to move checks from the treasury to the collection department?

Because 2: Until two years ago, the treasury and the collection department were next door to each other in the home office. Treasury put bricks of bad checks on a mail cart and pushed them through a door to Collections twice a day. When Collections relocated, we started using interoffice mail.

Why 3: Why did we stop the twice-a-day delivery of rejected checks to Collections when we switched to interoffice mail?

Because 3: Just before Collections moved out of the home office, the mail room manager advised the collections manager and assistant treasurer that he needed $300 to buy a few sets of colored mailbags to be used for bad checks, which could then be specially handled and put on twice-daily courier runs to Collections.

Why 4: So, why didn't we use the colored mailbags, as the mail room manager suggested?

Because 4: No one present had a budget of $300 to pay for colored mail bags; so they agreed to use regular interoffice mail instead.

Why 5: Why did they choose to use interoffice mail rather than seek funds to purchase colored mailbags?

Because 5: Because no one wanted to request a supplemental budget of $300 for mailbags.

When the assistant controller, who was a member of the team, heard this, he left the conference room with an unhappy look on his face. He used the phone in a nearby vacant office to call the budget office and add $300 to the mailroom budget for mailbags to expedite collection of returned checks. When he returned, he explained that the two days' float on the bad check balances had incurred more than $250,000 per year in interest expense on the company's line of credit. Later, when the company's CFO was asked if he had spotted the increasing receivables trend, he said that he had noticed receivables climbing but attributed it to increasing sales volume and changes in customer payment behavior.

In hindsight, saving $300 by not buying colored mailbags—which added $250,000 per year in extra interest expenses—is absurd. But that absurdity arose from basing a superficial decision about a practical problem on assumptions and opinions, rather than on facts. To break through the confusion between surface symptoms and deeper causes, remember the motto a successful executive displayed on a plaque above his desk: In God we trust, all others bring facts.

Real root causes do not make logical sense because they lead into a twilight zone of carelessness, randomness, futile best efforts, wasted good intentions or worse. So, when you're asking why during a root-cause analysis and you get answers that make logical sense, keep drilling until you uncover absurdities. Often, the key to a chronic problem is something as simple as replacing an absurd root cause with a sensible prevention step. Finding the root cause is often the hard part.

Root cause analysis is a powerful tool for cutting through confusion about why a problem keeps reoccurring. But it only works when people answer why questions with hard facts. Sometimes, there is no definitive answer available. So you'll need to make some guesses. When an informed hunch may help you to break through confusion about what's really going on, or about what the real solution is—make sure to test your guess on a small scale. Here's an example that shows a simple test of such a hunch.

TEST HUNCHES BEFORE BETTING ON THEM

This example was given to me by a young man participating in a process-improvement training program.

While a student, this man helped out in his family's restaurant in a city in Massachusetts. The family had operated their restaurant for many years with a loyal customer base, and they took pride in serving good food and keeping the place spotlessly clean and sanitary.

At one point, the restaurant developed a bug problem: roaches in the kitchen. The family immediately called a "bug man" to deal with the roach problem. Unfortunately, the bugs returned soon afterward. The family called the bug man again, and the cycle of bugs and bug man went on for a few months.

One day a new cook started work and learned about the recurring bug problem. The new cook suggested to the restaurant owner that the bugs might be hiding in the cardboard boxes in which supplies were delivered. To test the cook's guess, the kitchen staff left all cardboard cartons outside the back door when delivered and brought only cans and bottles of food inside the restaurant. Once they did so, the bugs disappeared and did not return. So, the simple test of the new cook's deeper insight solved their bug problem until they could switch suppliers.

In this example, no pricey or difficult-to-undo changes were needed to test the guess. Sometimes, though, a guess or hunch points to a need for expensive changes, so implementing the idea all at once in a "big bang" can be risky. A small-scale test designed to fail fast—if it's going to fail, why not keep it small—is a great way to prevent the more embarrassing and costly failure that could result from a big-bang implementation based on a hunch. A carefully designed small-scale test can tell you a lot about whether a change has a fatal flaw or real merit. You learn either way. Here's the story of a hands-on, small-scale market test.

An oil company that lagged its competitors in gallons sold per gas station in major markets asked our consulting firm to review their marketing approach and help reduce confusion about what their marketing strategy should be.

Our consulting team interviewed the client's marketing managers and met repeatedly with its advertising agency. They studied the client's two-foot-high stack of recent market-research studies on gasoline buying behavior, and interviewed gas station owners and other players in its distribution channels. The time to present preliminary conclusions and recommend next steps to the client was a few weeks away. All the data gathering and market research did not point to any specific root cause for the company's disappointing gasoline sales. Also, time had run out for gathering and analyzing historical data on how different variables correlated with sales volume.

Nonetheless, the senior consultant on the project, a former high level market research executive, arrived at several conclusions and one theory. He wished to recommend a particular strategy to the client, but there was no evidence supporting his hunch. He asked: might crowded pumps be reducing gas sales? At that time, filling stations had relatively few pumps compared with modern gas stations. Only a few discount gas stations had a large number of pumps—three or four times as many pumps as our client's stations. The project senior consultant's hypothesis was that, other things being equal, more drivers would pull into a station with empty pumps than one where the pumps were occupied with cars.

I had experience with statistical design of experiments, so the senior consultant on the project asked me to work with Dave, a marketing specialist, to design a quick and dirty experiment to test the station-crowding hypothesis. Dave and I had to design and run an exploratory test, evaluate its results, and prepare a report in time for the team's client presentation weeks away.

We came up with an experimental design concept. We would select a projectable sample of gas stations and compare their sales during time periods when the stations' pumps were crowded to sales during time periods with empty pumps. To run the experiment, we needed to control how crowded or empty the stations' pumps were, and test for significant differences in sales per hour between crowded and empty time periods. The what-if assumptions we used showed that a large experiment would be needed. The senior consultant ruled out even recommending a large test, and instead told us to design and run a small-scale pilot test at one station just to demonstrate the feasibility and potential usefulness of a larger, more definitive experiment.

Our new pilot test calculations showed that data from sixteen randomly chosen half-hour observation periods (eight periods of crowded pumps and eight periods of empty pumps) would give us reasonable odds of detecting the large impact that the senior consultant hypothesized. To produce statistically meaningful results, the test had to be run at a large station on a busy street during a high-volume day. The bad news about our pilot test design was that any findings about the impact of crowding on gas sales would be valid only at that one station on the day of the test. So, this test would only show that running such a test was feasible and give us real data to use in estimating the size of a full-scale test to produce results useful for making decisions.

The team's senior consultant gave us the go-ahead for a pilot test. Dave found a gas station willing, for a stiff fee, to let us run the test during a peak gasoline sales period. We chose random half-hour time slots to make the station crowded or empty of cars. The random design reduced potential bias due to time-of-day and traffic variation. Our one-station, one-day experiment had about a ninety percent chance of detecting an impact of station crowding on gasoline sales if the impact was as high as the senior consultant's highest estimate.

The test lasted for a nine-hour day, divided into eighteen half-hour time segments. The "big Y" outcome measurement was the total gallons of gas sold during all empty pumps time periods versus the total gallons sold during all crowded pumps time periods. The "little x," or experimental variable, consisted of the number of empty gas pumps available during each crowded or empty test period.

The "crowded station look" consisted of cars parked at six out of eight pumps—we selected the two available pumps at random during each crowded time period to eliminate bias due to pump visibility. During the crowded periods, only the two randomly selected pumps were empty at the start of that half hour and were the only pumps that real customers could pull up to. During the "empty station" periods, team members removed all dummy cars to a parking lot across the street, leaving all pumps empty except cars belonging to real customers.

Data from this small field test let us estimate the impact of crowding on gas sales at this one station. The estimated impact tended to support the senior consultant's hypothesis, but was not large enough to be statistically significant, even for that one station and day. However, we had shown the feasibility of running such a test and had the operational information and experience needed to design and propose a larger and statistically projectable test of station crowding on the client's nationwide gasoline sales. The client decided not to run the larger test, and instead implemented other recommendations.

This simple pilot test of a previously untested hypothesis was quick and low cost, and it helped the project team show the client how to resolve a confusion of possibilities. With this test, our team examined just one potentially significant factor in explaining why the client's gas sales weren't higher. The test was too small to lend statistically valid support for testing wider changes in station design, but it showed the way.

When we conducted this test, market experiments of this sort were uncommon and many managers considered them less reliable than simply basing decisions based on analyses of sales and market survey data. Market tests had been standard practice for many decades in the direct response (mail order and catalog) industries. Now, experiments are widely used, especially by Internet and web marketers, and are part of a profession now known as marketing analytics, which tests new products, processes, sales-training programs, marketing and political messages, and the like.

There are, however, a few caveats to keep in mind with such testing. Any field experiment, to produce statistically valid results, must be designed by a statistician who is knowledgeable about experimental design, working with a person who is equally knowledgeable about whatever is being tested.

Tests must be designed to "fail fast". When the change being tested does not work as predicted the test must stop quickly. Such a fail-fast approach limits disruptions from testing, and provides facts as a basis for decision or for further inquiry. Running designed fail-fast pilot tests limits risk. Two or three fail-fast tests can discover what works and how to avoid what doesn't work without risking a big expensive failure. So, when uncertainty and confusion reign, and you have only hunches about what's really going on—design and run pilot tests to maximize success and avoid "big bangs," always.

CONCLUSION

As a new organization member, you can expect to be plugged into confusing situations that you need to make sense of quickly. The stories in this chapter introduced a kit of vital tools for sorting out confusing processes and challenges when you are new to an organization. Using tools and advice from this chapter and appendices will help you replace initial confusion with a clear, factual understanding of what's really going in your organization. This understanding adds leverage to your motivating skills and abilities discovered in Chapter 1 and Appendix A, making you an even more valuable member or coach of the crew. Appendix C uses a flowchart to show an inquiry-based approach for appreciating and resolving confusion.

After dealing with personal, "new kid" confusion about where you fit and what you're fitting into, the next section tackles confusion that arises when individual crew members try working together to guide their ship toward better destinations.

Section II: Working-Together Confusion

Three chapters in this section deal with three categories of confusion that arise when individuals try working together in groups and organizations. In general, working-together confusion arises from failures of accountability at some level. At first there may be confusion over where your organization is headed and what course will take it there—who is steering the ship and toward what? Chapter three relates stories about guiding and how managers either accepted or failed in their duty to steer their organization toward a better future.

The second type of confusion arises over what motivates organization members to do their work—what's in it for each of them and for the company as a whole? To continue the metaphor does the captain of the ship trust each person to do his or her job because each job is vital to the ship's safety and mission? Has the captain ensured that each person is well trained and accountable for doing his or her job right? Or do those in charge of an organization trust in incentives and fear to motivate the crew? Chapter four's stories show how monetary incentives may boost performance measures, but produce unwanted side effects.

The third type of working-together confusion arises when people of an organization ask "*Who* did something wrong?" and seek a scapegoat—rather than asking "*Why* did something go wrong?" or "*How* did our process let us down?" to find root causes that can be prevented or removed. Managers who choose to blame poor outcomes on people, while tolerating error-prone and uncontrolled work designs, confuse blaming with real problem solving. They perpetuate their own confusion and the damage it fosters.

Chapter five is about how those in charge set their organization's course and serve as role models for those they supervise.

3

Confusion About Who's In Charge and Where You Are Headed

LEADERSHIP AND DIRECTION

Top managers of organizations rarely appear confused about where their organization is headed. But ask employees what's important in the organization and how they know it is important. Employees' answers usually differ from what their senior managers promote. Employees cite recent promotions, firings or bonuses that signal what topside considers the right direction. When top managers say one thing but reward another, they foment employee confusion and cynicism about where the organization is headed.

The following preview highlights lessons in this chapter about reducing confusion over leadership and organizational direction as you assume a senior management role:

1: Resolve confusion about where your organization is heading with answers to questions such as: What's our purpose? Why are we here?" Your organization's purpose must legitimize it within the larger organization, industry, economy or society that contains and sustains it.

2: Appoint lookouts to spot, assess and prepare for waves of change that may impact the organization. When trends emerge such people may help their organization convert threats into opportunities by designing a distant future and then working to realize that design in one or two years.

3: Identify work that distracts senior people from fulfilling the organization's purpose and mission. Offload it to people better able to do it. Managing all parts of an organization as a system for achieving its purpose is a full time job.

4: Rely on three plans if your current organizational situation becomes unsustainable. Plan A is to stay on course and hope the ship doesn't sink. Plan B is to organize the organization's people to figure out what must change and then coach them in making those changes now. Plan C is to make changes the authoritarian way. Sideline those who favor Plan A; coach and support people capable of pursuing Plan B in order to make Plan C unnecessary.

5: Move on if an organization's top managers say one thing and do otherwise. Those who adapt to such a culture may go down with the ship.

6: Create good examples of essential behaviors to replace confusion about what is essential with clarity. Leaders like Army generals sometimes hand out medals and sometimes kick troopers in the butt—both behaviors focus people's attention on the essentials.

7: Lead self-managing professionals such as research scientists and engineers the way a great teacher helps students excel. Work with and motivate them to find ways to accomplish far higher goals than they did before they met you.

8: Keep actions and words consistent because, to those who follow, a higher-up's actions speak louder than words. Strive to model good examples of behaviors you seek from those following your lead.

9: Convert butterfly feelings about facing challenges into enthusiasm about learning by doing. Start with small changes; pilot every new thing; learn from failures in order to expand and sustain what worked. Share credit with those who help. A better future depends on how much and how fast you learn, and how many people are made better off by that knowledge.

10: Accept problems that others are too busy or too confused to face as opportunities. Cooperate with others to seize each opportunity and become the leader you were looking for. If taking initiative is discouraged in your current organization, ask yourself if it is time to seek a new organizations that values initiative more highly.

For people to make the right choices when facing waves of change they must have clarity about their organization's purpose. With clarity of purpose to guide their decisions, each person's effort aligns with and promotes the whole organization's progress. When times change, it takes well-coordinated teamwork to overcome confusion and keep the whole organization on course.

The next section shows how one leader's answer to fundamental questions about mission overcame confusion about how to measure improvement in a very large organization.

HOW AN ARMY GENERAL CHECKS HOW HE'S DOING

For the following story, readers unfamiliar with the Malcolm Baldrige National Quality Award should know that the U. S. Department of Commerce issues criteria and guidelines for assessing opportunities for improvement in organizational management systems. (NIST)(2015–2016) In past years, military organizations tailored these Baldrige Criteria for use in assessing their own organizations' opportunities for improving management systems.

An army command requested my services in training examiners for their in-house performance improvement assessment. Part of my work involved briefing the General in command on the assessment process. The purpose of my two-hour briefing was to prepare the general to kick off a daylong workshop for his staff. In turn, the one-day workshop was the run-up to a major training program for fifty others in the command. The briefing's content was a "general officer level" overview of the Army Performance Improvement Criteria (APIC)—a Baldrige-based organizational assessment, improvement and recognition program then being used in the U.S. Army.

The briefing occurred while the general ate breakfast at a local restaurant near the base. I sat opposite him, turning the pages of a briefing book as I spoke. For the first half hour or so, the general ate and listened. He asked a few questions until the subject of measurements came up. Then the General stopped eating and said:

"When I get up in the morning, I look myself in the mirror while I shave and decide how I feel. (Long pause) And, how I feel is how we are doing."

Surprised—I had no idea where this was leading—I responded,

"Is that so, general?"

He continued,

"I'm tired of deciding how we are doing based on how I feel. How does APIC say I should decide how well we're doing?"

Aha, this was familiar ground—so I answered,

"Well general, most organizations use measurements to determine how they are performing."

"Measurements," he said, "That's interesting, and where do we start?"

I answered: "General, when you set up measurements the usual place to begin is with your organization's mission or purpose."

The general looked surprised and his facial expression suggested that this was an "Aha" moment. He paused and said,

"Our mission! Of course, that's it. We need measures that tell us how well we are accomplishing our mission."

I agreed, paused and went on with the briefing.

About half an hour after the briefing ended, the general and a room full of his staff reconvened at the nearby training center. The general was scheduled to make some brief remarks to kick off the training. In the short time between my briefing and the general's kick off remarks, he pulled together a powerful extemporaneous kickoff speech for twenty or so high-ranking officers from his command staff.

The general told his staff why he was enthusiastic about the APIC/ Baldrige assessment and improvement process. He emphasized that the organization's mission was service; that he wanted measurement of how well the organization was accomplishing its service mission to be a key element in their organizational performance improvement efforts. He ended his talk by challenging all the officers to lead the assessment and improvement program throughout the command. Then, unexpectedly, he stayed in the training room and participated for an hour or more in the opening small group exercise to clarify and understand the command's organizational mission as a basis for aligning all organizational efforts and outcomes.

This experience revealed a lifelong commander who felt accountable and, judging by his extemporaneous kickoff speech, listened carefully, He had realized that he and his organization needed measurements of the outcomes they were accountable for. The idea of viewing organizational performance by measuring how well it fulfilled its mission and purpose filled in some gap in the general's view of how his organization was doing.

The general had reframed his organization's mission in terms of accountability for helping the U. S. Army fulfill its missions. In less than an hour he shared his insights with his command staff. Then to emphasize how important that mission was, he stayed longer than scheduled to provide an example and to observe his officers translate their organization's mission into behaviors to achieve it.

The next story shows how a retired naval officer saved an old-line bank from aggressive new competition. He involved everyone in his organization in working toward a distant future, then coached them in creating it *now*.

WHEN TIMES CHANGE, LOOK TEN YEARS AHEAD AND GET THERE SOONER

Top managers who focus mainly on daily routine and assume that the future will take care of itself confuse their future with their past. Two months of clear sailing across the Pacific does not ensure there's no typhoon ahead. Here is how Bill, a retired Navy Commander, replaced confusion about the future with clarity and action.

After Bill retired from the Navy he took a job running the bank's operations center. He chose operations because he had run things in the Navy, liked that type of work, and felt that he would fit in the bank's operations management. During his first few months running operations Bill spent time listening to people and closely observing every unit that reported to him. He wanted to understand what they did, how things ran and why they ran that way.

As a retired naval officer, Bill commanded respect from people working in his operations. However, he had no experience in banking, so he asked questions that no manager in the bank had ever asked. Bill joked that he was the only person in the bank who did not already know all the answers.

After studying the bank's operations for several months, Bill realized that the organization was old, founded in the previous century. Its operations had once been totally manual. However, as new banking equipment was developed, management mechanized labor-intensive operations. The bank's products and basic work had remained the same, but machines did that work faster than before.

Bill realized that no one had thought about how to run the various operations better than they were already running. He also knew that his organization's sleepy attitude would have to change. After decades of restrictions on banking competition across state lines, powerful New York banks would soon be competing for his bank's wealthiest and most profitable retail customers.

So, Bill convened several days of planning meetings with all the managers from his operations. He had decided to use a planning process he had learned in the Navy. Each department in the operations center identified major trends affecting their department and the bank's customers, services and operations. Then they projected each trend ten years into the future. Working in teams, Bill coached his managers in imagining how those trends would force the bank to operate in ten years. Finally Bill led them in working out action plans to implement ten years of change.

Bill then described how his first operating area went through this process. The area processed all deposits, withdrawals and other items and rendered monthly checking and savings account statements to customers. Each account was separate; the bank had no information links to link all of an individual customer's accounts and banking assets to each other. Many customers were high wealth individuals, aggressively sought by the banks that Bill's institution would soon be competing against.

During Bill's planning session, the managers of this area identified two trends: increasing competitive pressure to attract deposits, and increasing customer demands to be paid the highest competitive interest on their idle balances. Projecting these trends forward led to the conclusion that the bank would be forced to link all customer accounts together and automatically move idle customer balances to a customer-designated interest bearing account as interest rates changed. This sweep capability, as bankers refer to it, allows customers to avoid visiting the bank to check rates of interest, and then manually transferring idle balances from low-yield accounts to an account with a higher yield.

Bill coached departmental teams in putting their plans into action successfully, but instead of a ten-year schedule, he asked the teams to plan for completing all changes in one year.

It worked. As time passed, Bill was promoted into positions of progressively higher responsibility. In each new job he repeated his rapid update. As Bill rose up the ranks of bank management he repeated this approach in each business area and transformed the bank into a highly focused competitor specialized in meeting the banking needs of high-net-worth families in its markets. Eventually, the bank's Board of Directors recognized his accomplishments by electing him Chairman and CEO, and he was still envisioning how the whole bank had to operate ten years ahead.

This retired naval officer turned a sleepy traditional bank about to be overrun by large, aggressive rivals into a formidable competitor, even against much large players. Bill accomplished this partly because he led people instead of viewing himself as a banker. He came into the bank with command experience, which he supplemented by observing work and listening to people. The Navy had also taught him how to organize major change in a hurry. His people, in turn, realized that Bill respected their knowledge and experience and responded to him by using what they knew in order to win.

Sudden changes that violate people's hidden assumptions about what insiders consider the right way to do things can cause anxiety and confusion.

In the past, when the current status quo was new, the assumptions justifying that status quo made sense. However, departing from the status quo asks people to ignore what have become over time unconscious assumptions that make the current way things are done feel right. So, many people feel anxious when change threatens their deeply hidden assumptions.

Looking ten years ahead freed Bill's people from anxiety and confusion arising from the assumptions that fortified commitments to the status quo. Once Bill's whole crew was clear on what their future could be and had to be ten years on, it only took a year or so—to make that future real.

New competition from outsiders can cause sufficient confusion to sink an organization. Here is how a highly successful CEO in a fast-paced technology business reduced risk and confusion caused by different waves of change approaching at the same time.

WATCH FOR "WAVES OF CHANGE"

I was wrapping up an interview of Brad, the CEO of a New England high-tech firm, fifteen minutes early. On impulse, I asked if he was willing to use the extra time to share his views on leadership. Brad was available until the end of the hour, so he agreed to chat about leadership in his organization.

Brad said his primary job as the organization's leader was preventing his company from succumbing to what he called the "New England Syndrome." He said that waves of change are always coming at organizations from changes in markets, competition, demographic shifts, economics, regulation, technological change and more. Many of the once great businesses that started in New England—firms like Digital Equipment, Wang Laboratories, Polaroid Corporation, Data General, Gillette (which merged with Proctor and Gamble) and others—either failed or were acquired. The New England Syndrome he said "is that they all disappeared under one wave of change that each missed."

Brad then explained how he stays aware of changes by visiting his company's plants in Europe and Asia as well as its customers and suppliers the world over. He had just returned from several weeks visiting competitors in

Asia. He participates regularly in McKinsey's CEO Roundtables and serves on Boards of several publicly traded companies. All this activity produces insights into potential new trends and waves of change.

Once Brad spots a new trend he explained that he discusses it with people all over his organization. When he finds an individual with the interest, experience and willingness to take the lead on understanding that trend, that person attends conferences, follows relevant journals and invites outside experts to brief upper managers on each area of change. Brad stays in touch by listening to updates on information and insights these folks have gathered. His aim is to avoid missing each wave of change by understanding it in time for his company to benefit from each wave.

"As long as I lead this company, we are not going to miss a single wave of change. It is my job to make sure that we don't succumb to the New England Syndrome." Then Brad smiled and changed the subject.

He explained that he has a ten-year-old daughter, and a few weeks earlier her school participated in the Take Your Daughters and Sons to Work Day. His daughter came in to work and spent a day with him in his office. Brad told her that it was a busy day packed with meetings and that he was pleased that she was interested in his work. He was happy she wanted to sit in his office, and she should just sit quietly and listen to what went on.

That night, while driving his daughter home, he asked her how she liked being in Daddy's office while he worked.

She answered:

"Daddy, I came in to your office with you because I thought that I would see you work; but all you did was talk for the whole day—I never saw you do any work."

Had Brad really changed the subject when he began reminiscing about his daughter's comment? He obviously felt accountable for how well he carried out his responsibilities. His schedule and activities suggested long hours, lots of travel, and hard work in addition to talking and listening.

Even people, like Brad's daughter, who are close to a vigilant, caring and self-accountable leader, may not appreciate how hard such a person must work to make sense out of confusing threats. The CEO's own daughter saw her father chatting with people and was disillusioned. She thought she would see her father use physical effort, perhaps because he often came home from work very tired.

But the hard part of her father's job as CEO was to have conversations that clarified concerns and confusion about changes inside and outside his organization. His responsibility as CEO was to engage members of the organization in important conversations about threats and opportunities in order to avoid the fate of other organizations that missed just one wave of change.

As CEO, Brad alone was accountable for how well all parts of the organization worked as a whole. Each new threat or opportunity or challenge put him in a pivotal role. On the surface, Brad's method of finding leaders within the organization to take ownership of threats and opportunities may not have seemed strenuous. However, replacing complacency and confusion with shared meaning, real teamwork and renewed capability and innovation is hard, important work.

LEADERS WHO GET OUT OF THE WAY

We have seen how Brad reduced confusion caused by waves of change. Now let's look at how one individual built his one-man startup into a huge industrial enterprise. He avoided organizational confusion during this growth by handing accountability off to one new coworker at a time as he scaled up the organization.

Leonard Poole, the founder and CEO of Air Products and Chemicals, spoke at the Wharton Business School in the mid Sixties. Poole told an audience of students and faculty his personal story, which had begun with selling industrial gases such as oxygen and nitrogen to steel makers and others. His employer delivered the gas to customers in heavy steel cylinders that were costly to transport. Poole imagined building on-site gaseous liquefaction plants at large customer locations that would cut shipping costs, increase flexibility to meet peaks and valleys in demand, and offer other benefits.

Poole told how he financed his new venture (from his wife's pension savings, if memory serves) and detailed how he hired his first employee. Poole was a salesman who had not gone to college. He needed a smart engineer to design and develop the portable gas liquefaction plant he envisioned. So he sought out the dean of engineering at a local university, explained his plan and asked the dean to recommend the smartest young engineering student graduating that year. The dean introduced Poole to his top student. Poole hired the young engineer as the only other employee of Air Products and Chemicals beside himself, and they developed the air liquefaction plant they needed to start up the business.

By the time Poole spoke at the Wharton School, his firm had grown into a huge industrial enterprise with thousands of employees in the US and overseas. After he spoke, the audience dispersed and Mr. Poole was standing alone at the side of the room. No one from the audience of faculty and B-school students was with him. The reality that one man had grown such a huge company from scratch fascinated me, so I walked up, introduced myself to him and asked how he had grown Air Products and Chemicals.

Poole said that when he started the company, he was alone and did all the work himself. As the business developed he identified activities that he was spending time on, and then searched for people who he could trust to perform them better than he could himself. Then he assigned the activities to those people. This was how the Air Products and Chemicals organization grew, one responsibility, one person at a time, beginning with that first engineer. Leonard Poole's answer was so simple, and clear, that over fifty years later it still stands out for its simplicity.

Creating accountability right for each job from the start, and then stepping aside to let others do what they do best, lets senior managers focus on how the organization is doing as a whole. Leonard Poole apparently scaled up his business without scaling up confusion. Establishing accountability for results, and getting out of the way of those who achieve them, reduces confusion when change comes to a large, troubled organization—as the following example from international banking shows.

Vince had just been appointed head of the Bank's troubled International Banking Division. Although he had no previous international banking experience, he had a proven track record as a tough, no-nonsense, profit-oriented manager who had started up and grown several of the bank's largest business units and turned around several other problem businesses during his long career. This time Vince accepted his biggest challenge so far—to turn around the International Banking Division.

On the recommendation of one of his former managers, Vince interviewed and then hired me as a consultant to form and coach teams of bank personnel in diagnosing and redesigning the international lending process. To kick off our effort Vince asked me to speak to the bank's annual international executive planning meeting, which brought overseas branch heads and international subsidiary bank presidents back to the home office for a week of long range planning. That year's planning week was going to be a bigger deal than ever, because many participants would meet Vince, their new chief, for the first time.

My half hour presentation was the next to last item on the first day's agenda. Vince introduced me and I gave a slide presentation on our approach and timetable. My hope was to reduce people's confusion and anxieties about what would be happening. After the presentation there was time for questions, but there were no questions. A cocktail hour followed and the bar opened. I watched as people began milling around, socializing and chatting with each other.

Just as I began looking for a way to slip away unobtrusively, Vince walked over to me and said quietly: "This is an important project. I am counting on it to produce major results. You may run into problems as you go along. If you do, I want you to come to me immediately. My door is always open to you, and I am your problem solver."

I did not know Vince personally at that time; but people who had worked with him for many years had told me that he was a man of his word. Consulting assignments often place a consultant in ambiguous and confusing situations. Although a client with substantial authority had retained and was paying me, the project's success depended on making needed change without invoking or exercising that client's authority. Ordering people to change things would breed insecurity and risk aversion among organization members. But it turned out that we never needed to ask Vince for help "solving a problem" in the months that followed.

A few months after the kickoff at the international planning meeting, our diagnostic team had identified what needed to change, and it was time to work out how to effect that change. Vince chose about thirty individual bankers from all around his organization to participate in several cross-functional teams. These teams were coached in working out who, what, when and how to make the changes that our diagnostic assessment had found during a week of action planning sessions.

Vince kicked off the planning sessions by telling the room full of people that he had great confidence in them. He also gave me a plug by saying he had heard good things about the team-based change process we were following. But, in line with his reputation, Vince put everyone on notice that he already had his "or else" option in mind when he said: "If you cannot get the results we need the democratic way, then I will get them the authoritarian way."

Vince took his sponsor role seriously—he monitored progress weekly, gave feedback and encouragement and stayed out of the way. During implementation, over a dozen project teams implemented scores of changes. To coordinate teams and projects, an internal consultant from the bank, who had worked on this effort from its first day, made a weekly visit to each action team, checked on progress and problems and reported each team's status to Vince. After each weekly briefing, Vince visited each of the dozen or so teams in person to acknowledge those that were doing well, and to ask any teams that were slipping how he could help them get back on track.

As a sponsor of drastic change, Vince was truly a problem solver—he established accountability and stayed out of the way. Each problem was either solved by those who understood its root causes, or immediately brought to Vince's attention. There was no confusion while making the changes, because people who defined the changes knew that Vince would hold them accountable for success and would help them solve problems blocking that success. This project succeeded without causing disruption; one year after the project ended one of the bank's top international executives said that implementation of the action plans "had been a non-event."

This organization was in serious trouble when Vince took it over; he needed to develop and implement drastic change quickly. Everyone working for him knew his reputation as the bank's problem solver. Instead of choosing one of the mighty consulting firms to solve international banking's credit problems he opted to sponsor a highly visible, high-risk process improvement effort by relying on his own people and the structured change process that they followed. Vince avoided much fear and confusion by giving everyone a choice between becoming part of Vince's solution or being part of Vince's problem.

The next story shows how top management of an organization defeated their own agenda by demanding improvement from their teams while they themselves failed to be the problem solvers for those they led.

LOOK OUT FOR LEADERS MODELING RIDICULOUS BEHAVIOR

There is a simple recipe some senior managers follow to create confusion in the organizational ranks: "Say one thing, and do another." Here's an example.

Several dozen process-improvement teams were trained and within one year completed projects producing over eight million dollars in audited savings. However, many team members complained about problems with their management sponsors. Some improvement sponsors refused to allow teams enough time to solve their problem. Others ordered teams to skip pilot tests of process changes and rush into "big bang" rollouts of new and untested processes. As team member complaints increased, voluntary team formation and project success rates declined. Top management responded to these complaints by mandating that before a manager or executive sponsored an improvement team she or he must attend a one-day training seminar in team sponsorship.

The morning session of team sponsor training walked twenty or so senior managers through a typical team process improvement project from beginning to end. The goal was for the managers and executives to become familiar with what team process improvement is and what tools it uses.

The afternoon session involved participants role-playing "team meets sponsor" scenarios in pairs. Each pair contrasted a "good sponsor" scenario against a "bad sponsor" scenario. Four or five class participants acted out each scenario while the rest of the class observed and documented examples of good and bad sponsor behaviors on sticky notes. After each pair of role plays, the class divided into small groups to discuss good and bad sponsor behaviors and then took turns presenting their insights to the rest of the class.

When a participant selected to play the role of team sponsor read his role sheet, he complained in a loud and angry voice that this role was horrid. He could not possibly act as badly toward any team he sponsored as the role sheet called on him to behave. It was absolutely out of the question. He ranted on: surely no team sponsor who acted this badly worked in our company; these scenarios must be based on other organizations. The bad sponsor's behavior was so terrible that no improvement team in this organization would ever work for this sponsor.

This outburst was so unexpected and disturbing that I nearly panicked. To quiet his complaints, I offered to reassign the bad sponsor role to someone willing to play it and let him play a different role in the next scenario. At this he quieted down and reluctantly said that as bad as this role was, he would try to be the bad sponsor. With that, the rest of the class observed and took notes as the planned scenario unfolded.

As scripted, those playing the team members presented their progress, explained their problems to their (pretend) sponsor and asked for his support or help. However, every time the sponsor responded to a team question or request, all the participants in the room laughed. This was puzzling. I was listening intently and had not heard anything in the dialog worthy of such hilarity.

During the break, I asked a class member what was so funny about the answers the bad sponsor made to the team's requests. The answer was that the man playing the team sponsor role was a gifted mimic. During the scenario, each answer he gave to a team request was a pet "put down" used by one or more senior manager. All class participants recognized who the pretend sponsor was mocking and found his performance hilarious.

The "sponsor's" annoying, loud and inappropriate protests that their management would never act as badly as scripted, set up a parody of management behaviors that people in the class could recognize and enjoy. The awareness that this performance ridiculed their bosses made me feel sad that bad behavior by some senior managers may have defeated the purpose of the training by increasing cynicism among its participants.

As a leader, reduce confusion by checking that your behavior is consistent with how you ask others to behave. One way to do this is to have a neutral observer (perhaps an independent executive coach) tally how well your words and actions model your organization's values and purpose. Then act on your coach's feedback. Use such a behavioral feedback approach with great care, however. The next section shows how another top manager generated confusion and cynicism when he talked the improvement talk but didn't walk the talk.

LEADERS BEWARE—YOUR ACTIONS SPEAK LOUDER THAN WORDS

The kickoff of a corporation's "excellence" transformation program began with a three-day top management development program on performance excellence. During training, the top 55 leaders from the CEO down assessed their current management system against the Baldrige management system model. At the end of the training, the participants organized into teams. For example, the CEO, his direct reports and other senior officers formed an executive leadership team. The heads of Marketing, Sales, Customer Satisfaction and Field Service joined the customer-focus team led by the top marketing executive, and so on.

Each action team assessed the strengths and opportunities for improvement in its designated area and developed action plans for improvement. After the training, all the teams met and began carrying out their plans with help from an experienced improvement coach. After several months of follow up on action plans, the improvement coach called me to say she was leaving the firm. She said she had recommended that the company retain me to continue coaching the excellence effort until her permanent replacement could be found.

I was willing, and everyone involved from the CEO down knew me from the original training and self-assessment. The firm hired me to continue coaching their effort on a month-to-month basis, until they appointed a new coach. On her last day the outgoing manager briefed me on developments since the training, which had ended several months earlier.

The coach had used participation in team meetings and conference calls, along with progress on tasks completed, to measure progress. At the start, participation was high and all teams made significant progress implementing the tasks in their plans. After a few months, though, the CEO and other senior executives began skipping team meetings and conference calls. They also began to pay greater attention to upsets and work-related problems, which forced managers reporting to them to work in fire-fighting mode.

Before she resigned, the outgoing coach had surveyed all 55 participants about why participation on improvement had dropped. Her analysis of survey results listed 25 significant problems, which she shared with me. She also handed over files of survey data and a copy of a presentation of survey results that she had made to an "executive steering team." With that, I was in the hot seat.

On my first day, an experienced manager helped me perform a spider-web analysis of the 25 issues the survey found to be interfering with progress. We drew a Pareto bar chart of out-arrow counts for all 25 problems on the spider web diagram. The Pareto diagram's 25 bars started with the highest out-arrow count bar on the left, and ran downhill like a ski run to the lowest out-arrow count bar on the right. The three tallest bars on the left showed which three problems were hurting progress the most. These three problems drove almost all disengagement: (1) conflicting priorities between "the requirements of my day job" and "spending time on the excellence transformation;" (2) lack of senior executive involvement in reviewing team progress; and (3) the executive steering team fails to help individual teams resolve problems they encounter that block progress.

Several survey respondents also commented that they knew managers who had gotten into trouble (including one who was fired) when day-to-day performance slipped, but no one had gotten into any trouble for failing to fulfill obligations on the excellence implementation teams. After reviewing the spider-web analysis with my management contact, he arranged for me to brief the CEO on my analysis of survey results.

The meeting with the CEO began with me explaining the survey (the former coach's work) and the spider-web analysis of the survey data. After I had walked the CEO through the analysis of one problem (out of 25) on the spider-web diagram, he silently studied the diagram for a long moment. Then he looked up and said: "If I understand this diagram correctly, it says that to find out why the excellence program is in trouble, I should look at myself in the mirror." I replied that I would not have stated the root cause quite that way because we should always look for the "what" and "why" and avoid assignments of blame. Without further comment, our meeting ended. A few days later my management contact called to say that the CEO had cancelled my coaching contract.

This experience made me wonder. What might have happened if the CEO realized that solving day-to-day operating problems and leading his dedicated and capable management team in systematic prevention of future upsets were not an either-or choice. Could he have found a way to balance both progress on management system improvements and resolving and preventing day-to-day operational problems?

When performance falls short of an organizational leader's expectations, leaders should look themselves in the mirror to understand their role. Here is how a great leader taught a lesson in self-preservation with a kick in the butt to a future New York cabby who forgot to look out for himself.

WHEN TRUE LEADERS CARE—IT MAY HURT

As the cab pulled away from the Shuttle Terminal at LaGuardia on the way to a Wall Street destination the cabby asked where I had flown in from. When he heard that I was from Boston and worked for Arthur D. Little (ADL) a consulting firm near Boston, he asked: "Is that the outfit that General James

Gavin works for?" I told him that General Gavin was our Chairman of the Board, to which the cabby replied,

"Your boss kicked me in the ass once."

I thought that I had misheard the man so I asked: "Excuse me, what was that? What did you say?"

The cabby answered:

"Your boss kicked me in the ass once when I was in the 82nd Airborne during World War II. I jumped during the Normandy landing on D-Day. After I landed, I took cover behind a hedge. I was looking around for other members of my unit when, whack—someone gave me a sharp kick in the ass. I turned around to see who the hell it was and there was "Jumpin Jim" himself—General Gavin—looking right at me.

Gavin said to me, 'Soldier, if you want to keep that, keep it down,' and then he moved away."

I told the cabby I had never heard General Gavin referred to as "Jumpin' Jim." The cabby replied that everyone in the 82nd Airborne called him Jumpin' Jim because General James Gavin always jumped with his troops. When I asked him what his troops thought of General Gavin he answered:

"We knew he cared about us."

Why had the cabby small-talked his way into sharing an experience from his youth, years earlier? He wanted me to appreciate that working under a leader who cared sometimes felt like a kick in the butt when a trooper became confused. With that kick General "Jumpin' Jim" Gavin showed leadership that was real and personal.

Great teachers go beyond caring; they sense and resolve confusion in those they teach. In this regard some great teachers can be role models for leaders who must resolve confusion in those they lead. The next section shows how.

OUR FIRST LEADERS: GREAT TEACHERS

Leadership is a buzzword that often conceals confusion. Here is how a room full of scientists and engineers increased clarity on leadership behaviors that energized their research efforts.

During an executive development program for top managers of a large research and development laboratory a heated discussion erupted about how they lead their R & D organization to excellence. Most of the forty plus members of the class were Ph.D.'s in scientific or engineering fields and had strong feelings about leadership, which apparently they had never discussed. So they were questioning what values, traits and standards of behavior the laboratory's leadership should encourage in role models for systematic improvement of excellence in the lab's research and design outcomes.

As senior staff members in a large research lab, all the participants had shared the graduate student experience of research leadership by their best teachers. I wanted to end their debate and restart their discussion about research leadership on familiar territory. So, I wrote the heading "MY BEST TEACHER" at the top of a blank flip chart page and asked everyone in the room to think of the best teacher each had ever had.

After a few minutes, class members began naming their best teachers' qualities. One person called out, "My best teacher really knew the subject she taught." So I wrote that under the heading. Another said, "Mine was passionate about the subject he taught." Within minutes the following list was on the flip chart page:

MY BEST TEACHER

- Really knew the subject
- Was passionate about the subject he taught
- Made the subject interesting and exciting
- Made me want to learn more about the subject
- Set high standards
- Demanded my best work
- Was extremely critical
- Made me work hard
- Cared whether I was learning
- Was available when needed and gave me helpful criticism

- Was helpful when I needed help
- Explained confusing subjects clearly and simply
- Related the subject to real problems

When the flow of ideas dried up, I used a felt tip pen to cross out the word TEACHER and write LEADER, while explaining that the characteristics of their best teachers were also the characteristics of leaders who were able to guide and inspire research. The teacher who excelled at stimulating interest, curiosity, collaboration, experimentation and learning was a role model for leading scientists and engineers. Each class member had at least twenty years of education so their best teachers were the top ranked teachers from many.

These outstanding teachers had developed future engineers and scientists by setting high standards based on wisdom, upholding those standards, generating enthusiasm, encouraging, helping and coaching students through confusion. The great teachers encouraged their students to aspire to higher goals than they would have set without that encouragement. Then the teachers helped each student learn and develop in ways that let them exceed their highest aspirations. Great leaders do all those things for those they lead.

The parallel of great teachers with great leaders may not apply in all situations, but it resonated with that class of scientists and engineers for whom independent critical thinking was a lifestyle. For them leadership came in the form of wonder, enthusiasm, ambition, encouragement and learning—not directives and commands. By refocusing the class's understanding of leadership behavior in their research setting, this exercise replaced confusion with concrete behaviors they could adapt and emulate to stimulate discovery by helping, trusting and supporting each other's research.

Confusion in mid-organization has convinced some ambitious people to take leadership into their own hands when legitimate to do so. The next section shows how organizational confusion stimulated many energetic people working in mid-organization with little formal authority to lead people on pathways out of confusion.

BECOME THE LEADER YOU HAVE BEEN LOOKING FOR

Most graduate students in my courses are mid-career managers working in large organizations. They return for graduate studies to gain knowledge and new skills they need to tackle larger challenges and add greater value in their work. Unfortunately, many students of process improvement expressed frustration with leadership in their organizations.

Toward the end of each semester, top performing students in class after class made private comments such as:

"I'm tired of waiting for the top management to set direction and lead. Please tell me how I can lead from the middle of my organization."

"How can I take the initiative for necessary changes when my department head opposes any change that does not come down from higher ups?"

"How can I establish the legitimacy of changes I know we need to make when I have no authority in several areas that must be involved in those changes?"

"I thought my department suffered from poor processes. But studying process improvement made me realize that we suffer from a lack of leadership. I conclude that I must become the leader I have been looking for."

Each manager/graduate student saw opportunities for improvement in organizational "white spaces" where responsibility for action had fallen between boxes on organization charts. Some had already taken ownership of problems and opportunities in the "no man's land" between functions on a chart. Although these students lacked formal authority or informal empowerment to foster changes, they were eager to step outside their formal responsibilities, with some coaching and guidelines on legitimizing their leading initiatives without authority from mid-organization.

During each semester students used process-design tools and systems thinking methods to turn knowledge from literature research and past experiences into a detailed Leadership from the Middle (LftM) process. Students started the design process by completing Is/Is-Not tables similar to Figure 4 to clarify what each person's opportunity to lead from mid organization without formal authority is (and is not).

They also created a similar table to use in engaging others they would lead in defining a "Goldilocks" opportunity—not too big, not too small, but just right.

IS	IS NOT
• For good people who care about the success of the whole organization enough to take risks.	• For those who care only about self interest and getting credit
• Ethical ways to develop new skills	• Proven way to get promoted
• An extra effort, outside your regular job responsibility	• Something that will hurt your regular job performance
• Connecting and collaborating with others (people/units/agencies)	• US versus THEM
• Learning from many small successes and failures	• Instant home runs and "batting a thousand"
• Informal and loose circle of people willing to collaborate and help each other at the start	• A team at the start
• Risky and therefore stressful (butterfly feelings)	• Sure to succeed
• Adaptive and evolutionary using cycles of trying, inspecting what happens and learning	• A preplanned, rigid project on a fixed schedule
• Areas of change that many concerned people believe will make things much better.	• Going it alone or "rocking the boat"
• *Starting by understanding why people feel the status quo is "the right way to do things."*	• *Blindly accepting hidden assumptions buried in their thinking.*
• Drilling down to root causes by asking "What?" and "Why?" but never "Who?"	• Acting out of panic or confusion or finding fault and blaming people
• Negotiating with give and take by relying on trust and influence	• Using power to command change

Figure 4 — What Leadership from the Middle IS and IS NOT

Figure 5 shows a high level flowchart of one such process. The class developed requirements that each stage of the Leadership from the Middle (LftM) process must meet. Then they created comprehensive checklists of tasks that met those requirements in each stage the process of leading from mid organization. Each individual student then tailored the generic checklists to his or her leadership opportunity or challenge. Students discussed their initiatives and their experiences and problems in class throughout the semester. Because many students had ten or fifteen years of experience, class discussions added great value to insights obtained from the literature. Appendix F — Leading from the Middle of Your Organization (LftM) provides greater detail on the ideal process design developed in a typical class.

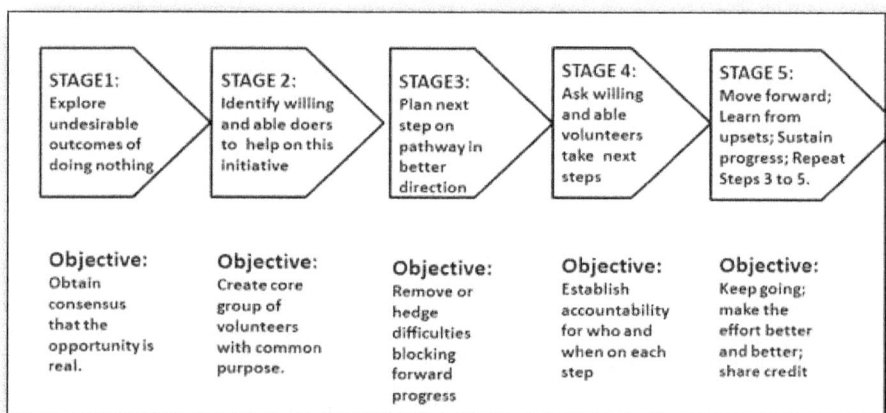

Figure 5 — Stages of a Leadership from the Middle Process

Leadership from the middle speeds up innovation and adaptation when top leaders encourage such initiatives. In five years of leading this seminar three or four students in each class have worked their way through significant success stories, and many more students were on promising paths toward future successes. A significant number of students have earned promotions based on successful initiatives on which they took the lead. The following example of leading from the middle of an organization (LftM) comes from a woman who was a member of the fourth LftM class in 2013.

An LftM student was responsible for educational programs in a non-profit organization that helps at-risk urban youths. Among other programs, the organization provides college scholarships to deserving college-bound youths. The class member realized that members of the Board of Directors had differing views on scholarship policy. Members representing donors funding the scholarships wanted to offer substantial scholarships that could have a major impact on the most deserving applicants. A second faction wanted to spread the scholarship money as widely as possible by granting small scholarships so that as many youths as possible could start their college educations. Board members had strong feelings on one side or the other.

The class member decided to begin leading from mid organization to help resolve this policy debate. She used an incremental approach based on the LftM process designed in class. Over three months, she formulated a plan, focused on a feasible scope and enlisted a helper responsible for the scholarship program to work with her. First she organized and ran focus groups of three segments of scholarship recipients: current students, alumni and those who dropped out of college. Using focus group inputs, she developed a survey, reviewed it with the manager of the scholarship program, and e-mailed the survey to all previous scholarship recipients for whom e-mail addresses were on file. She also surveyed past change incidents in the organization, and aligned her effort with the organization's mission and planning goals.

After analyzing the survey responses, the LftM student briefed the organization's Board of Directors on her findings. Most scholarship recipients preferred spreading available funds over as many recipients as possible, as this approach aligned with the organization's mission. Open-ended comments by past scholarship recipients showed a mature attitude toward the wide distribution of scholarships. However, a significant number of respondents said they would have liked the opportunity to compete for higher scholarship amounts.

Board members welcomed this first-hand input from scholarship recipients. A subcommittee of the Board read all verbatim survey responses, including many "thank-you" comments from past scholarship recipients. The past scholarship recipients' high level of approval of the status quo—small scholarships that maximized the number of scholarship recipients—resolved the Board's debate about scholarship policy.

Now the organization is seeking sponsors to fund a second layer of larger scholarships for highly qualified applicants. Within two years, the woman who took this initiative was promoted to the position of Outcomes and Evaluation Manager for the whole organization – a significant increase in her responsibilities.

CONCLUSION

From army generals to naval officers, from research scientists to middle managers enrolled in graduate programs, from world class industrial CEOs to International Bankers—leaders at all organizational levels coach those they lead by replacing confusion and random actions with cooperative change for the better. These leaders negotiate and focus systematic efforts on helping people learn and grow.

Stories in this chapter have shown how leaders looked ahead to better organizations; better ways of helping people work together; better futures for coworkers, customers and business partners; better ways to anticipate and benefit from future threats; better service to customers than competitors deliver; and better returns to investors. Few ever referred to their perspective as "a vision." They each faced forward and set courses for better and brighter futures for their organizations and themselves; then they helped people solve the problems and remove the roadblocks preventing progress.

The next chapter shifts the focus to individual contributors. It invites you to consider what's in it for the people of an organization to excel at their work. In chapter four we will look at the innate drives that motivate great performance and how the mistaken belief that money motivates top performance often produces more confusion and problems than it solves.

Confusion About What's In It For You

WHY MOTIVATION WORKS WHILE INCENTIVES FAIL

The fourth type of confusion common in work environments arises from a fundamental misunderstanding of what motivates individuals to work toward organizational and personal goals. People often confuse incentives with drives. A drive, such as self-enhancement, is an inner hunger for a favorable view of yourself and your actions which those around you also share. This drive differs from a monetary reward or incentive, which feeds people's greed. Drives such as self-enhancement are similar to hunger, they cannot be ignored.

The following executive preview summarizes lessons about distinguishing between motivation and engagement of head, heart and hands versus striving to drive employees' work performance with incentive pay:

1: Ask whether your pay schemes distract attention from important operational signals such as: unwanted employee attrition; customer attrition, processing effort that adds no value, unfair supervision, or failing to innovate in ways that keep old customers loyal and attract new customers.

2: Recognize and reward those who resolve bottlenecks blocking achievement of the organization's mission and purpose. Expect unpleasant side effects when you dangle rewards in front of people who lack real methods and the capacity to deliver better outcomes.

3: Avoid managing by magic—do not demand results when there are no means to produce them. Prevent damage caused by linking incentives to performance targets that are beyond people's and processes' capabilities. People's drive to look good and desire for incentive payments may tempt some to resort to tricks, game outcomes and create the illusion of results better than what is possible. Instead, build better processes that produce the results you seek.

4: Ensure that people work in lean, well-maintained and consistently improving processes that attract and satisfy customers. A new pay scheme is not a process improvement. Process performance in sales, and many other areas, depends on factors such as customer expectations, people's job skills, practices, the process followed, process outcomes and then, perhaps pay.

5: Do not waste the creativity of your workforce. Paying piece by piece for completed work sounds like a direct way to right size pay for performance. However those doing the work know more about their work than anyone else. When costs are too high, a simple and direct approach—training and leading your employees in reducing waste—is powerful. The mind is power.

6: Invest in prevention and you will get what you pay for. Put a stop to upsets, errors, and operations and services that spontaneously combust. When you reward those who thrive on crises and fighting fires, you will have lots of upsets, errors and "fire-fighting." The return on investing in prevention is many times larger than the losses incurred and bonuses paid to fight preventable fires.

7: Appreciate and thank people when they make special efforts. Most employees who work with others to achieve stretch goals prefer being thanked by people they respect to receiving bonuses.

Two students recently graduated from Penn with master's degrees. One earned an MBA from the Wharton School and started work on Wall Street at a salary and bonus of about $180,000; the second earned a MS in Psychology and began work as a school psychologist at an annual salary of about $60,000. Does the three-to-one difference in their salaries show which graduate is more engaged in her work?

Management folklore says that about ten percent of employees are "money-driven." When these one out of ten are asked what they want out of work, even those who are already well-paid say more money. Perhaps if the young MBA is one of the money-driven ten percent, her high salary may induce her to work harder and better. The other ninety percent expect fair pay for their work. Assuming the school psychologist assesses her salary as fair, does the fact that it's lower than her Wall Street counterpart cause her to work less diligently or care less as she counsels youngsters who need help? What do you think?

> More than twenty years ago the editor of a professional journal for benefits and compensation managers asked me to write an article on the role of compensation in improving organizational productivity. In my twenty years of improving productivity and quality of service organizations, incentive compensation had never come up as an effective way to improve processes and boost productivity. Some people lack motivation to improve; but more lack managers and supervisors who can actually teach and coach them on how to improve.
>
> The editor strongly agreed: "Yes—productivity does not arise from compensation systems. But senior executives routinely ask benefits and compensation managers to design and implement incentives to improve organizational productivity and profitability."
>
> The article, entitled, Paying for Productivity: A Concept Revisited, appeared in the summer 1987 issue of *Compensation & Benefits Management*. It showed how confusion caused by viewing incentive pay as a quick fix engendered a long list of productivity woes and realities that managers capable of actually improving organizational performance must address.

Often top managers look at incentives after management has failed to change work in ways that make it easier and less error-prone. Work performance begins with fair compensation of people for their work. However improvement takes training and coaching of those doing the work in how to use their knowledge, thinking and creativity to change that work for the better. Here is how a confused insurance CEO's belief in incentives delayed facing the reality that his company's productivity problem endangered its existence.

WHY DID MORE BONUSES YIELD LESS PRODUCTIVITY?

An insurance company's sales force was suffering from skyrocketing attrition of experienced sales people, and sales were on a sharp downtrend. The CEO had started decades earlier as a salesman, and with the conviction of a good salesman explained that the productivity problem was due to unenthusiastic selling efforts when he asked for help solving his "sales force productivity problem."

Two years earlier the CEO had recruited a senior executive from a leading sales incentive firm and put him in charge of "sales promotion." The new sales promotion executive installed an incentive scheme that rewarded salespeople who produced year-to-year sales gains each month. If a sales rep's July sales this year were 25 percent higher than last year's July sales, the rep earned a large bonus. For months that showed year-over-year sales increases smaller than 25 percent reps earned their salary but no bonus.

The first year with new incentives sales rose a few percentage points, but, while many reps earned substantial bonuses, the sales force turnover skyrocketed. Within two years the incentives added $40 million to annual selling expenses but total sales volume was below pre-incentive levels. Worse yet, many of the company's top sales people were leaving to work for competitors. The company was temporarily saved because its investment earnings offset operating losses. Interviews of a cross section of field sales reps and sales managers turned up the following insights.

When the incentives were new, sales reps pushed hard to earn bonuses, but the flow of leads and prospects stayed the same. So, sales people could not sustain a sales pace high enough to max out their incentive bonuses every month. A few figured out that they could look at their sales rate in the first week of a month and their prior year's total sales for that month and ascertain whether they had a chance to max out that month's bonus. If the first week of the month's sales were high and the prior year's sales for that month were low, a rep would close as many sales as needed to max out the bonus. But, if sales in the first week of the month were low and the prior year's sales for the following month were also low, sales reps shifted as many sales as possible to the next month to maximize next month's bonus.

Timing sales to game the bonus system worked like a charm. After two years every rep in the sales force of several thousand was timing his or her sales to max out incentive earnings. Also top-producing sales people were joining competitors at a fearsome rate, "for the same reason they joined the company—a better future and an income," as one resigning rep explained.

No one in top management was aware of how the sales force was gaming sales. But interviews of sales people also revealed something else. The company's product line featured whole-life products but the market was shifting to universal and term life policies that offered higher amounts of insurance coverage at lower monthly premiums. The top producers who were leaving had figured out they could triple their incomes by selling term and universal life policies, which were much easier to sell than expensive, lower face-value whole-life policies.

The CEO's theory of unenthusiastic sales effort and his reliance on incentives had caused confusion and delayed discovery of the root cause of poor sales productivity by two years. Fortunately, one of the sales productivity improvement plans the company's team developed was to field test a more competitive product in several market areas that suffered from the worst "sales productivity" problems.

One of the company's subsidiaries already offered a universal life policy in a few states. So the company met with regulators to qualify salespeople in several of their worst performing markets to sell those universal life policies. Within months, sales reps that had previously been considered marginal producers doubled or tripled sales with no incentives other than commissions, which also rose. The company acted on these tests results, which saved it from being acquired.

The insurance CEO had been confused about the cause of poor sales performance, and therefore how to achieve better sales performance. He assumed that setting higher targets for others to achieve would make them sell more. Wishing for more sales by the magic incentives did not and could never solve the real problems making sales worse. The next story shows how a confused executive responded to his bonus formula with magic instead of by championing improvement.

MAGIC IS NOT A MANAGEMENT METHOD

Magic is the illusion that a surprising outcome can come about without any means to produce that outcome—like pulling a rabbit out of a hat. In other words, it's a trick. Here is an example of an executive who confused magic with managing.

A new logistics executive was hired away from a large conglomerate to operate a distribution system. After a poor start, he proposed a multi-million dollar investment in a new warehouse management system to replace a system that had been installed just four years earlier. The firm's executive committee tabled his proposal and formed a cross-functional team to diagnose the warehouse's processes and recommend improvements rather than buying another new system. After hard work the cross-functional team arrived at the following diagnosis.

Shortly after the new head of logistics arrived, the industrial engineers (who reported to him) presented to their new boss revised productivity standards for several warehouses. The newly hired executive reacted to the new standards by ordering the industrial engineers to raise their productivity targets by twenty percent. The head of industrial engineering protested that the revised standards were already tight by competitive norms, but the new boss overruled his objections with claims that the warehouse workforce was not working hard enough.

The new standards were loaded into the warehouse management system and the warehouse workers, who knew none of the background, immediately discovered that they could not keep up with the higher work pace. When overloaded workers fell behind by mid-morning, some began skipping items that customers had ordered. To cover this, they reported those items as out of stock, even though they were actually on the warehouse shelves. Eventually, the whole warehouse work force adopted this hush-hush ploy of skipping work to make their picking quotas and kept it secret even from their supervisors.

This resulted in a sharp drop in warehouse service levels to customers, which the new management blamed on the warehouse inventory management system. Reporting items out of stock, when they were actually on the shelf, made physical inventory records inaccurate. So a staff of four auditors was hired full time to audit and update inventory records. Also, damage from omitting items from orders rippled through to customers, generating higher costs and demoralizing people across the organization.

When the team reported its findings to its executive sponsor (who outranked the logistics manager) they found out that the new logistic executive's bonus depended on increasing warehouse throughput. When his arbitrary goal setting resulted in widespread problems, he tried deflecting attention away from his ignorance of warehouse operations by blaming the warehouse workers and rigging the warehouse management system to speed them up.

The new logistics manager's actions confused magic with management. Management magicians demand better results in the belief that people will magically produce those results. When people do produce surprising results, more often than not, they do it the same way that magicians do—by inventing new tricks that fool those watching.

If you ask managers who set arbitrary targets, "How will your people achieve those results?" do not be surprised if they answer, "That's their problem." Few management magicians can describe practical methods for hitting the higher targets they demand. Their confusion arises from ignorance: of how to lead those doing the work in using simple tools and methods to improve processes; and to boost results by cutting wasted effort, delay and error.

Sales people and managers are not the only folks in organizations who can be confused by incentives. The next section shows how a confused management paid incentives that distorted the working of a heavy equipment manufacturing plant.

HOW TO RUIN AN ORGANIZATION WITH REWARDS

A second form of management by magic ties rewards to desired outcomes without ensuring that people have whatever they need to achieve those outcomes. Here is an example from manufacturing.

Our team was diagnosing why parts made in a heavy equipment manufacturing plant often failed to arrive on schedule for assembly into finished machines. Because of the delays, rows of partially assembled machines sat in the final assembly area, each wearing red cardboard tags tied at locations on the machines to make it easier to install missing parts when they arrived.

To solve this problem, the plant hired five fulltime expediters, each of whom worked from a weekly "hot list" of parts needed in the assembly area that week. "Hot" parts were parts that delayed completion of a machine scheduled for assembly that week because they were not available in the assembly area. Each expediter started in final assembly and backtracked through the factory along the route of each such part, looking for batches of partly finished work. When the expediter found the delayed parts, he or she ordered the supervisor in that area to finish those parts and rush them to final assembly.

At the expediter's order, each supervisor "broke the setup" for whatever they were working on to set up and complete a batch of hot parts. Hundreds of these daily interruptions had thrown the factory into turmoil. Each expedited part interrupted the regularly scheduled production of other parts, wasting production capacity, and delaying the parts that were scheduled to be made that day.

To find out why, the team sorted data from a year's worth of weekly hot lists to find out which parts showed up most often in the past year. The hottest parts were expedited in half or more of the fifty weeks studied (there were no hot lists for the plant's two-week vacation period). Even though this plant had not assembled a complete machine from on-hand parts in several years, no manager could explain why so many parts had to be expedited.

A team member worked with Bill, an accountant who knew the factory, to follow the trails of the top twenty hottest part numbers through the plant and count the number of unfinished units on hand by location. Their search was made harder because hot parts were often buried under loads of other parts or hidden out of sight. After much searching, the pair tracked down all in-process inventories of the twenty hottest parts.

Bill and the team member had expected frequently expedited parts to be scarce. Instead they found more than a year's supply of work in progress for all twenty parts. This was really confusing —why weren't these parts being finished and sent to the final assembly line as scheduled? After showing the hot part data to supervisors in areas with the most chronically hot parts on hand, one supervisor explained what was going on.

Several years earlier, management had installed a piecework pay system to control labor costs. As each new part was designed, an industrial engineer estimated the labor needed to make that part and then converted the time estimate for each operation into a labor cost, called the piecework rate for that task. Each worker was paid the piecework rate for each operation performed on a part. Payment was made whether or not the parts were of good quality, which was a separate issue. However, the industrial engineers set some piecework rates too generously, and others, called "short pay" rates, were set too low.

A skilled operator could earn a day's pay with just a few hours' work on parts with generous piecework rates. But rates on short pay parts were often set so low that an operator who worked eight hours might be paid for just three hours of work. All operators knew which parts were which, and no operator would work on short pay parts unless his or her supervisor gave a direct order. But because forcing people to work on short pay batches poisoned a supervisor's working relationships, no supervisor would force people to work on short pay parts just to keep another department on schedule.

When an expediter came along and directly ordered the supervisor to make enough parts to get that week's final production out the door, blame for forcing someone to sacrifice a fair day's pay shifted from supervisor to the expediter. The expeditors were like tourists in the plant. They had no close working relations with anyone actually making parts. So, supervisors blamed the expediter for ordering workers to work on short pay parts. The supervisor also spread the financial pain of short pay by asking operators to take turns working on hot parts. The team also learned that workers hid batches of short pay parts that arrived in their area so that expediters could not find them.

Relying on drives such as greed and selfishness by incenting people with money bonuses or incentives stimulates dark-side behaviors capable of producing chaos and confusion. As a last resort, people maximize their incentives even if doing so is ruinous. Incentives seem to be easy management tools. But in reality, money talks so loudly that it may drown out warning signs and overpower common sense and integrity.

This plant's managers had confused their assumption that workers would not produce unless their pay depended on it with reality. In reality, without supervisors who coached and led workers in thinking through and making improvements, the plant would always be unable to compete against other manufacturers that respected and benefited from the thinking of their workforce. This plant, (with several thousand jobs) like many others, was put out of business by foreign competitors. Foreign managers learned from inspiring Americans like Frank Polkinghorn, W. Edwards Deming and Joseph Juran, of the need to deal directly with the realities of workers and work.

When people see money, they focus their attention on the money and equate maximizing payoff with doing their job right—even if it bankrupts their employer. The next section shows how this confusion spoiled well-intentioned bonus and recognition programs in a bank.

STOP ENCOURAGING WRONG BEHAVIORS BY REWARDING THE RIGHT THINGS INSTEAD

Reward and recognition programs send powerful signals to people in organizations. If all the rewards and recognition go to those who work hard fighting fires, and no one recognizes fire prevention efforts, firebugs will prosper. Confusion arises because reacting to problems when they pop up is visible; however, work that prevents problems is not.

An assessment of opportunities for improvement in a bank's management system revealed that the bank operated about two dozen reward and recognition programs. However most of the bank's reward and recognition awards worked against improvement. The human resources department records showed that over ninety percent of hundreds of the thousands of dollars in bonuses paid that year had gone to people who had put out fires. The bank rewarded people for heroic efforts cleaning up after problems and disasters.

Paying nine people bonuses for putting out fires for every one employee rewarded for preventing fires makes little sense, because the firefighting will never end. There were too few rewards for preventing process upsets and errors. The people who kept the bank out of trouble day in and day out were "just doing their jobs".

The briefing of the bank's top management reported this finding as an opportunity to refocus the bank's reward and recognition programs on quality assurance and prevention of customer "ouches." When the CEO heard this recommendation, he turned to his HR director and asked if there were data on bonuses, incentive and recognition awards. The HR director reported that data on all such activity was available monthly and broken down by department and reasons for awards.

Right then, the CEO told his management team that he expected them to award at least 25 percent of all monetary reward and recognition to employees who took initiatives that reduced error rates and service problems before they impacted customers or bank operations. He also asked the HR department to monitor and report to him monthly on the total of reward, recognition and training spending on prevention versus total spending on awards for cleaning up after damage was done.

Two years later, the bank's Vice President of Service Quality spoke at a service quality conference. The speaker opened by saying he was presenting results from two years of effort spent following up on feedback from a Baldrige assessment the bank had run on its management system. To my surprise, his first slide credited the author with performing that assessment. The banker presented charts and graphs showing impressive improvement trends in bank financial results, customer satisfaction, service levels and favorable cost trends. Many improvements were probably sparked by the greater recognition of employees whose prevention and improvement efforts had formerly been invisible and unrecognized. The people who assured high quality service, prevented problems and improved customer experiences were finally being recognized for working toward excellence.

Prior to this assessment, the bank's reward and recognition incentives were trapped in the WYSIATI (What You See Is All There Is) fallacy. Trouble attracts attention, while preventive efforts are out of sight. Rewarding visible firefighters added cost and damaged value for customers and bank profitability. In contrast, rewarding people who found new ways to prevent upsets added value and cut costs by delivering more nearly trouble- and error-free services.

A survey of over 10,000 employees of a consumer products company asked employees when they felt their work was most valued. The top four responses were: 1) When someone important to them, such as a peer or customer, said: "Thank you." 2) When they were asked for their input or for help. 3) When they had a chance to work on something they liked; and, 4) When they were a member of a winning team. Fewer than one hundred of the 10,000 employees responding mentioned pay or promotions.

CONCLUSION

If you answer the question, What's in it for me to work here? by stating that your job pays well, then consider your answer a red warning flag. Don't confuse high pay with producing real value for yourself and those who depend on you. Organizational cultures are shaped by the "4 Ps"— pay, promotion, privilege and punishment. The examples in this chapter have shown just how confused people become when bonuses, rewards, privileges and incentives send wrong or conflicting messages.

The fourth "P", punishment, consists of blaming, fault finding and making threats to job security. This negative force uses fear to shape people's perceptions of which behaviors are not legitimate. Fear discourages risk taking and experimentation, which in turn reduces learning and produces lower returns.

The next chapter deals with a behavior that causes much organizational confusion —blaming and scapegoating. The sections of the chapter invite you into classrooms, boardrooms, client offices and international banks to see how to replace blaming, fear, cover-ups and confusion with genuine problem solving. Replacing blame by finding the root causes of trouble leads to solutions that lessen trouble, improve morale and replace confusion with clarity on how to solve problems.

Confusion About Who Caused This Mess

ROOTING OUT CAUSES OF ORGANIZATIONAL PROBLEMS– WITHOUT BLAMING

O rganization members who seek someone to blame for the mess they are in and then point fingers at scapegoats are not facing reality. They are like members of a ship's crew who feel safe and snug standing high on the rear deck of a ship, blaming the forward deck crew as the ship sinks bow first.

The experiences in this chapter spotlight organizational confusion caused by going hard on people while going easy on critical processes and practices. These experiences came from a supermarket chain, an international bank, a large Internet service provider, an electronics manufacturer, a real estate organization, and a professional football coach. The following executive preview summarizes one or more lessons from each of this chapter's stories.

1: Go easy on your people and hard on your processes. When problems arise, first ask, "Where did our process let us down and why?" instead of asking who to blame.

2: Go and see for yourself. Gather facts about problems first hand; always ask for proof when people offer opinions and guesses. When seeking root causes of trouble make your motto: In God we trust; all others bring facts not opinions.

3: Avoid pushing the punishment button of the 4 Ps (Pay, Promotions, Privilege and Punishment) when things go wrong. Instead, pass the heat up and the credit down.

4: Strengthen capability and accountability for ensuring that things go right; recognize those who quietly prevent things from going wrong.

5: Assure quality work through such proven approaches as: a right sized workforce, job aids, quality checklists, clear work instructions, agile work designs, job skill training, one-point refresher training, coaching, cross-checks, redundancy and error proofing, and listening to and constantly using customer feedback to spark creativity and innovation.

6: Get a head start on making every customer happy. Select and train people who are emotionally "hard wired" with traits that serve customers well. Seek people who feel energized by helping customers. Avoiding poor hiring decisions is one of the best ways to prevent "people problems."

7: Avoid embarrassing individuals when customer service slips. Avoid ranking individuals to show who is letting the team down. Instead retrain and coach the whole team in how to excel with one-point training in the right way to please customers.

8: Insist that root-cause investigations be based on data, facts and direct observations of problems that re-occur. Write answers to why questions in red type when they are opinions or guesses. Write factual answers in black type. The ratio of black to red predicts problem-solving effectiveness.

9: Assure quality by error proofing work in tasks that rely on human effort. Human errors committed during processing roll through the rest of a process and damage customer experience.

10: Expect any process operating normally to produce random static in the form of variation in outcomes. Variations that deviate significantly from normal static—upsets—are worth investigating to find the root cause. Finding and removing root causes of upsets prevents them from happening again and often opens the door to improved process outcomes.

11: Paying managers to praise or punish employees for random defects in process outcomes hurts morale and wastes effort. Ranking employee performance on the basis of random ups and downs in process outcomes creates a lottery.

12: Do not confuse people you trust personally with people whose first-hand knowledge you trust when making important decisions. Even trustworthy people express opinions and make guesses. For important decisions, rely on first-hand knowledge of the employees accountable for outcomes.

13: Take the advice of an NFL Football coach. Avoid putting people in "blame frames" when coaching changes and improvements. Instead use "learn frames" to coach people to improve, and they will excel when they work in "win frame" mode.

DRILL DOWN, DON'T BEAT DOWN

After several months of coaching, a process-improvement team made a mid-point progress report to its sponsor, Gil, the chain's CFO. The team had been working to find ways to reduce supermarket store maintenance expenses, which were higher than industry benchmarks. After their presentation Gil asked the team to repeat the presentation to Harry, the chain's CEO and Gil's boss.

The team's presentation to Harry took place during a regular executive committee meeting that Harry chaired. Each team member gave a show-and-tell on the parts of the project that he or she had worked on. Midway through the presentation, Tom, a mechanic, was explaining a chart when Harry, the CEO, interrupted him. Speaking in an irritated tone of voice Harry said, "I know who's to blame for that mess," and began naming and blaming a scapegoat for the problem that the mechanic had just described.

The CEO's accusatory tone surprised and momentarily upset me. Our team of mechanics, system analysts, finance specialists and a store manager had worked hard gathering facts on the store maintenance process. We had analyzed over three years of cost and sales data, and had actually drilled down to find the root causes of a mess of interrelated problems the CEO was now blaming on a person who was not even in the room.

Harry gave no facts to back up his finger pointing—his comment was pure blame. Leaving the accusation unchallenged would undermine our project, create fear on the team, and halt real improvement. So as the team's coach, I heard myself speaking calmly, emphatically and off the cuff, directly to the CEO.

"Harry, on our team we avoid making blaming statements, and demand facts that point us to root causes. These causes usually are either problems in our processes or lapses in selecting and training employees to follow those processes correctly. Any team member who makes a blaming statement in one of our meetings has to wear a black hat for an hour. I have some black hats out in my car. If you want to blame people for our problems, then I'll go out and get a black hat for you."

Calling blaming by its name felt like the right thing to do—otherwise who needed a coach? If the CEO's blaming behavior went unchallenged, team members and others throughout the organization would be fearful of seeking real causes of chronic problems. Surprisingly, Harry was silent in response to the black hat offer. Perhaps the idea that problems have root causes surprised him. Just the word "problem," and the mechanic's description of it, seemed to trigger Harry's fault finding and my reaction. Harry invited the mechanic to finish his presentation and all the remaining team members also performed well.

Publicly embarrassing your client's boss is not an accepted consulting practice. Surprisingly, this spontaneous reply to Harry's blaming did not end my consulting engagement. My client, Gil, never even mentioned this incident to me and I continued training and coaching process-improvement project teams for that company for several more years.

Seeking root causes of problems requires going hard on the work and easy on the people by asking: "Why did our process let us down?" or "Why is our process not working for us?" instead of, "Who did it?" or "Who messed up?" Using the Five Whys to discover the reasons some process let us down avoids finger pointing and blaming, which breed fear and confusion in the organization.

The improvement team gathered and analyzed facts and data on store maintenance practices at the stores with the eight highest and the eight lowest maintenance costs in the entire chain. They gathered store data on twenty or more factors that the team listed as possible drivers of store maintenance expense. Among the many findings, one example stands out as memorable.

Repairs on automatic meat slicers in deli departments correlated with maintenance costs in those stores. One team member, a mechanic, did a root cause investigation and found that all the stores with high slicer down-time and expense used high-pressure scalding hot water for nightly sanitation cleaning. All the low cost stores used other methods. The mechanic called the slicer manufacturer's customer service unit and found out that sanitizing slicers with scalding hot water melted the lubricants out of the machine's bearings, causing the slicers to shake themselves to pieces with use. The manufacturer's customer service representative referred our mechanic to specific warnings in slicer maintenance manuals against using high-pressure hot water to sanitize a machine. The manual also recommended an alternate sterilization procedure that caused no damage.

The team's root cause investigation found that the chain had no standardized store maintenance practices on any in-store equipment. Drilling down deeper still, the team found that no person either in store management or the maintenance department was assigned to set up and deploy proper preventive maintenance routines to keep new store equipment working. The mechanics only responded to stores when things broke and needed fixing. So people working in each store tried to maintain the equipment by doing what they thought was best.

This root cause made no sense, so the team tried replacing it with something that did make sense. They created a manual of best practices and pilot tested their new maintenance approaches. The maintenance team retrained all managers in one high-volume, high-maintenance-cost store. The team did not have to wait long for proof that the new practices improved store-level accountability. The pilot store's maintenance costs plunged.

Within six months, the controller analyzed maintenance costs in the pilot store and estimated chain wide savings based on actual cost savings in the pilot store. In its second presentation to Harry and his executive committee, the team shared the controller's analysis and recommended a chain-wide store-maintenance cost prevention program. Upon hearing the total savings estimate, Harry interrupted the presentation, turned to Gil, the CFO, and ordered Gil to cut the annual budget for maintenance the next year by the full amount of the team's savings estimate—a seven figure sum.

The assistant controller quickly explained to Harry that the team's estimated savings were based on our one store pilot test. The full savings could only be achieved by deploying new maintenance practices in every store department of the chain, which was impossible in a single fiscal year. This satisfied Harry.

This team implemented changes in store manager training, maintenance processes and maintenance information systems, which eventually brought the chain's expenses in line with the benchmarks. Not a bad return on an investment of twenty or so weekly three-hour team meetings involving two process analysts, an assistant controller, a store manager, four maintenance mechanics and a process-improvement trainer and coach.

Top executives who confuse blaming a problem on a scapegoat with actually solving that problem are common. When senior executives in an organization play blame games, the result is fear, risk avoidance and eventually a crippling organizational culture. None of these outcomes improve the organization's competitive performance.

BANISH BLAMING BY FINDING ROOT CAUSES

When people at the top of an organization blame and point fingers at scapegoats they set a bad example that others in the organization may follow. When blaming and scapegoating goes unnamed and unchallenged, it generates fear, lowers morale, dampens improvement efforts and helps to ensure that poor outcomes and adverse trends continue un-prevented.

Ray, the CIO of a big information service firm, formed a team of his senior technical managers in a project. The project team's objective was to discover why Information Technology (IT) reliability, which had improved steadily for four years to benchmark levels, abruptly crashed in the fifth year, wiping out four years of steady improvement.

During the year in which reliability slipped, Ray's management team blamed many causes. Each finger pointed outside the blamer's area of responsibility. When customers escalated their complaints to the company CEO, Ray asked for help in getting his managers to focus on the root cause of sinking reliability.

Ray's cross-functional reliability improvement team included senior people from all IT specialties and functions. The day-to-day leader of the team was the manager of the Rapid Response Unit (RRU), a cross-functional team of technical specialists. The RRU provided round-the-clock diagnostic and remedial support on major outages and was located on a high floor of a skyscraper. The RRU's dazzling physical plant and high-tech paraphernalia resembled the bridge of a starship in a sci-fi movie.

The reliability team's objective was to get to the root cause of the reliability problem with some coaching and help in performing statistical and reliability analyses as needed. During initial team meetings, members blamed the reliability meltdown on departments represented other than their own. As coach, I noted all the causes of outages people had mentioned and prepared a data analyses plan to gather use facts to confirm or refute each suspected cause.

The RRU maintained a database of all outages, from the moment of detection until the outage was finally "closed out" after verification of corrective or preventive action on it. Each individual outage was severity coded by scope and duration, so for example, "severity-one" outages or "sev-one" outages as they were called, "deprived a thousand or more on-line customers of access to system functionality for fifteen minutes or longer."

An analysis of all the RRU's data on severity-one outages showed that the RRU was not finding the root causes of major outages. After each severity one outage, that exact same type of outage was highly likely to reappear in the near future. These reoccurrences proved that either the root-cause analysis or the preventive action taken to nullify that root cause, or both, were ineffective.

After the analysis, Ray replaced the RRU manager as team leader with Tony, a vice president reporting directly to Ray. Tony activated data gathering modules in operating systems and telecommunications network control software, and obtained data on the number of software changes and updates by time period. After several months of accumulating detailed operating data, we began using those data to test the explanations that team members had offered for different types of severity-one outages.

One by one the data refuted all the explanations for falling reliability, and the team was left with an empty bag. Finally, after several months of effort that were not adding value we sent a draft of our detailed technical findings to Ray and he scheduled a final presentation.

Instead of a small audience at the final presentation, more than a dozen people from all parts of Ray's IT organization met in a large conference room. One by one we presented analyses and graphs of data that clearly ruled out excuses and attributions of blame that people had offered to explain the growing reliability problem. By the end of the presentation, the analyses of facts had let the air out of the finger pointing and excuses. Unexpectedly an acrimonious argument broke out around the conference table.

Loud remarks flew back and forth. Some people mentioned "the Joe meeting," which meant nothing to me. Eventually, everyone was arguing right in front of the boss, Ray; the meeting was out of control. Time ran out and Ray stalked out of the conference room without saying a word. I felt embarrassed and clueless about what had happened.

Back in Tony's office he explained that Joe had been Ray's deputy in the IT organization until about a year earlier. One of Joe's many duties was improvement of system reliability. At the start of each day, Joe required all IT department managers to meet in his conference room to review all high-severity outages during the previous twenty-four hours. The meeting opened with all participants sharing the facts they had on each outage. Joe listened and assigned people to investigate further and report their findings in the next day's meeting. During the second half of each daily meeting, Joe listened to explanations of root causes and assigned accountability for devising and implementing preventive measures for each type of outage.

This explanation suggested strongly that the four year improvement trend in uptime and reliability had resulted from Joe's following up on every single major outage by demanding facts and sound preventive measures. In his daily outage meetings, Joe had insisted on an investigation and on immediate corrective, preventive and quality assurance actions—or else. When Joe was transferred to a new position, his daily outage meetings stopped. Without Joe's meeting every morning, accountability for error prevention, process discipline, cross-checking and training to combat human error relaxed and faded. Blaming and finger pointing replaced Joe's insistent demand for a culture of prevention.

As Tony finished his explanation, Ray walked in. I apologized to Ray for the way the meeting had broken down. He stopped me and said that he knew all along that the loss of Joe's focus on prevention and process discipline had caused the slide in reliability. However, he had no facts to back this up. Worse, his direct reports disliked the Joe meetings, and aggressively pushed back every time Ray asked them to reinstate them. Now that Ray could finally rebut all arguments that daily outage meetings wasted time he would reinstate strict accountability for use of error prevention disciplines—which had disappeared when Joe left.

All processes operated by people are subject to human errors. Humans commit errors randomly, at stable and predictable rates depending on skills and task complexities. Consequently, error prone tasks in processes must be neutralized by process designs that prevent or catch and correct inevitable errors before they damage customers. Fault-intolerant processes in fields such as nuclear energy, submarine operations, and commercial aviation daily prove beyond doubt that operating incredibly reliable processes is possible even if error-prone humans play key roles in process operation and control loops.

Once Joe left, Ray left his position vacant, and no single executive was directly accountable to Ray for overall reliability. This accountability vacuum explained why severe outages grew so rapidly that four years of steady improvement were undone in one year. The loss of one leader created a lack of accountability in place of the prevention culture that Joe's daily outage meetings had enforced. The functional managers filled the accountability vacuum with confusion by trying to shift responsibility for preventing problems away from their units.

The next section shows how lecturing employees and asking them to try harder causes many times as much waste and trouble than simply giving the employee a simple tool to know when trouble is real and requires action.

HERE'S HOW A TOOL TO SPOT BAD OUTCOMES MADE A HARD JOB EASY

Tools that really improve quality and productivity must also make each worker's job easier.

On a process walk-through at a food manufacturing plant, there was a woman monitoring the weight of jam jars coming off a filling line. She used special tongs to pick up four jars of hot jam in one grab. After putting the four on a digital scale, she calculated the average weight per jar and the weight difference between the heaviest and lightest jars. She wrote these measurements on a chart and plotted points on diagrams next to her scale.

When asked what she was doing, the woman said she was monitoring the jam filling operation to make sure it did not produce short-weight (underweight) product. She surprisingly added, "I love my control chart," and explained that she had done this same job for eighteen years. Before the control chart she found her job very hard. If the weight in the jars went up, she was supposed to reduce the flow of product slightly and vice versa if the weight went down. She pointed to a knob she used to adjust the flow and said that for sixteen years she had never been able to get that knob just right.

Every month or two, a manager would visit her on the job and tell her that she had made a run of short weight product. The manager would lecture her on the importance of her job and how the company counted on her to keep tight control over product weight. She added in a bitter tone of voice that no matter how hard she tried to adjust the flow rate she could never get it just right.

She explained that two years earlier a newly hired quality manager showed her how to plot data from the samples of jars she weighed on a form known as a control chart. The new quality manager also gave her new work instructions. She was never to adjust the flow control valve. From now on her job was to simply take her measurements and stop the filling line if one of her measurements went above or below horizontal lines drawn on her chart (which are called process behavior limits). This new job was easy.

When asked what happened after that, she said that since she had begun charting the jar weights, she almost never had to stop the line. Once in a rare while, when a weight plotted on her chart fell above or below the behavior limit lines on the chart, she just stopped the line and called her supervisor. Usually her supervisor would clear a piece of fruit that had become stuck in the jam supply line. When product became stuck in the line supplying jam to the machine, jar weights went haywire, which was why she had to stop the line immediately.

Later, I told the quality manager about my encounter with her "number one fan for statistical process control" on the jam filling line. The manager said that before she arrived, the plant had a high over-fill percentage and also serious cost problems with short-weight product.

Short-weight products cost the company a lot of money, because the firm either donated the product to charity or relabeled it as "short weight" and sold it to jobbers at a discount. Training the woman to use a control chart stopped her constant tampering with the fill rate and was saving about $50,000 per month. The quality manager had found that more than ninety percent of the weight variation before introducing the control chart was due to the worker's constant tampering with the flow valve.

Managers like those who nagged this woman on the jam line to try harder to adjust her filling process had blamed the worker for random variation in process outcomes over which she had no control. They did not understand that all processes outputs vary randomly. As a result, when a work process runs normally almost all outcome variation is due to random causes lurking in the process or the work being processed. In service processes, variation often arises from customer to customer variation in wants, needs and expectations. In a production process such as filling jam jars, the variation was caused by chance factors that were unknown to the woman monitoring jar weights.

Without an understanding of random variation, workers misread normal, random up and down process variation as signals to do something. The frequent tampering with the filling valve in response to random ups and downs inflicted huge costs on the plant. By providing a simple graph showing normal versus abnormal variation the plant eliminated this self-inflicted waste. It also made this woman's job easier and less frustrating.

We've seen how one quality manager enlightened a diligent but frustrated worker about process tampering. The next section shows how a top manager taught his work force about processes.

AN EXECUTIVE ROLE-PLAYS THE QUALITY GURU

Some executives kick off process-improvement programs with an announcement at an all-hands meeting or by sending an introductory e-mail to all employees. However Ed, a general manager, surprised everyone in his organization with his process-improvement kickoff. Ed re-enacted the late Dr. W. Edwards Deming's red bead demonstration, which highlights examples of managerial confusion like process tampering and blaming workers for outcomes they do not control. (Deming, 1993) Recall how managers harangued the lady filling jam jars for sixteen years in the previous section, before a new quality manager cleared up their confusion.

The morning Ed was to kick off his process-improvement effort, he arrived early for the all-hands meeting he had scheduled in the company cafeteria. He carried in a large cardboard box and began placing its contents on the table at the front of the room. His props included a large glass bowl filled with hundreds of white marbles within which were mixed a few red-painted balls, a ping-pong paddle with a checkerboard pattern of twenty holes drilled into the flat paddle, and a flip chart pad.

As Ed finished arranging his props on the table, his audience of employees arrived and filled the room. He began by explaining the process-improvement initiative to his workforce. He wanted everyone to understand how work processes cause variation. He explained that management had to define responsibilities for monitoring, controlling and reducing unwanted variation and inconsistency in their service quality. He was going to run a demonstration to make these concepts real.

Ed, playing Dr. Deming's role, told his employees that he was in charge of a start-up firm, the White Ball Company. He was hiring people to fill several jobs, and everyone in the cafeteria was a candidate for a job. Then he said White Ball's new hires had to be top performers; the company wanted "grade A" employees. In addition, White Ball employees had to be motivated to do their best for the company.

Ed picked several "new hires" from the audience and asked them to come up to the front table. As they stood around the table Ed explained that they had been hired because they were above average and ready to do their best. Next, he explained that White Ball's company mission was to produce zero defects—which meant 100% white balls. Ed used the paddle to stir the balls in the urn and thoroughly mix the red balls among the white.

Ed went on lecturing his "team" on their business objective—turning out 100% white balls—and exhorting them to do work as a team and do their best to accomplish that objective. Next Ed showed one "willing worker" how to use the paddle to fish a sample of twenty balls out of the urn without dropping any marbles. Oh-oh, there were a few red balls among the white balls on the first paddle of twenty. So Ed reminded the worker that he was hired to do his best to fulfill the objective of 100% white balls—and suggested that he had let them down by producing some red balls. Ed then designated another worker as a "quality inspector" and showed her how to count the red (defective) balls and the white (high quality) balls and report the worker's name and quality data (red and white ball counts) to the "data analyst."

Ed then positioned another new employee (the data analyst) at a flip chart, which had rows for worker names and columns for the defect count (number of red balls), number of white balls (high quality) and the percentage defect rate (equal to the red ball count times by 5 percent). The data analyst wrote the quality inspector's data for the first worker's production in the top row of the table for all to see. Ed then had the supervisor return the first day's ball production to the urn and stir the balls.

A second willing worker took a turn fishing a full paddle of balls out of the urn. The quality inspector counted and called out the number of red (defective) and white (defect-free) balls to the analyst, who wrote them on the flip chart next to the worker's name, calculated the percentage defective and entered the result on the flip chart. After all four of his "production workers" had completed the process sequence, Ed declared their first workday over.

Next, Ed coached the supervisor in motivating his workforce. Pointing to the production numbers from all four willing workers on the flip chart, Ed asked the supervisor which worker was the most valuable. The supervisor named the worker who drew the fewest red balls as the top performer. Then Ed asked the supervisor which worker needed improvement. The supervisor designated the employee who had the highest red-ball defect rate as "needing improvement, which is the same as a C-grade." Ed then coached the supervisor in reviewing the performance of the worker who he had designated a "grade-C employee." Ed coached the supervisor in praising the top performers and warning the worker with the most red balls that White Ball Co's A-grade workforce could not tolerate C-grade employees for long.

Then White Ball Co ran three more "days" of production, worker after worker, sample after sample, inspecting and recording data, ranking workers from best to worst—and praising, scolding or threatening workers at the end of each simulated day. When the demonstration ended, all participants returned to their seats.

Now Ed became the teacher. He graphed the defective data percentages on a new flip chart to show how the defect rate varied, and asked: "What happened to the defect rate?" Answer from the audience: "Well, it varied from lot to lot, but it stayed around the same level for all workers during the four days." Had the defect rate improved? "No, it had not." Ed asked, "Hadn't White Ball Co. tracked defects and demanded improvement from employees whose quality failed to measure up? Why didn't the supervisors' warnings and praise improve the defect rates?" The audience was silent on that one. Ed persisted: "Where did the defects come from?" Someone in the audience said that red balls were already mixed into the urn of white balls before work began, so they were built into the process and just popped up at random.

Next Ed asked why inspecting quality in a product after it was produced was a bad idea. Someone replied that the process for putting balls into the urn had determined the quality of the product (for better or worse). Ed then explained that to ensure 100 percent white ball quality those on the scene needed to investigate the root cause of the red balls and use that knowledge to change the process by which red balls were getting into the urn in the first place. Could White Ball Co. achieve 100 percent quality by asking all employees to do their best? Someone answered—no.

One by one, Ed drew out the points that Deming had stressed to managers and supervisors of operations. The objective was for them to see their real jobs as teachers, trainers and coaches of process change and improvement. Ed explained that supervisors had to train their people on each task of a process. If the output of the process fell short, then the supervisor needed to lead the workforce in finding the causes of defects and follow up by changing the process to address those causes—and repeat the cycle of prevention and corrective action as needed.

Ed summarized other points: common tactics such as ranking employees by process outcomes and blaming people for random process variation only served to ruin moral and motivation. Praising the top performers and punishing the bottom when those rankings were based on random variation in process outcomes was just a crapshoot that made everyone feel bad sooner or later, but never resulted in lasting improvement,

Ed finished his review of the demonstration with a pep talk that related Deming's points to the improvement program he was kicking off. He took a few questions and then his audience went back to work.

As Ed picked up his props, I praised his performance and asked where he had seen Deming's red bead demonstration. He said that his wife had taken a course from Deming and had suggested that Ed kick off this process-improvement initiative by playing the video. But Ed liked the video so well that he decided he wanted to re-enact the demonstration himself.

After the kickoff, Ed's process-improvement program went well. As executive sponsor, Ed had shown his people that using process variation to improve process outcomes produced quality by preventing causes of poor quality. If workers use a lousy process, no matter how hard they tried, the results would be lousy. Once workers learned to find the causes of process upsets and poor quality, they could make changes to prevent those upsets in the future. So, unless workers and managers redesigned their work, quantity and quality of work outcomes would not improve.

Ed, courtesy of his wife, showed that he understood process variation and the need for the workforces to learn how to reduce unwanted process variation. The next section introduces a production supervisor who used one-point training to help a conscientious worker overcome confusion about the right way to do his job.

TO ERR IS HUMAN: TO PREVENT ERROR TAKES PROCESS DISCIPLINE

An important benefit of following a process is that process steps can be designed to prevent small problems from snowballing into large problems. However, ensuring that all hands follow such a process is a challenge for managers.

Henry managed the final assembly department in a large Internet equipment manufacturing plant. Once day, Henry interrupted our meeting to take a call about a problem on his shop floor. When the call ended he invited me on a tour to see his operation. As we walked, Henry said the call was a complaint that two network routers had been shipped to the wrong customers. Each unit was built to customer specifications, but each customer had received the other customer's equipment. Both customers were major buyers of equipment, so senior management wanted Henry to explain how such a shipping error had occurred and what steps he planned to take to prevent such an error from ever happening again.

When we arrived in the final assembly area, Henry walked me step by step through the assembly process, from the stockroom where all components used in the assembly process were stored, through the assembly process, to where the machines were put into shipping boxes and sent off to the shipping department.

The assembly line was a wide rubber conveyor carrying a parade of routers in some stage of assembly, each of which passed by a dozen or more cubicles. As routers passed each cubicle, a technician used tools and test equipment to perform tasks in the assembly process. Henry walked me down the row of cubicles in the direction the routers were moving, explaining the process as we went. He pointed out job aides, lists of tasks in plastic envelopes hanging on the wall in each cubicle, and occasionally showed me how the job aide documented the work being done in that cubicle.

At the end of the line, Henry greeted John, who was working there, and then introduced me and asked if John would mind us watching him work. John's job was to prepare and box each router for shipment to the customer.

It was fine with John for us to watch. He was in the middle of his work routine, so while we waited for him to start work on the next router, Henry went over the job aide for this cubicle line by line so we would know what to expect. The job aide listed:

Final shipping workstation tasks:

1. Advance one router onto the lazy Susan table.
2. Press the "print" button on the line printer.
3. When the printer stops, tear off the multipart form.
4. Orient the router on the lazy Susan so that the back is facing you; place the foil equipment nameplates on the spaces provided, making sure to orient the label using the guide lines on the router cabinet.
5. Apply the equipment labels,
6. And so on.
7. And so on.

As we watched, John began working on the next router. He went over to where finished routers were waiting on rollers and advanced two routers into his work area. The first he positioned on a lazy Susan turntable at the end of the conveyor, the second he parked at the end of the conveyor behind the first. Then, he pushed a button on line printer twice. The printer clattered as it printed a multipart form that included a bill of lading, a shipping label, packing lists, a set of metal foil nameplates, and other documents. The printer filled in two of these forms. When printing stopped, John tore the two forms off the printer, and went into action.

Working fast and steadily, John separated and applied various printed labels and nameplates to both routers. At the push of a button, a large overhead contraption lowered a cardboard shipping box down over the router on the lazy Susan. John removed paperwork from one of the printed forms and placed the documents in envelopes, which he stuck on the outside of the shipping box. Then John closed and sealed the box and pushed it off the lazy Susan onto another conveyor that took the boxes directly to the shipping area. Next, John guided the second router onto the lazy Suzan and repeated his routine on that one.

As the second router went on its way to shipping, Henry asked John why he packed two units at once, given that the job aide called for working on one unit at a time. John answered that he used to follow the job aide exactly. But as volumes increased he could not keep pace with the assembly line feeding him work. By trial and error he learned that doing his job on two routers at once let him keep up with the line. Henry thanked John for letting us watch, and we went back to Henry's office.

On the way back to his office, Henry shared his diagnosis and the corrective action that he planned to take. The shipping error was probably caused by working on two routers side by side instead of one at a time as the job aide stipulated. Because John printed two sets of documentation at once, the likely explanation was that the documentation had been accidentally switched between the two routers.

Henry said nothing to John because John alone could not correct the problem. The entire process required review. All workers on the final assembly line were cross-trained to do jobs further down the line. If work backed up to their workstation due to a bottleneck further down the line, they were supposed to stop their work and "flex" forward one workstation until the work station falling behind (in this case, John's at the far end of the line) got the help it needed to catch up.

Each time such a bottleneck incident occurred, the people who flexed forward were trained to place a small red adhesive dot on a huge flowchart of the assembly line taped on the wall. Each red dot showed where that bottleneck had appeared in the line. Once a week, Henry and his assembly team reviewed the dots on the chart and decided how to shift work tasks or adjust staffing to restore even throughput along the whole line. This is called an agile work design and is a self-adjusting work process to ensure that everyone has an equal workload.

Henry's diagnosis was that the agile work design was short circuited by John's desire to keep up with the faster work pace. When John departed from his job aide work did not back up, which would have brought upstream people forward to help John out. Because no one flexed forward, no one placed a red dot on the process flowchart each time a bottleneck developed. So, Harry and the rest of the work force were unaware that John was routinely overloaded. The root cause of the router shipping mix-up was that John mistook his inability to keep pace with the assembly line for poor job performance, when in fact it was a process problem.

Henry's planned corrective action was to retrain the whole assembly team, including John, in the importance of following their job aides even if their work backed up. The assembly team needed to be reminded that backups were the signal that workload and staff needed rebalancing. Henry planned to rebalance John's workload and use one-point training to restore and reinforce the agile work design.

The next section shows how one-point training every day for everybody in an organization can create a culture of excellence in service without shaming and blaming. It also shows how one-point training cured a tough, discourteous skeptic of his doubts about the effectiveness of one-point training.

THE SECRET TO OUTSTANDING SERVICE QUALITY, PART 1

When things go wrong in a well-designed process, the cause often is that people have confused trying their best with following a sound process the right way. Fifteen or twenty minutes of simple, punchy one-point training of all people working in a process by their supervisors can reinforce and restore sound work practices without shaming or blaming individuals for service lapses.

About mid-afternoon on day two of a professional development seminar on how to use the Baldrige Award criteria to assess improvement opportunities in service organizations, the class was going well with one exception. One attendee kept up a steady stream of heckling. He made snide and skeptical comments out loud. Everyone in the class of twenty or so (including a team of six managers from outside the US) could hear his skeptical and offensive remarks. The heckler's behavior was embarrassing, and I had spoken with him off line several times, to no effect.

The Ritz-Carlton organization had been recognized with a well-deserved Baldrige Award. In class I used examples from the hotel chain, whose systematic approach to maintaining service levels uses continuous refresher training after any slippage in service. After an explanation of how the Ritz-Carlton's "daily lineup" used customer feedback from all hotels to schedule daily one-point refresher training of the workforce in every department in every Ritz-Carlton hotel, the class heckler snorted, "Oh, yeah, and tell me another one."

Just as he made this comment, a banquets waiter came into the seminar room and began setting up our afternoon break. I approached the waiter, explained what our class was about and asked if he would speak to the class for a few minutes about the daily lineup in this Ritz-Carlton hotel. The waiter replied that it would be his pleasure. He finished his task, walked to the front of the room, faced the class, tidied his white jacket, and spoke in a confident tone of voice suited to the room and size of audience:

"Here at the Ritz-Carlton Hotel Company every employee in our hotel is trained at the start of each shift in what we call the "daily lineup." Usually each supervisor gives the training to his or her department, but sometimes when the topics are specialized a hotel training or service quality person delivers it. This morning when my shift began, the banquets supervisor delivered today's training to our banquets team. Today's training topic was 'Our responsibility to protect the safety and security of our guests and the property of the Ritz-Carlton Hotel Company.' This morning's training covered seven points. Point one was …. Point two was . . ." And so on.

After the waiter presented all seven points, he paused and said that he would be pleased to answer any questions. No one in the class asked anything. That waiter—speaking without preparation or notes—had exceeded my highest expectations. Arriving to perform a simple service for our class, he had given an impressive live demonstration of a world-class training process. I thanked him, turned toward the class heckler, looked him in the eye, and said:

"Now Mr. _____, you had a hard time understanding this training system earlier. If you have any questions about the daily lineup, here is your chance to have your questions answered. Please ask them of the waiter, now!" If looks could kill, the heckler would have at least been wounded. For the first time in nearly two days, the man was silent—and that ended his hostile and disruptive heckling for the rest of the seminar.

At that time Ritz-Carlton Hotel Co. trained every employee every day in a systematic, carefully targeted fashion. The training points were chosen based on customer input and process outcome data, not by opinion or guess.

No matter how sound an organization's processes or its measures of quality outcomes, or how carefully its employees were selected so that their aspirations, character traits and personalities fit the demands of their job, supervisors and managers need to reemphasize "gold standard" practices daily. At Ritz-Carlton, continuous training on how to be "ladies and gentlemen" serving ladies and gentlemen maintained the proficiencies needed to carry out that mission—to ensure every guest was treated well in whichever hotel location they stay.

Now that you have seen how workplace leaders of an international hotel group reduce confusion and sustain service excellence for hotel guests, you may wonder if it is possible to duplicate such a success on a small scale. The following story shows how a bank branch manager used "golden rule" training to replace confused feelings that blaming can cause when customer service slips.

THE SECRET TO OUTSTANDING SERVICE QUALITY, PART 2

Conscientious service workers who take criticism from upset customers to heart become demoralized. So how do you replace low morale caused by criticism and blame in a small work group with something uplifting and effective? Here's how a bank branch used mystery shopping report cards to maintain excellent customer experiences.

Mystery shopping is a market research service in which trained survey takers act as customers in a service establishment such as a bank branch. These "customers" are unknown to branch service personnel so they are called "mystery" shoppers. Mystery shoppers are trained and willing to complete comprehensive surveys after each service experience. Mystery shopping data lets bank managers obtain in-depth feedback on diverse customer service experiences in their own as well as competitors' branches.

Jeff was the head of the bank's retail banking division when the Research Director of the bank's market research vendor called with good news. The market researchers had analyzed historical data service quality scores from over 5,000 bank branches and found that one of Jeff's branches was top ranked on service quality among all 5,000 branches for several years without ever slipping in rank. The caller congratulated Jeff and asked if he and a colleague could visit the branch and meet with its manager and staff. Jeff checked with the woman who managed the branch and she agreed to host these visitors as long as they arrived an hour before her branch opened.

Jeff and his visitors arrived as agreed and were met by the branch staff. After the visitors congratulated the branch manager and her staff on their outstanding service achievements, they presented the manager with a certificate recognizing the branch's exceptional record of excellence.

Next Jeff and his visitors met with the branch manager to find out how she kept her branch's performance so consistently high. She explained that she managed customer service according to the Golden Rule—"Do unto others what you would have them do unto you." She and all her staff continually experienced poor customer service outside their branch. She explained that she had turned branch employees' "positive paranoia" about "quality audits" into reminders that each customer interaction was an opportunity for their service to shine by treating the customer as they themselves would like to be treated.

The branch's monthly mystery shopping reports rated customer experiences on 55 service elements. For example, one service element was whether or not branch employees sincerely thanked each customer by name before the customer left. At any sign of slippage on a service quality element, she and her branch staff came to work a half hour earlier than usual for refresher training on just that service element.

Each early morning training session opened with a discussion of how the staff personally would prefer to be served when they were customers. Next, they role-played customers experiencing service that made them (in their roles as customers) feel as happy as customers would wish to feel. After retraining on that single point the branch opened for business. Throughout the month, all branch employees retrained on any service element that had slipped in the prior month's mystery shopping report.

The bank branch manager had used survey feedback to identify service elements for which immediate refresher training was needed to maintain the branch's extraordinary service quality. For years, month after month, the branch had produced service excellence. When the visitors asked about turnover, the manager stressed the need for careful hiring. Was the constant training worth the time and effort? Any answer would be a speculation—but studies of banking customer switching behavior show that banking customers change bank branches because of poor service experiences.

The next section shows how resolving confusion about who to trust when approving a loan stanched loan losses. This story is another example of confusion caused by the WYSIATI trap. What a banker sees in a loan application that prompts her to make that loan is often not all there is to know about that loan.

WHEN ALL SHARE RESPONSIBILITY NO ONE IS ACCOUNTABLE

Chapter three introduced Vince as a leader and go-to problem solver for improving a troubled international banking unit. In this incident, Vince's challenge was to clear up his boss's confusion about knowledge and accountability. Vince's boss was the Chairman and CEO of the bank. He formed a team to diagnose the situation as follows.

The bank's dozens of overseas branches operated like conventional banks in the countries they served. So for example, the branch in Singapore lent to Singaporean companies either in USD (US dollars) or local currency.

Unfortunately, at the time of this incident, US bank loans to borrowers in economically distressed geographic regions were souring for all major US international lenders. This bank's international units had several billion dollars in what had become risky loans made by overseas branches to local borrowers.

Small loans were approved in the country of origin. However, approving the bank's largest international loans (called "jumbo loans") required review and approval at all six levels from the local branch that originated it, up the international lending hierarchy to the home office International Credit Committee under Vince. International jumbo loans went one step higher, to the Senior Credit Committee chaired by the bank's Chairman and CEO (Vince's boss).

The basis for requesting and approving a loan was a document called a loan application (referred to as a "credit" within the bank). Each credit contained factual data and analyses needed to make credit approval decisions based on local assessments of the borrower's capacity to repay, which translated into the bank's risk exposure if that loan was made. The uncertainty in lending is deciding how able a borrower company will be to repay its loan with interest when payment is due. In international lending at that time, uncertainty about whether country central banks would allow loan repayments to be converted into dollars and repatriated back to the parent bank made matters worse.

The diagnosis found unexpected political dynamics and confusion in this credit approval process. Small loans were no problem, but large, potentially profitable jumbo loans had become the source of financial pain. Local lenders had found that "tweaking" credits was needed if they wanted their larger loans approved at higher levels. So they hand crafted proposals for large loans in ways that played to the biases of participants in higher-level approvals.

An additional source of confusion was introduced by ambitious, well-educated and hard-working officers who worked on country desks in the home office. Country desk officers often came from the overseas branches originating the loans. These bankers hoped to return home eventually as senior branch officers. When jumbo credits arrived on their desks, these bankers sometimes rewrote them. This rework was supposedly to improve the English used in the application, but it tended to enhance the odds of home office approval of reworked credits.

By interviewing participants at all levels in the loan approval process, the team learned that the Chairman (Vince's boss) believed that the more experienced the lenders who approved a large credit were, the lower the risk of that transaction becoming a bad loan. Unfortunately this deeply ingrained belief was not backed up by the facts. Our interviews revealed that the various levels of authority involved in approvals had partial or zero firsthand knowledge of some of the ten different sources of risk the bank evaluated on jumbo international loans.

The team's diagnosis was that Vince's main problem was a lack of accountability. So many individuals at all six levels of lending authority had signed off on what ultimately became troubled loans that accountability was lost due to confusion about who to go to and what to ask them to do differently. The reality was that no individual or organizational level was clearly accountable for assessing each type of risk presented by a credit. All of this was spread over thousands of miles, dozens of languages, countries and individual central banks, which controlled currency flows.

The diagnosis presented data and analysis of each approval level's firsthand knowledge of each of the ten types of risk. For example, the country branch had no first-hand knowledge of the bank's country risk, which was determined at the International Credit Committee level. Also, members of the International Credit Committee in the home office had no first-hand knowledge of the borrowing customer's markets and sales outlook or the local central bank's policies. The diagnosis produced a grid with six horizontal lines (each labeled with one of the six organization levels) and ten vertical lines (for the ten types of risk present in jumbo credits). Circles were drawn at each row and column intersection.

From interview data the team shaded circles at each row and column intersections to show that organization level's (row) estimated first-hand knowledge of the type of risk represented by the column at that intersection.

So, a blank circle in a row and column indicated that the organizational level at that row had zero first-hand knowledge of that source of risk. A completely filled circle at a row and column intersection indicated that the organizational level represented by the row had the bank's entire first-hand knowledge of the source of risk corresponding to the column.

When the grid was finished only one combination of two rows had solid dark circles across all ten risk types. This showed that a combination of just two organization levels out of six had firsthand knowledge of all ten risk elements, which in turn implied that two approval locations possessed the entire bank's knowledge needed for assessing riskiness of jumbo international loans accurately and factually.

Under the existing approval process, Vince faced dozens of troubled large loans that had been approved by experienced bankers working at all six approval levels. All these partially informed approvals amplified confusion and destroyed accountability once a loan went bad. These findings produced hot reactions, political fireworks and a year of delay until Vince won the Board Chairman's approval of a streamlined two-level international loan approval and risk accountability process. If a loss occurred due to any one or more risk types, the process firmly established 100 percent accountability at the branch level for six causes of loan losses, and full 100 percent accountability at one home office level for the other four types of risks.

Process-improvement teams often must clarify confusion over responsibilities within complex processes. In this case, requiring six organizational levels to approve loans gave the opinions of many less informed personnel equal voice with the bank's best informed people. As a result individual accountability for troubled loans became confused.

AVOIDING DECISIONS THAT OTHERS WILL REGRET FOR DECADES

Just as confusion over accountability can grow up and down a vertical organizational chain of responsibility, confusion can also grow across a horizontal chain of specialized functions when accountability falls into cracks between organizational silos.

Organizations typically define accountability within functional silos, which might lead you to expect less organizational confusion. But the following experience shows that problems in "white spaces" between functional boxes on an organization chart confuse people about who is accountable for what.

A real estate organization designs, builds, owns, operates and maintains many large office and residential buildings. Tenants complained that its maintenance function often failed to respond promptly to their "building too hot" and "building too cold" calls. So the maintenance managers formed a process-improvement team whose members included experienced controls repairmen, a customer service supervisor, a tenant relations manager, maintenance planners, a maintenance supervisor and a process-improvement coach.

Service calls on complex building climate controls are not simple "see-a-broken-thing, fix-a-broken-thing" repairs. While flowcharting their as-is process for diagnosing and repairing controls, the team learned that skill levels varied widely from one repair technician to another. Individual repair people dispatched to a building were often unable to diagnose and repair the building's controls malfunction. Often different specialists had to make several time-consuming repair calls to restore a building's controls to normal.

Controls repair people need training to keep up with changes in building control systems. But in this case they did not get that training due to cost, lack of backup while control specialists were in training, and so on. So, a few control people were trained on some systems—but no individual repair person was trained to diagnose all types of control systems installed in the company's buildings.

Building control technology, so critical to energy efficiency, was advancing rapidly. The firm's engineering department had narrowed its list of control manufacturers for new buildings down to three vendors able to meet energy efficiency targets. Team members discovered that maintenance hadn't trained anyone to diagnose and repair those three vendor's building controls. To make matters worse, twelve different types of legacy control systems were still running in older properties.

The company's design and engineering departments were unaware of how their decisions impacted future building maintenance staffing needs and costs. As long as engineering and design units stuck to their knitting, only the controls repair staff and the company's future tenants would be upset. Without some action to close the disconnects between design, engineering, and maintenance functions, confusion about accountability would grow.

All departments reported to a senior executive who was several layers of management removed from day-to-day technical and operational considerations. That senior executive sponsored a co called "heavy weight" team of the heads of architecture and design, engineering, construction and maintenance to solve the problems surfaced by the improvement team.

Design decisions about a building determine at least half of the total cost of owning and operating a building over its useful lifetime. Every maintenance cost that designers do not prevent in a new building raises the owner's future repair costs for up to thirty years, until the building is remodeled or sold. It will take years of experience to learn whether improved executive visibility, coordination and accountability along the "design-build-operate-maintain" value chain yield a better balance of future maintenance expenses against potentially higher initial cost of constructing and owning the building. However, overall savings can only be realized if upper managers enforce cooperation in the white spaces that separate organization functions. Whether increased cooperation across the white spaces succeeds will become known in the future.

In this case, confused accountability and invisible gaps in cooperation between departments working on widely differing time scales created unhappy tenants and high maintenance costs. Serious cooperation among top leaders and their departments are needed to ensure that lifetime operating and maintenance costs for new real estate are factored into today's design and construction decisions.

In the next section a professional football coach coaches a winning team without blaming by pilot testing every new play over and over again during scrimmages to remove all confusion.

STAY OUT OF THE "BLAME FRAME," STAY IN THE "LEARN FRAME"

A coach's story parallels the "golden rule" one-point training approach of the bank branch manager in an earlier story.

A professional football coach gave a guest lecture to a class of graduate students studying coaching. The coach told the class that when his team is playing in a real game against real opponents, coaching is impossible. Everyone on the team is immersed in what the coach called a "win" frame of mind. When team members are in win frames, players focus on winning the game, looking good to each other and to the coach, and not looking bad or having the coach blame them for messing up a play that went wrong.

The coach explained that effective football coaching on new plays happens during scrimmages. The coach divides the team into offensive and defensive squads and explains the new play. The offensive and defensive teams take their positions at the line of scrimmage and run the new play against each other. The coach watches the play unfold until he spots players making errors. Then he blows a whistle and all the players stop where they are and face the coach.

Next the coach asks each player: "Where are you supposed to be?" Some players are where they should be. Others answer the coach's question or say they do not know and the coach tells them. The coach explained that with the play stopped and all players paying attention, the team is in "learning frame." Once the coach gives feedback to each misplaced player, the team runs the play over again. The coach and team rerun the plan-try-check-and-correct sequence until the team runs the play like clockwork every time.

When members of a team are in a "learning frame" of mind, every mistake highlights what went wrong and gives the coach an opportunity to provide feedback that helps the players avoid mistakes. The scrimmage continues until everyone on the team runs the play the right way. As individuals learn, the whole team's performance improves.

At work people often adopt a win frame of mind. Each person wants his or her peers to have a favorable view of the person's performance and perhaps to obtain favorable notice from higher ups. So when coaching people who are changing from an old way of doing their jobs to new processes or procedures, those sponsoring and coaching change must create an organizational "learning frame."

The least confusing way to create a learning frame of mind is to stage a test run of process changes or new skills in an environment away from people's day job. A short, fail-fast pilot test or prototype of something new avoids stressing people. It replaces the need to look good with the opportunity to make mistakes and learn from them without embarrassment. As the coach explained, scrimmages test new plays until players learn their way out of confusion.

In the workplace pilot tests should be planned to avoid disrupting regular work. Pilot tests allow for dry runs of each new way of working until it is safe to develop how-to training in that work. By studying their own mistakes without fear of embarrassment, people invent and master better ways to produce winning outcomes.

CONCLUSION

When blaming and punishing replace problem solving, organizational confusion results. Blaming drives defensive reactions that crowd out efforts to find and remove deeper root causes. To prevent blaming, managers must support training and development of the skills of root cause problem analysis. In addition managers must hold themselves and those they lead accountable for crafting and implementing real solutions that remove or prevent root causes.

Managerial leaders impact problem solving, as the lack of such leadership shows.

Encouraging learning in your organization can be a powerful protective frame that replaces fear and anxiety of failure with learning, which yields greater knowledge, understanding and personal growth. For your organization to have a better future, it must pursue a mission while also coaching all hands in the day-to-day work of sailing toward that mission.

This chapter concludes Section II—Working-Together Confusion. The section has shown how leaders in management answer the legitimate questions, "Where are we going?" "How will we get where we are going?" "What's in it for me to do my best work?" and "Can I trust you if we run into difficulty?"

Your best work may not earn you your largest bonus, but it may make you feel contented to work at your best. Work that engages your head, heart and guts can make you proud. Your duties to yourself in an organization are to accept responsibilities, face goals and challenges, plan actions, trust and help others, take risks, and be satisfied by learning from experience as much and as fast as you can and using what you learned.

Section III, the final section of this book, deals with confusions at the team and whole organization levels. Chapter six highlights and clarifies confusions about who to involve on teams and how to work with and support teams so they succeed. Chapter seven addresses organizational level confusions. Chapter seven shows how management systems sustain continuous organization-wide learning and improvement in pursuing an organization's mission.

Section III: Making-Things-Better Confusion

Members of organizations must choose between generating helpful or negative confusion. Helpful confusion about why things went wrong stimulates inquiry, learning and change for the better. It seeks understanding of root causes as a basis for designing and testing ways of making things better than ever. In this section helpful confusion arises from improvement efforts which accumulate and provide vital change and improvement capabilities.

Members of organizations that generate negative confusion, avoid accountability, and employ blaming when problems appear. As a result they never learn about the art and science of improvement. The resulting negative confusion drives chronic poor performance through lack of ability to solve problems. Seek work in organizations whose managers encourage helpful confusion, and hope that your employer's competitors generate corrosive negative confusion.

In this section we look at how helpful confusion results from improvement efforts. Chapter six focuses on team-based improvement projects. Cross-functional teams carrying out improvement projects are basic process-level building blocks in systematic organization-wide improvement. Chapter six addresses pragmatic lessons learned by unraveling confusion about issues such as team member personality traits and skills; the need to train all team members in a common language and kit of tools; and the need to follow a roadmap to achieve process design or improvement goals.

Chapter seven highlights examples of organization-level clarity that connects an annual planning cycle to cross-functional process improvement teams. Those teams involve the right people to ensure the success of their improvement projects. Each improvement team's success breaks through a performance bottleneck in achieving planned results. Such a cycle repeats year after year, with those who contributed to success each year being recognized and promoted to greater responsibilities.

Improvement is just a set of skills that develop through coaching and use. Some sections in Chapter seven deal with confusion arising from treating improvement as a "one and done" program. This confusion arises from a false assumption—that an organization can make one big push, hit a few improvement home runs in its worst problem areas, and then return to business as usual and prosper.

A major cause of such confusion arises from assuming that the sum of improvements in random parts of an organization equals a better organization as a whole. Chapter seven shares experiences from organizations that improved organization-wide performance—one carefully targeted improvement project at a time.

6

Confusion About How To Pull Together

LEARNING TO TEAM UP FOR IMPROVEMENT

Jackie Robinson said that the number of lives you touch is a measure of your personal worth. If so, working with or being a member of improvement and implementation teams is sure to enhance the worth of your work life. Serving as a member or coach of a cross-functional team can yield peak experiences.

Here is a preview of lessons learned from working as a member or coach of improvement teams, which will help you exceed what you can accomplish alone.

1: Form, charter and train improvement teams to improve end-to-end performance of strategically important service and administrative processes. Select team members skilled in all process steps, train them in using improvement tools and provide coaching.

2: Address concerns of new team members and stakeholders joining a team before they raise them by anticipating and answering questions such as: What are we supposed to do? Why am I on this team? What's in it for me? What will happen to me? How do I know I can trust you?

3: Develop professional, personal and social skills by sponsoring and serving on cross-functional teams. Teams using simple, proven tools to carry out an improvement project make improvements by using facts and finding root causes in a structured sequence. Sponsors of such teams learn how to support their success.

4: Build a new team's experience and capability with small or medium-sized processes before working on large projects. As team members share experiences, the team as a whole learns who knows what and who to trust for each challenge in a new situation.

5: Select process-improvement team members from the people available, even if an ideal team is unavailable. An ideal blend of seven types of skills helps cover common situations a team runs into as it takes a process-improvement project from start to finish. When possible, stack the deck by including three "Atta boy/Atta girl" team members for every "Yeah, but" member.

6: Include a "plate breaker" with deep knowledge and integrity who may use humor to point out unpleasant truths others may prefer not to hear. Dissatisfaction with the current situation motivates people to deal with realities they may otherwise avoid. Cross-functional teams tend to shape members' behaviors through peer pressure, so productive conflict must be deliberate.

7: Avoid wasting any time of busy people whose expertise your team needs. Teams borrow valuable human resources from elsewhere in the organization. Use a structured approach and take steps one at a time while respecting all points of view on your team. Then thank everyone who contributed and show gratitude for their contributions.

8: Find out first-hand what each problem is (and is not.) People sometimes use the name of a solution to label their problem. For example, the label "methods and procedures" once described a wide variety of challenging process control, quality and productivity problems in white-collar service operations.

9: Teach improvement skills to those who do the work and make it possible for them use those skills to improve their work. A workforce able to use such tools as the Five Whys, flowcharts, checking if each task adds "more customer value for less cost," and pilot testing prevents errors, removes bottlenecks and ensures a smooth flow of work. It is also more efficient and effective than asking process-improvement experts to learn details of work processes.

10: Ensure that team members have the time and job flexibility to attend all team meetings without jeopardizing their job performance. Provide backup coverage during absences from regular work. Absenteeism from team meetings damages team morale and signals that missing team meetings is acceptable behavior.

11: Maximize project success by tackling an entire process from A to Z. Breaking all difficult tasks into smaller, easier tasks minimizes the odds of action plan failure. When faced with an outsized risk, engage your team in hedging, escalating or neutralizing the risk of failure.

12: Engage team members in identifying their motivating skills and invite members to work on tasks that need those skills. Form small specialized sub teams for metrics and data analysis, "voice of the customer" focus groups and surveys, cost-benefit analysis, implementing "quick hit" corrective and preventive actions and tasks that need not involve the whole team.

13: Invite executives with stakes in an improvement team's success to serve on a steering team that meets with the team monthly. Serving on a steering team lets senior people guide the improvement team, check its progress and solve problems. Junior team members benefit from their visibility to senior management.

14: Design and run small, fail-fast, pilot tests of new approaches or processes. When a pilot reveals upsetting unknowns, shut the test down quickly, study its outcome, learn and adapt.

A group of people becomes a team by working toward a shared objective that demands skilled effort and input from all members. Teams usually begin by assessing their current process or operating reality. As they map the current process and document its problems and challenges, team members often become discouraged. Coaching them in using simple tools usually replaces discouragement and confusion with progress toward their improvement objectives.

The sections in this chapter show how team members replaced confusion with confidence based on step-by-step progress toward goals. All who train, coach or sponsor teams need to design team meetings that engage people in working together toward goals that all members want to achieve. Team meetings should be planned and run efficiently so as not to waste members' time.

FROM "METHODS AND PROCEDURES" TO LEAN-SIGMA IMPROVEMENT TEAMS

In the 1970's powerful database and telecomm network technology had not yet become available. The service boom forced managers in growing service organizations to seek help with what they called "methods and procedures" problems in service workflows. The term "methods" was borrowed from industrial engineering studies of how workers performed production work. The term "workflow" at that time was common in large operations to mean informal streams of white-collar administrative and service work moving between specialists, such as orders going from sales people through order processing, or insurance applications going from underwriters to policy production specialists. Each specialist had been trained by the previous worker. Each did his or her best, but the whole operation often produced poor results.

Managers of workflows usually had few or no measures of in-process performance. As a result they had limited control over the outcomes of the workflows they managed. When managers attempted to use factory-focused approaches on service and administrative operations, their efforts failed. Unlike factory work, the value of administrative tasks—such as reading, reviewing, assessing, deciding, questioning, validating or supplying information and so on—was invisible. Quality, in terms of freedom from error, was achieved by double-checking, inspection and reworking errors – there was little systematic prevention.

At first managers and those seeking to improve processes relied on advice from professional systems analysts and consultants instead of relying on their most experienced employees. Gradually, however, confusion over how to improve intangible service processes was resolved by replacing "either-or" with *both* employee teams *and* improvement specialists as trainers and coaches of employee teams. Neither employee teams nor professional systems analysts alone could replace wornout workflows with well-designed processes. The next section outlines the structure of successful service process-improvement teams that evolved from several decades of improvement projects.

ROLES TEAM MEMBERS PLAY—INCLUDING "PLATE BREAKER"

Usually sponsors pick team members with track records, positive attitudes and a willingness to work with others. Loners or those with negative attitudes usually perform poorly on team projects aimed at improving how work is done. Team members also should be selected for their record of finishing tasks they take on. Guest specialists may attend team meetings now and then, but a core team is expected to remain stable for the duration of its improvement project, typically four to ten months (depending on process complexity) or until process changes are deployed and outcomes improve.

A review of experiences with dozens of team projects has shown that almost all major breakthrough ideas came not from senior people but from members who were closest to the work: customer service agents, help desk managers, maintenance mechanics, warehouse clerks, office workers and so on. Lower ranking team members live with process problems daily and have the motivation to think about how to make them disappear. Junior contributors were not necessarily young, but were usually lower ranking, eager to learn, ambitious for recognition by higher-ups and hardworking. Importantly, they delivered on team assignments as promised.

The following roles evolved from over forty years of experience training, coaching and leading hundreds of process-improvement teams:

Executive sponsor—Improvement begins when the top management team identifies and links gaps between actual and "should-be" performance to processes that must improve. This usually takes place during annual strategic planning. Next an executive is chosen as the owner accountable for improving each bottleneck process. That executive becomes the sponsor of an improvement project to close his or her process's performance gap.

For example, the top marketing executive might own the sales process with a target of doubling the new business per salesperson. The process owner forms a team to improve the sales process and defines the scope of that team's charter. Such a team charter covers first diagnosing the process needing improvement from start to finish, and then outlines tasks of an improvement project to achieve performance targets defined during annual planning.

Steering Team—When a process uses resources from several functions that report to different managers, those managers form a steering team chaired by the executive sponsor to whom they all report. Steering teams for fast-moving projects usually meet every week for half an hour with the team and its coach. However, most steering teams meet with their improvement team for an hour or two each month. In steering team meetings all improvement team members may interact with senior managers. In turn, the senior managers become familiar with individual team members and their performances, which often benefits team members.

Each month, an improvement team briefs its steering team on progress and problems, and obtains guidance and support. Senior managers need not be full members of an improvement team. Senior management members of teams may make sincere commitments to the team effort, but during projects that may run six months or more, senior team members experience overloads that force them to slip commitments and miss team meetings. Failing to keep commitments and being absent from team meetings wastes time, adds delay and damages morale among other team members. Absenteeism signals that "day job" priorities are more important than what the team is working on. Wasting people's time in team meetings is fatal for a team's success.

An executive sponsor may use the following roles to guide the choices of team members from available people. In summary the seven roles beyond team sponsor and steering team for successful process-improvement teams are:

Core Team Leader – either a volunteer from the team or a member appointed by the team's sponsor, whose challenge is to maintain the team's focus on its objectives throughout diagnosis, process improvement and deployment;

Core Team Members –people from the process workforce who together have end-to-end expertise in the process needing improvement from suppliers of inputs to customers who depend on outputs. The size of an improvement team depends on the number of specialists needed to understand the process from start to finish. Each team member should have two or more years of experience in the processing steps he or she represents. Also customers or customer contact employees with first-hand customer contact and deep understanding of what customers care about should be core team members. Service process-improvement core teams often have between six and twelve members with 80 to 200 years of combined experience in the process to be improved. A team member who has worked for two or more years in each of several functions may represent several functions if that member's knowledge is still up to date.

A core team of six members meeting for two hours per week averages twenty minutes of "air time" in which each member can speak and be heard. If the process of interest demands a larger team, core team members may also serve on specialized sub-teams. Sub-teams help ensure that each member averages at least 20 minutes of air time per meeting. Any core team member may also play one or more of the following roles:

Rocket Scientist – a team member with good spreadsheet and database analytical skills. This person may lead a data analysis and metrics sub team to gather customer and process data and perform analyses.

Sergeant Major – someone who likes to do things, is well respected by the executive sponsor, and is experienced and trusted by coworkers working in the old process. The person in the sergeant major role is the point person for piloting a new process, and later for deploying it in the actual workflow.

Plate Breaker – someone dissatisfied with the current situation, with deep experience and knowledge of what is wrong and a low tolerance for whining, blaming and excuses. Plate breakers know the facts and call things as they are. A sense of humor is essential for poking fun at painful truths without giving offense, by making humorous comments that get the team laughing while facing painful realities. Plate breakers tend to succeed best in organizations run by a plate breaker.

Guest or Consultant – part-time members with specialized statistical, computer and IT, training or other types of specialized input, may participate in core team or sub-team activities when needed.

Team Coach or Facilitator –an outsider or experienced process-improvement professional who has deep experience in human resources, operations, quality improvement, or information technology. Coaches help the team leader and team overcome difficulties as they complete steps in an improvement project. Some coaches may also help design each team meeting to eliminate wasted time. So-called six sigma "Black Belts" may serve as coaches if they have led several large service process-improvement projects with some success.

A team coach accountable to the executive sponsor helps ensure the integrity of team assessments of the value added and the criticality of process tasks. Non-essential, non-value-added tasks will be removed from the process value stream. Essential non-value added tasks, such as safety or regulatory compliance, belong in supporting processes that supply just-in-time inputs as the main value stream demands them. Coaching is also helpful during pilot testing and deployment of a new process and may help integrate new processes into control, corrective and preventive process maintenance, training, and other supporting infrastructure.

The above roles on a team are not rigid positions and should never be used as labels for members of a team. If you sponsor a process-improvement team you can only involve the individuals you have available—whether or not you fill all roles. Once the team's members are selected, they become the team. Most teams measure up when supported with training and skilled coaching.

In early process-improvement work during the 1970s, even naive cross-functional teams produced tremendous results on improvement projects. They were patterned on multi-disciplinary operations research teams and followed a structured process that took people from confusion in the current state, through a sequence of team activities that mapped out the desired future state and a step by step action plan for migrating to the future state.

Working with people on teams teaches respect for the talent, cooperation, enthusiasm and creativity of an organization's workforce. Taiichi Ohno (who developed the Toyota system of lean production) insisted that the mind is power and that wasting the talent of the workforce was the greatest single waste in organizations. Yet managers who ignore the experience and intelligence of their workforces lose opportunities to lead and coach workforce members in solving problems and improving their work outcomes. Lean competitors are unlikely to pass such opportunities up.

Organizations that depend on teams for two or three annual improvement cycles evolve an important team-level dynamic. Team members who worked together in varied situations develop a type of self-organization called "transactive memory." Transactive memory arises among members of a group as they learn which skills each member excels at, and team members trust each other to perform as appropriate in new problem situations. Transactive memory reduces formal coordination of team members and enhances overall team performance. Research on transactive memory in consulting, sports and other teams found that the performance advantage arises when members work as a system that automatically responds to cues with learned responses which the team accumulated from past experiences in similar situations.

Now that you have seen the ideal roster of improvement team members that has evolved over many years and teams, the next section shows how to ensure such a team's pathway to success by paving the pathway with low risk, low difficulty steps.

ADMIT IT: CHANGE IS SCARY

Participating on teams helps satisfy deep human needs to cooperate and connect with others for the common good. Members of successful teams participate in accomplishments far beyond what they could achieve alone. Teams enable individuals to combine individual pockets of knowledge in new ways that yield progress, innovation, accomplishment, satisfaction and eventually good feelings, as cooperation and improvement replace messy fragmentation and confusion. However, even the most successful teams do not start out as teams. They begin as groups of people who may not even know each other. At the start, future team members may wonder about answers to the following questions, even if they do not ask them:

Why ME?
What's going to happen to ME?
What's in it for ME to change?
What help will YOU give ME or what will you do to ensure that changing will not hurt MY performance?
What results or changes will come of this?
Why should I trust YOU with all of the above?

No individual ever poses all these questions at once. But all have been asked so often that, if you want people to work with you on making change, it makes sense to be ready with real, frank and honest answers. Failing to anticipate and answer important questions opens the way to fill the information vacuum with made-up answers far worse than the truth.

In most organizations, it is safe to assume that during the first few hours of a team's first meeting, its members may feel fear, anxiety and confusion at being invited to work outside the comfort zones of their day-to-day routine. So, giving straight answers to fear- or anxiety-inspired questions helps build mutual respect and trust. Members of your organization must see change as legitimate. Explanations of a proposed change must make good sense to all who are affected by it. Organization members must feel that the change is the right thing to do under the circumstances; and that it will make all who are impacted better off than they were before the change.

Even when the honest answer to a question about the future is, "I don't know; we will have to wait and see, and deal with whatever we run into," that answer is right. You and the questioner are in the same boat. You must invent change as you go. When you lead change, care enough about the people you work with to give real answers to their important questions. Acknowledging that change is scary and keeping your promises reduces people's confusion and fear. The next section shows how a path from the status quo to a better future can be made of small easy steps that maximize your chances of success.

MAKING ACTION PLANS EASIER... AND EASIER... AND EASIER

No matter how well staffed your team is, or how hard and well the team works, success in achieving its goals is not an accident. Teams can ensure success by identifying, and then preventing or removing difficulties from their plans, one at a time. Reducing risks and confusion by simplifying all difficult tasks plans for change is sometimes called "baby stepping."

Many people confuse successful change with taking a few big risks. The opposite is true: success avoids big risks by breaking them into smaller but more manageable low-risk baby steps. The confusion arises from the fact that an improvement project requires several steps to succeed as planned, one after another. So, for example, some might feel that succeeding at four out of every five steps in a plan implies the steps are easy. The confusing thing is that an action plan that includes ten or fifteen such easy tasks is almost sure to run into trouble or fail.

For example if all ten tasks of an action plan have four out of five odds of successful completion, that plan will achieve its goal on average 11 percent of the time. If a more complicated plan depends on success with fifteen such tasks its odds of success fall to just one success in 28 attempts or about 3.5 percent. Since a typical improvement team may need to carry out dozens of tasks, it is vital to ensure that each task has high odds of success so that all tasks from start to finish can succeed. The following story shows how teams can reduce the risk of failure in their plans for change.

After several days coaching members of six software development teams in using process-improvement tools to plan their software projects, the last step was for each team to agree on a project action-plan. These action plans were to be entered into standard project management software and used to monitor and manage the progress of each project.

The project planning template was a table with a row for each planned task and columns for such task data as duration, person-days of effort, predecessor and successor tasks and a final column for a task difficulty rating from one to ten. The six teams each filled in their project planning templates with their planned tasks and the data on each task.

For the difficulty ratings, all six teams calibrated a ten point scale based on a range of recent actual tasks and projects they were all familiar with. Then, each team used these difficulty benchmarks to assess and rate the difficulty of each task in its project plan. A simple, low risk task was rated 1 out of 10, which a high difficulty task likely to fail was rated a 9 or 10 out of 10.

All six teams filled in difficulty ratings on their tasks and shared their ratings. Each team had rated one or more tasks as a ten on the ten point difficulty scale. The teams then were asked to break each seven or higher rated task into as many smaller, easier tasks as needed so that all tasks rated a 3 or less on difficulty. Four of the six teams were able to simplify their most difficult tasks and arrive at a project plan with all low risk tasks. Two teams, however, had at least one killer task rated at difficulty 10, which they could not break into smaller, easier tasks.

The first of the two high-difficulty tasks was, "obtaining executive approval of customer's final software requirements" rated at 10. They explained to me that the customer executive who had to approve final requirements for a software system that the team was building had refused to give final approval. As time passed, in desperation, the team leader had begun development without final approval on specifications and the team had already invested more than a million dollars of development effort based on software engineers' guesses about what the final requirements would be. This team's ten rating red flagged the need to escalate the issue of customer approval of final software specifications to the highest executive level in charge of software development.

The second team had been forced by a change in company strategy to use a new and unfamiliar software technology on their project. They rated the difficulty of first use of this technology at ten out of ten. Use of the new software technology was nonnegotiable. It was part of a planned shift in the company's software engineering strategy. So this team redesigned their project plan to include two parallel development projects. Using the new software approach was Plan A—high difficulty with high risk of failure—rated ten. However, plan B, a low-risk development option, used familiar technology to build the exact same system. They rated all steps of Plan B at difficulty of 3 or less.

The team's revised project plan was to seek approval to work on both plans A and B in parallel until Plan A, using the new technology, progressed to a point at which completion risks and difficulties were much lower. At that point, they would abandon Plan B and reassign its resources to speed up Plan A. This approach would cost more, but would ensure an on-time delivery by hedging the very high risk of using the new and unfamiliar development technology.

While baby stepping can reduce risk by breaking down tasks to minimize their difficulty, other project failure risks depend on confusion over which team member should do each task. The following section shows how a group of people about to work on a large project avoided that pitfall.

TEAM LEADERS AS MATCHMAKERS

Even if a team has removed all difficulty from a project plan, the potential exists of assigning team members to roles based on job skills rather than on genuine interest. As a result, an effort that might have been a labor of love turns into just plain labor. Here is how a team leader invited team members to volunteer for tasks in a project plan based on each member's most motivating skills (from the motivated skill self-assessment presented in Appendix A) as well as the skills which each task demanded.

A team of 20+ members was formed to design and build a single customer web interface to replace six independent customer web interfaces. Fran, the project manager, was senior executive from finance, and her team included people from several business units and product lines, as well as members from finance and from software development. This was a large and complex project, even for such a seasoned team.

Fran sponsored a three-day, process-improvement training program using the team's actual project as the working example. This gave team members hands-on experience using each tool as they learned it. At the end of three days of training, the team's project planning was complete. Team members had placed more than 140 sticky notes on a wall-sized chart, each with the name of a discrete task from the start of the project to its completion. The team arranged the notes in time sequence from project start to finish and connected the tasks with arrows showing which later tasks depended on completing earlier tasks. The last step was for the team leader and team members to agree on which team members would be responsible for leading or working on each of these tasks.

Team members had come from many business units and functional areas, so Fran was not personally familiar with many of her team and agreed with my suggestion that she let her team members pick their task assignments based on their individual motivating skills. This meant that all hands needed to complete the skill self-assessment template in Appendix A. Fran wanted to let team members work on tasks that they would enjoy so much that they would work on them even without pay. No one objected to this sky-high hope, because after three days of hard work they were relieved that the end was in sight.

To ensure that the list of activities in the success-motivated skill table included all types of activities needed by this project, Fran read out each task name and the skills or activities that the task required. The remaining team members checked that each skill appeared in the assessment table. A few skills were not listed on the preprinted tables, so everyone used blank rows at the end of the table to add these skills.

After assuring everyone that no one would have to share their personal data with anyone else, the team members took an hour to self-assess the skills they had used most often in highly satisfying work assignments. One systems analyst finished in record time. It turned out that she had labeled and rated skills for just three highly satisfying work experiences because she was only part-time. These were all the highly satisfying projects she had worked on at this company. She then included satisfying experiences with previous employers and volunteer activities that she found rewarding and completed her self-assessment on a larger sample of satisfying experiences.

Another eager software developer had checked about two thirds of all tasks (rows) in the first three or four columns he had analyzed. After a reminder that he should check off the skills he had made heavy use of in each satisfying job or experience, he agreed to limit himself to the top five or six most-used skills in each experience column. In less than an hour everyone had identified their most satisfying skills, and it was time for team members to decide which project tasks to work on.

Some people find running things satisfying, while others are happy working without taking control. So in addition to volunteering to work on any task by writing their initials on the sticky note for that task, each person was asked to write the letter "L"(for leader) if they were willing to lead that task; or the letter "P" (for participate) for tasks they just wanted to work on. People walked along the project plan on the conference room wall, initialing the sticky notes of tasks they wanted to volunteer to work on. They made their choices surprisingly fast and everyone was back in his or her seats in about fifteen minutes. Perhaps after working on planning the tasks for nearly three days, their familiarity helped team members recognize those tasks that would let each do his or her most satisfying work.

After everyone sat down, Fran read the whole plan out loud, task by task, naming the volunteers for each task. Ten out of the 140 sticky notes had no volunteers. For each of these Fran named an individual and asked her or him to take on that task; no one objected. None of the 130 or more tasks that attracted volunteers had two "L"s. Perhaps people with a strong desire to lead had run around initialing their preferred tasks with an "L." Or perhaps after someone volunteered to lead a task, late-comers sought other tasks to lead. With all team roles thus assigned, the training program ended and I lost touch with the team.

More than two years later I met Fran during a visit to the organization. She told me that her team had completed the project successfully and on time. The new Web interface and organization-wide access and security controls they put in place were a big hit with customers, who no longer needed to sign into several independent Web sites to use all the company's product lines.

In less than two hours, this team had examined their own motivating skills and used their self-understanding to volunteer for some 130 tasks, leaving only ten unassigned. To the credit of the project leader, by basing task assignments on this project on her team members' most motivating skills and willingness to volunteer, Fran had reduced confusion and hassle. In the next section, you will see how a confused CEO undermined his own leadership team by showing that he mistrusted his own people.

HEY, CEOS: TRUST YOUR TEAMS

Trust and respect for members from the workforce starts with top executives and works its way down the levels of an organization. Here is an example of what happens when that trust is absent.

A consulting team was making a sales call at an office equipment company that discovered it had a paperwork problem. The four-member team was ushered into a large meeting room where Leo, the company's CEO, and six or seven members of his executive committee were seated at a large conference table. Leo opened the meeting with the following story.

Leo had hosted a recent sales leadership conference. During the cocktail hour an old friend of his, from when both had worked together as salesmen, walked up to him and said that he "had a bone to pick." The two sat down at a table and the sales rep opened his briefcase. As they sat, the salesman began taking paper forms from the brief case one at a time and explaining to Leo what each was for.

The first form was for ordering a fast-selling type of equipment, the second was an equipment lease agreement, the third was for ordering supplies, another for a service contract, and another and another and another. Leo got the point and asked how many forms his friend used. The salesman did not know the answer, so the two of them counted all the different forms he carried in his brief case—there were 38. Worse, these were just the forms that the salesman used most often to serve his largest customers. He often carried other forms for specialized customer needs.

Leo asked how many forms the salesman used on a typical sales call and was told that a dozen or more different forms had to be filled in for a sales call with a high value customer. What's more, the salesman could not spend an hour of face time with the customer filling out all the paperwork. So he left most of the forms blank and asked sales administrators (admins) in his field sales office to fill in the missing details. The admins often did not know the correct answers, so ordering error rates were sky high. His customers also complained about being hassled by admins calling for missing information and many customers delayed payment on erroneous orders. The whole thing was an incredible mess.

Leo told the consultants that he checked this story with several other sales reps at the conference and became so upset by what they told him that on impulse, in his keynote speech to the whole sales conference, he made a promise: he had just learned they had a paperwork mess on their hands and he was going to make it go away—end of story.

Several executive committee members sitting at the table with Leo looked embarrassed as they heard him tell this story to yet another consulting team—for the third or fourth time that day. Then, our team presented our proposed approach for addressing this problem. Each team member made a short presentation. We described our cross-functional team approach to redesigning administrative processes such as the sales and order administration process that was driving Leo's sales force crazy.

When Leo heard that we planned to help his executive team pick members of their staff for the cross-functional team he interrupted with a question:

"Do you expect me to believe that you can bring a room full of my people together on a team and expect anything useful to result?"

Leo's question and tone took the consulting team by surprise. It embarrassed the executives at the table by belittling the people reporting to them. Leo's reaction to working with teams of his company's people could have doomed our approach. After years of forming and working with teams of client employees even our least successful client teams had never failed to make at least some improvements.

The consulting team had already provided Leo and his executive committee with a list of big name clients who had agreed to vouch for us and our team approach. So, confident in our references, we guaranteed to Leo that, given the right tools and coaching, his people would do the job. And, if he doubted our approach he should check our references for confirmation. We also explained that he had no choice but to rely on teams of his own people because after we or any other consultants left, Leo's people still needed to implement improvements that would keep his promise to the sales force.

Whether or not Leo and Company checked our references, they did pick us for the assignment from among five heavyweight contenders. Our consultants and the client's employee counterparts formed a joint team to diagnose the causes and impacts of the paperwork issues. No surprise—the paperwork problem was just a symptom. The deeper root cause was an outmoded piecemeal approach to designing and building sales and order entry systems for a complex multiproduct, multi-division company. The "paperwork" problem was of the company's own making. The joint diagnosis led to forming several employee teams to carry out process-improvement projects. With coaching, Leo's teams cleaned up the sales process mess and made good on Leo's promises to the sales force.

Leo, a former top salesman who had risen to CEO, distrusted his subordinates. He had not heard about this problem from executives who were already aware of it. Instead he first heard about the problem from an old friend who was brave enough to bring bad news right to the top. While Leo trusted his old friend from the sales force, unfortunately he was hesitant to trust teams of experienced and well-qualified employees to solve a customer-visible and damaging problem. This project became a major success and the company's IT organization adopted our cross-functional team approach as their methodology for reengineering all administrative and service processes more than a decade before the term "process reengineering" entered the management vocabulary.

Leo's main confusion arose from assuming that no bad news equaled no problems. This organization's culture rejected escalating bad news from sales and field offices upward. So those who heard the voices of customers every day feared to relay bad news to the executives who were planning and setting priorities on system development. The ensuing information vacuum amplified problems as the rapidly growing office equipment business added new customers, products, services, supplies, leases,—without matching its systems to the growing complexity of its offerings.

Leo, the CEO, was confused by the lack of bad news and skeptical about how well his organization would solve its problem. The lesson: leaders in organizations that don't pass the heat from small problems up, and hand the credit for solving them down, will be surprised the way Leo was.

Now that you have seen how functional boxes on an organization chart can generate skepticism and confusion about the effectiveness of teams that link those boxes, let's look at how contributing to a successful improvement team can be the highlight of a typical employee's work.

KEEP MEMBERS WHO LOVE TEAM WORK COMING BACK FOR MORE

While setting up a training room for a class of process-improvement team members, a familiar looking man wearing a maintenance man's uniform walked in. His name, Carl, was embroidered on his shirt, and he looked familiar because he had taken this class two years earlier. Carl explained that some members of his improvement team had turned over, so all team members, himself included, had opted to go through training as a team.

Carl's story was that after the training his improvement team worked on reducing utility costs for the company's dozen or more buildings in a large industrial park. Carl's team began by installing power-measuring devices on the electric and gas supplies of all the buildings and major installations. He described how team members used tools they learned in training to analyze the use of power and gas, and then said that the team got great results, as evidenced by signs the team placed at entrances to all the company's buildings.

Sure enough, large cardboard signs with a life-sized stick figure named Electric Bill had been placed near all building entrances and exits. Each sign displayed a graph of year-to-year power consumption in that building and gave reminders of energy conservation tips such as using revolving doors to cut heat losses during winter weather. Carl explained that the Electric Bills (the name his team had chosen) were moving on to launch an awareness campaign to involve more people in energy conservation. He reported that his team had already saved $800,000 on the company's total utility costs compared with the previous year.

When asked if Carl enjoyed working on the Electric Bills team, he started by saying that he worked in maintenance. He left measurements, Pareto charts, brainstorming, and action planning to other team members because it was "not my kind of stuff." But when the time came to go out in the parking lots and climb up utility poles, Carl had begun to enjoy working on the team. When asked to explain, he said that the Electric Bills' data gathering and analysis had found that lighting the parking lots around the many buildings at night was one of the biggest costs on the company utility bill. (The firm's production lines operated around the clock with three full shifts.) His team decided to put timers and motion detectors on all parking lot lights to keep lights on during each shift change, but switch them off during night shifts unless the detectors spotted motion in a parking lot. Carl added that he was the team member who got to climb all the poles and install the motion detectors, which he enjoyed.

Carl described how this change had another unexpected benefit. The nighttime security force stared at banks of video monitors all night long, watching all parking lots and building entrances. With the new motion-detecting lighting controls, the screens of those TV monitors were dark during the night until something moved in a parking lot. Then the lights would come on, brightening the TV monitor and attracting the security guard's attention.

The security people liked the change and, since Carl's team had installed the motion detectors, no cars had been stolen out of any parking lot during night shifts. A minor side effect of the change was that wild deer passing through the lots at night set off the detectors. So security was considering putting chain link fences around the campus.

Carl, the maintenance man, was participating in his second round of training on tools and methods that he did not enjoy using. But as the maintenance department's volunteer on the Electric Bill team, he had made his own contribution to improving the company's energy efficiency. He enjoyed being the team's arms and legs for changes that saved such a huge amount of money. What's more, he was on the stage when the company CEO recognized the Electric Bill team's accomplishment before an all-hands meeting.

Participating on this team allowed Carl to work on what he enjoyed and be thanked for his role in the team's success. As a member of the Electric Bill team Carl had obtained what employees want from work—to be relied on, thanked, and given credit; and to see how his efforts benefited the company, its security force and the night shift employees whose safety and parked cars were more secure.

Months later, while walking to another team training session for software engineers, a familiar-looking man stopped me, asked if I was back to train more teams and then shook my hand and thanked me. He saw I was puzzled and explained that before team training everyone at his level in the company had his or her own way of conducting meetings. But, after years of training people from all over the company, thanks to process-improvement training, the managers and others had learned a common language and set of tools for solving problems. As a result, communication and cooperation in the organization had improved far beyond what it had been before the training.

Later that day, the same man walked by and a class member told me that he was the head of the company's software engineering division. After training about 2,000 people in this organization from 1991 to 2001, this chance meeting in a corridor was my first personal "thank you" outside of the classroom. The organization's training objective was to improve the tools skills of improvement teams solving workplace problems. No one realized that senior managers across this complex organization experienced difficulty and frustration as they tried to work with each other. This perceptive executive was grateful that providing a common vocabulary, set of tools and team approach to working across organizational lines had reduced confusion and expanded effectiveness.

Teaming and managing in a complex enterprise are both group processes. Yet an organization that willingly trained maintenance workers to be effective as members of an improvement team had simply assumed that its managers already knew how to succeed in groups or teams. In this case, leadership had confused high salaries and important titles with basic teaming skills and know-how that must be learned from a teacher.

WATCH OUT WHEN CHANGES MAKE "WINNERS" FEEL LIKE LOSERS

Those who build information systems to help managers can become confused and upset when a technology upgrade overlooks business behaviors that were obscured by weak reporting and controls.

An experienced information-systems analyst assessed the benefits of upgrading her organization's field sales reporting system. After interviewing sales managers and field sales people on existing sales information systems, she did a thorough job of documenting business and user requirements, costs, benefits and risks. Her conclusion was that upgrading the current system would satisfy management's needs for improved sales information.

The recommended upgrades avoided an expensive and difficult conversion to a new customer relationship management and sales management system. So both the systems and sales organizations gave the analyst the go-ahead to upgrade the system as she had recommended.

The upgrade project was successful from the project management and technical points of view. The upgraded reporting system passed user-acceptance tests for all requirements. But once the system was implemented in the field, some salespeople and sales managers began complaining about the changes. Over time complaints from some top salespeople grew.

The information systems (IS) team attempted to resolve the complaints with tweaks here and there, but objections remained. Then a number of influential users rejected the system upgrade altogether, and some refused to enter data into the upgraded system or use its reports. The IS department pulled the plug on the upgrade and reverted to the previous system, which made the people who were displeased with the upgrade feel vindicated.

At the request of the project manager and her supervisor, the IS department conducted a detailed project postmortem to obtain lessons learned from this embarrassing failure. After interviewing the software development team, sales executives, managers and field sales people who had used the upgraded system, the postmortem team found two different reactions to the now defunct sales reporting system upgrade.

A majority of salespeople and managers were satisfied with the upgrade—they had no problems. However some sales producers said they had had difficulty matching their pre-upgrade sales levels after the reporting upgrade and blamed their problems on time wasted using the new system. Other interviewees whose selling productivity had either stayed the same or improved after the system upgrade said they had been satisfied. Some also told the IS team that some salespeople were unhappy because the upgrade had eliminated ways to game the previous version of the reporting system.

Under the old system some salespeople were able to report better sales numbers than their actual sales. The upgraded system made these manipulations of orders visible, so the manipulations stopped. As a result, people whose sales numbers had previously looked good appeared to have lower sales. They began blaming the upgraded reporting system—which was understandable, because it revealed they had been gaming their reported sales.

The IS specialist had done her job from a technical and project-management perspective. However, the upgrade was implemented without a pilot test, which might have identified the hidden and non-discussable reporting practices by some salesforce members. Because reported sales impacted rewards, recognition and reputations, the upgraded system should have been phased in gradually so that people could adjust to the increased visibility of their activity.

No team can know what it does not know, and no team knows everything. So, running pilot tests is a safe way to find out what is unknown. This system upgrade omitted pilot testing because it was just an upgrade of a proven system. With no required way to report sales, some people exploited system limitations to improve their apparent sales performance. Sarbanes-Oxley legislation has since made situations similar to this less likely in publicly owned organizations.

In this case, confusion and eventual failure resulted because IS had tried to serve the needs of a sales organization it did not understand. Had the IS team included a few experienced salespeople as team members, and pilot tested their upgrade with sales people before releasing it, this confusion and its consequences could have been avoided.

CONCLUSION: IMPROVING YOUR FUTURE THROUGH TEAMWORK

If you sponsor a team to improve a critical process, pick team members who have a cooperative spirit and willingness to work together. Provide a new team with an experienced coach to help them use tools and follow a proven step-by-step improvement approach. Team members are confused for about the first third of an improvement project, and may become discouraged when faced with the current, messy reality. However as your team uses tools such as flowcharts, spider-web diagrams and root cause analysis, their confusion will give way to deeper understanding—and spark changes that will produce more value for customers with less waste.

In this chapter we've looked at examples of common confusions arising within and around individual teams. The next chapter shows how leaders can replace organization-wide confusion with an organization-wide system for pursuing a mission.

At the organizational level, committing random acts of improvement by tinkering with problems that hurt performance creates confusion and slows progress toward a better future. The next and final chapter shows how to elevate improvement from hit-or-miss random acts to a more complete, system-wide view of improvement in pursuit of accomplishing the organization's mission. Chapter seven shows how to view your organization's management as an organization-wide feedback and learning system. Such a management system focuses scarce improvement resources on removing bottlenecks slowing your organization's pursuit of its mission. The first experience with a pilot that connects planning to doing—checking and then deciding what to do next based on what resulted—pilot tests a cycle that is the foundation for most human learning and progress. Don't let the name of this plan-do-check-act cycle frighten you—it is a simplified scientific method.

7

Confusion About Random Versus Systematic Improvement

ORGANIZATIONAL SURVIVAL IS NOT MANDATORY

Confusion in organizations about purpose, strategy and change is common. People cannot be fooled by a lofty mission statement. An organization's leaders must prove the mission is real by the actions they lead —not just by their words.

Each organization hosts conversations among countless combinations of managers, employees and customers, functions, departments and suppliers. The rise of social media has made it possible for the static of misinformation and distortions to spread further and faster than facts. What emerges from all this chatter? More often than not, instead of coordinated and well-designed organizational action, the result is widespread clashes and confusion.

The following executive preview summarizes the main lessons derived from the sections in this chapter:

1: Define your organization's purpose and lead its people in building an organizational system for achieving it. As long as an organization commits only random acts of improvement, debates about what to do will create confusion. To avoid such confusion select improvements that relieve the top bottlenecks to achieving your organization's defining purpose or mission.

2: Ask and answer: why does your organization exist? A CEO tends to describe the organization in terms of what it does for its customers;

how it adds value to its products and services; or what the major functional components are. A fourth, rarely considered view—why the organization exists—can resolve organizational confusion at all these levels.

3: A high-performance organization may be thought of as a social system that multiples its members' effectiveness the way a bicycle multiplies a rider's pedaling—by a factor of five or ten times. All parts of an organizational system must work together to sustain excellence in achieving its mission, just as all parts of a bicycle work together to multiply mobility.

4: Engage and humanize your organization by naming types of confusion, feelings, drives, purposes and fears. Making sense of the mix of organizational and individual emotional drives and purposes is a challenge that must be faced in order to relate individual member needs and efforts to fulfilling the organization's purpose.

5: View your organization as a system in which no part is the most important part. The performance of the whole organization arises out of how well all parts cooperate and enhance each other's' performances so the whole achieves its mission.

6: Join an organization that involves people's hearts and minds in seeking answers to the questions: What can we do to attract more new customers, and to please all our customers as they have never been pleased before. How can we make our customers' dreams come true? Innovation is an emergent property of an organization functioning as a purposeful social system.

7. Expand opportunities for individuals to set higher personal and team goals, and expand skills and cooperation to achieve those higher goals. Within an organization, power-over, the ability to make people behave the way you want them to, must yield to power-to—helping organization members create, change and innovate in ways that achieve the organization's purpose.

8: Identify the character traits of high-performing employees and then select new employees who will excel because they share those traits.

High-performance organizations select individual members who value pleasing customers and coworkers above gaining personal rank and power over others, and then train and coach them to work in agile work designs so no individual is overwhelmed by inevitable upsets.

9: Focus more time on progress toward achieving mission and purpose and less on watching the financial scoreboard.

10: View your organization as a social system for pursuing a meaningful purpose. That social system must integrate plans, resources, changes and metrics into an annual improvement cycle for improving the organization's capability to fulfill its mission and pursue higher missions.

11: Prevent backsliding on improvements by monitoring outcomes and metrics for signs that process maintenance is needed. Building a process is like building a house. If you do not maintain your new house for too long, it will fall apart. The same applies to any process: without sustained and effective, corrective, preventive and improvement actions it falls apart.

12: Assess your organization's actual management system against a validated template. Such an assessment aims to spot gaps and approaches that fall short of what your template requires. Each gap or shortcoming in the management system is an opportunity for improvement in an organization's management system.

Even if an organizational diagnosis finds hundreds of opportunities for improvement throughout the organization, available resources are typically too scarce to pursue them all. So a diagnosis poses a practical question: which improvement opportunities should organizational leaders pursue when they cannot pursue all of them at once?

This chapter's sections show how managers and consultants have resolved confusion and disagreement over what changes will most improve organizational performance. Other sections show how executives integrated functions, processes, and structural components of organizations into organizational systems to serve economic and social missions.

Collaboration and teamwork are the social glue knitting organizational parts into a system for accomplishing organizational purpose. But collaboration and teamwork demand moral and social commodities that are not traded on any free market and cannot be outsourced. As Nobel Laureate Kenneth Arrow points out, when employees and contractors are hired they understand that employment is conditional on willingness to obey authority. However, those who join an organization also contribute valuable social and moral commodities beyond obedience to authority. These include mutual trust, honesty, loyalty and commitment to the organization's purpose which cannot be bought or even easily contracted for. (Arrow, 1974)

Everyone in an organization can describe aspects of their organization that could improve. The problem of choosing what to do from the list of all potential improvements is similar to the decision a scientist must make about which of many possible experiments to run to test a new theory. The scientist looks for the change that she believes will make the greatest progress, and designs and runs an experiment to test it. Then the scientist learns from seeing the result of the experiment. Repeating this cycle over and over again expands knowledge and understanding, which drives development. This sounds like an idealized model and it is. But like all ideal models it must be adapted by all organizations that seek to prosper and endure in an ever-evolving competitive environment.

In the next section you will see how the view of organizations as purposeful systems unifies conversations about what the organization should do, how it should do it, and what different activities it must engage in to pursue its purpose or mission. The section will also show how to start purposeful, unifying conversations about what actions are needed to resolve critical bottlenecks to performance, and to make those conversations ongoing and systematic.

CEO ELEVATOR SPEECHES TELL ALL

CEOs and general managers from all types of organizations attended executive seminars on organizational improvement. Individual executives often opened personal conversations by describing their organizations in simple, memorable terms (a sort of "elevator speech"). These CEOs' short organizational descriptions grouped into four categories.

The first type of organizational description was functional. It summarized what the organization did or what useful output it provided to those who relied on it. For example:

"We are an OEM supplier to the auto industry and we do whatever our OEM customers don't want to do themselves."

"We are a family business and I manage the company in a way that provides good jobs and incomes to members of my family."

"We are an international bank because our largest customers expanded overseas and asked us to serve their banking needs wherever in the world they did business.

The second type of description was of process, stating how the organization's sequence of work or processing activities added value.

"Our bank is a deposit in-gathering, money-lending and risk-managing institution."

"We are an order-taking, make, fill, ship, bill and collect business."

"We are our customers' purchasing agent. We find out what goods our retail customers want to buy, and we find suppliers that produce high quality at competitive prices."

The third view looked at the organization's structure, by identifying units comprising the organization.

"We have a retail deposit side that generates expenses and investable funds, and a credit and lending side that manages risks and produces income. We make profits by maximizing the difference between the two."

"We basically have a large retail banking side and a wholesale banking side."

"We are the world's largest startup and we organize ourselves around developing and building each new generation of systems."

These examples show that organizational leaders use different simplifications to reduce confusion. The functional view makes sense by describing how the organization's products and services are used. The process management view looks at operational flows as a value stream from start to finish. The structural view describes the design and building blocks of an organization by naming its basic parts.

None of these simplified depictions states why the organization exists. Such incomplete descriptions increase confusion by overlooking how improvement efforts relate to justifying and sustaining the organization's broadest goal, sustaining its existence as conditions change. The three narrow views overlook how improvement does or does not enhance an organization's pursuit of mission within its changing economic and social context.

The fourth and rarest description of an organization that a CEO could give is a thumbnail explanation of why the organization exists. This type of description depicts the organization as an inquiring system for discovering and fulfilling a basic economic, social or technical mission. In ten years of chats with CEOs and other senior executives have I encountered only three examples of this fourth group of organizational descriptions. The third example in the list below came from the CEO of a Baldrige Award winner.

"Our organization exists to improve the health of populations in the market areas we serve by providing excellent health insurance and other services that achieve our mission."

"We see our customers and suppliers as a team working together to find new and better products and services which let us generate and share benefits jointly."

"We are Ladies and Gentlemen serving Ladies and Gentlemen by providing genuine care and comfort to our guests."

No CEO who described his or her organization in terms of its mission used the terms "purpose" or "system" in describing it. But by defining why their organizations existed they integrated decisions about products, functions, processes, organizational and technical structure into a unified whole—an organizational system. Focusing on purpose makes sense of how function, process and structure must work together as a system so the organization adapts to changes that sink less adaptable competitors.

A systems view of the organization does not speak of *the best* function, *the best* process or the *best* organization structure without first referring to the organizational purpose. Only an organization's purpose provides insights into how good is good enough, how important is important enough, and what higher purpose to pursue if the current purpose no longer attracts and motivates stakeholders.

The next section presents an analogy to understand organizational excellence. This analogy shows how dynamic linkages of leadership, planning, direction, purpose, processes, workforce and customers fit into a management system. The management system pursues excellence in achieving the organization's purpose. But please be aware that a mechanical analogy for describing organizational performance omits social elements of an organizational system. Each organization's leaders must design and integrate social aspects of management into a system of purposeful individuals and units able to work cooperatively to harmonize and fulfill individual, unit and organization-level missions.

THE BALDRIGE BICYCLE ANALOGY FOR ACHIEVING EXCELLENCE

The Malcolm Baldrige criteria are a national advisory standard that summarizes the American consensus on what requirements leaders, managers, and organizations must meet to achieve world-class competitiveness. The U. S. Department of Commerce's National Institutes of Standards and Technology

(NIST) maintain and update the criteria, which are in the public domain. NIST revises them every other year and publishes them in booklet form. (For an explanation, please see Schaefer, et al. 2011).

In the fall of 1997 a client called me with an urgent request. He had been using the criteria for the Baldrige Award to assess gaps in his organization's management system. The caller was preparing a speech that evening to his local Chamber of Commerce on how his company used the Baldrige criteria to improve competitiveness in the challenging business environment that he and his audience faced at the time.

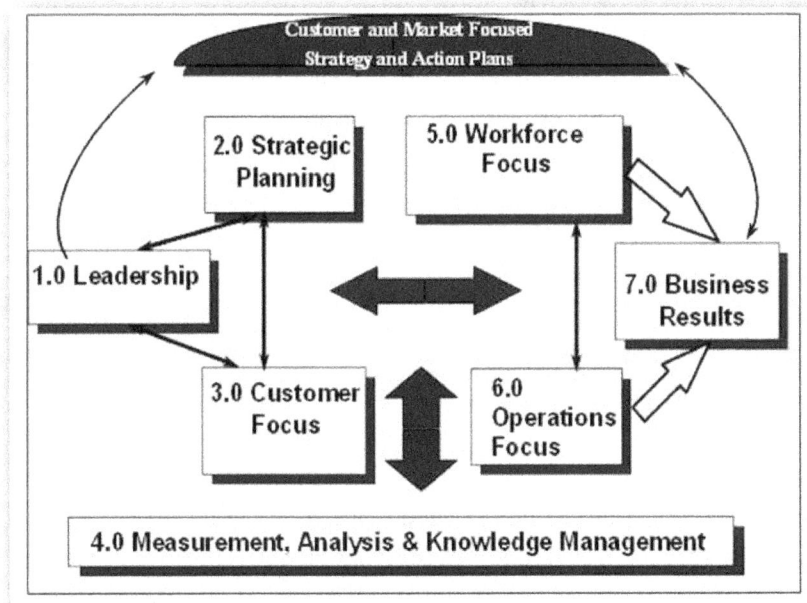

Figure 6 — The Baldrige System Flowchart (Simplified from Baldrige Criteria)

A few weeks before this call, the NIST had published a new system diagram in its revised Baldrige criteria. The diagram showed how major elements of a world-class management system fit into a whole-system perspective. When the caller saw the new system diagram, he panicked because he could not explain the diagram in Figure 6. So, we agreed to talk through the diagram and figure it out together from an understanding of each of the seven boxes.

Beginning on the left with Leadership at the leftmost corner of the triangle (called the strategic triad), the diagram's arrows show organizational leaders interacting and integrating their organization's strategic planning and customer-focused activities. So the diagram implied that top leaders worked with organization members to define a shared mission and vision of how the organization would achieve sustainable excellence for their customers (and other stakeholders).

During planning the top leaders set a market-oriented direction by answering questions such as:

If we cannot compete in all markets, which markets do we want to compete in? If we cannot serve all customers in our chosen markets, which customers will we seek to serve?

If we choose not to offer all products, which products and services will we offer and how will we ensure that they offer greater value to customers than competing products and services?

If not all distribution channels or service locations, which channels or locations will we use to reach customers?

If not all product or service configurations, which configurations do customers value the most and get greatest satisfaction from?

Annual planning conversations result in a plan for the next few years of organizational success in attracting and satisfying customers profitably.

After organizational leaders and members agree on their organization's mission and strategy, the leadership requirement asks how the leaders' actions and decisions set personal examples of excellence. How do they create values and norms that sustain high performance while respecting and responding to customer and workforce needs?

An organization's leadership aligns the behavior of all units and members of the organization in the direction of the organization's future. This is analogous to the way the front wheel of a bicycle steers the whole bicycle in the direction the rider chooses. The strategic planning box in the diagram represents how those leaders translate decisions about organizational direction into action plans that align efforts throughout the whole organization with the planned pathway forward.

Next, we began working our way around the triangle on the right side of the diagram (referred to as the result triad). This triad symbolizes how management in a high-performance organization focuses on motivating and satisfying the needs of its workforce to produce superior business results by improving processes. Measurement and analyses in such areas as sales, customer loyalty, product and service quality, employee and stakeholder satisfaction, productivity and flow of value to customers and users require approaches for process measurement and data analyses as well as improvement skills.

The flow of value and profit the organization generates in the result triad supplies resources to fund initiatives set by the strategic triad activities of planning, focusing on customers and leading in the left triad. All plans and opportunities in the left triad must integrate with appropriate implementation actions and process changes in the right triad.

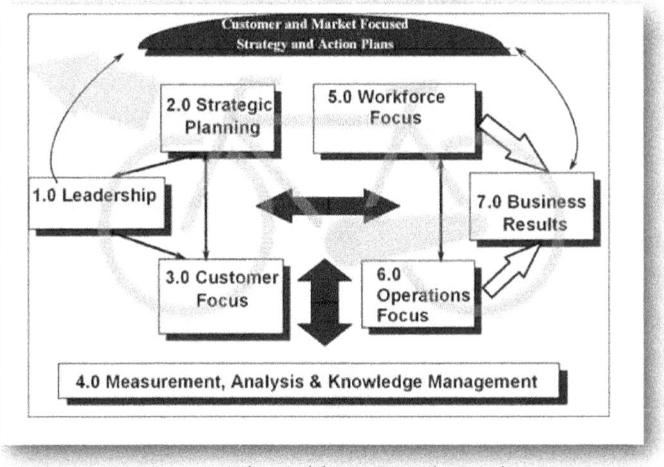

Figure 7 — The Baldrige Bicycle Analogy

With those insights, out of the blue, I told the caller, "Think of the management and organizational system as a bicycle." The purpose of a bicycle is to boost human mobility by converting pedaling motion into five to ten times as much forward progress. Looking at this diagram and imagining it as a bicycle (as shown in Figure 7—The Baldrige Bicycle Analogy) parallels how leaders of an organization gain a performance advantage by unifying their organization from end to end and top to bottom into a system for finding better ways to win races for satisfied customers.

A bicycle is designed to produce high performance (measured by mobility) by integrating three subsystems—the front wheel, the back wheel, and a frame that aligns all elements of the bicycle into a system. If any part of the system is removed, the remaining elements cannot generate high performance under some conditions. In the organizational system, the front wheel represents the Baldrige strategic triad. The pedals, chain and back wheel represent the result triad, and the frame connecting both wheels with the handlebars represents action plans for improvement as well as outcome metrics that tie the left-hand direction setting wheel to the result wheel on the right, so that all elements perform as a system. Later versions of the system diagram (in 2016) show the two triads and their integrating framework, resting on a foundation of values and key concepts. These values and concepts include: systems perspective; visionary leadership; customer-focused excellence; valuing people; organizational learning and agility; focus on success; managing for innovation; management by fact; societal responsibility; ethics and transparency and delivering value and results.

An organization's performance also depends on the environment it operates in, and the same is true of a bicycle in its environment. The race against competition is the path the bike takes along a given road. In the case of an organization, the environment also includes the competitors the organization is racing against in the markets it serves. The organization's environment includes communities and the society within which it operates and on which it relies for its talent, workforce and supporting infrastructure.

A high-performance organization monitors environmental changes to detect threats that could turn current strengths into weaknesses. If the rider enters a bicycle race against competitors, whether the race course is a long steady uphill grind, or a sudden high speed turn makes a difference in steering, balance and speed. In an organizational setting, unplanned developments may present risks. If the road the race follows ends at a deep river, the bicycle is no longer a high-performance system for racing over water. Also, whether an organization is massive like Toyota Motor Co. or tiny like a high-growth Internet-based social media start-up influences all aspects of its organizational system.

Sometime later, my client reported that his Chamber of Commerce audience liked the bicycle analogy. Since then the bicycle analogy and Figure 7 have been used to explain management systems to audiences all over the world. (Stankard, 2002).

Although the bicycle analogy may be suggestive, it is flawed for purposes of understanding an organization as a social system made of individuals. Anyone who has ridden a bicycle understands how riding a bike enhances mobility by moving its wheels several times as fast as the rider moves his or her feet on the pedals. As a mechanical system the improved mobility a bicycle delivers may perform diverse functions such as transportation, recreation, or competing in bicycle races. But a mechanical system cannot change the purpose for which it was designed—to enhance mobility. In other words neither a bicycle nor its parts can think for themselves or adapt to changes beyond a narrow range.

ORGANIZATIONS AS SOCIAL ENGINES FOR PURSUING PURPOSES

In organizations, collections of individuals and social groups choose what roles to play; what processes to follow; what functions to perform and debate and agree or disagree on; what missions are legitimate; and whether to cooperate with or compete against each other. An organization is malleable while a bicycle is mechanical. Individuals, departments, divisions, and a whole organization pursue many purposes. The bicycle analogy for an organizational system is an engineer's look at a social system.

Real understanding of organizations requires an understanding of how people feel, what they think and assume, and what those feeling and thoughts prompt them to say and do. The sociologist Robert Jackall refers to self-selected cliques of organization members as "sociological gangs." (Jackall, 1988) Unlike a mechanical system, an organization's parts (individuals and work groups) can think and feel and act on their own, guided by their individual purposes and surroundings. This living system can be a source of confusion that must be appreciated and resolved by encouraging and integrating learning and leading at all levels of the organizational hierarchy.

When organizations—whether businesses, unions, governments, charities or what have you—are understood as social systems, clarity can replace much confusion. That is not to say that all chaos, conflict, and indecent acts cease. Leaders must still work with organization members to agree on how all parts of the social system can work together as a whole and how to choose, train and motivate individuals who work within the organizational social system to fulfill its purpose or mission without sacrificing their personal values.

This section has taken a bird's eye view of how a high-performance organization uses its purpose and mission to set organizational priorities on actions. It is sad that few senior organizational leaders seem to think of the organizations they lead as social systems unified by working and other relationships. The next section shows how systems thinking by an air force officer clarified army officers' confusion about parts of a system.

WHAT IS THE MOST IMPORTANT PART OF A SYSTEM? ALL OF THEM!

To earn close to a maximum of 1,000 possible points in a Baldrige management system assessment all parts of an organization's management system must be effective, applied wherever useful, prevent problems rather than react to them, and generate outstanding results for all stakeholders relative to competitors and leading benchmark organizations. The gap between a management system's actual assessment score and 1,000 point perfection represent improvement opportunities. As mentioned in the Baldrige Bicycle story above, the allocation of the thousand points to individual parts of a management system, are revised from time to time. These revisions can lead to confusion as the following experience shows.

Several dozen officers from all three armed services attended a course in Cleveland to update themselves on the latest revision of the Baldrige criteria. Most attendees had been using the Baldrige criteria as a template for assessing opportunities to improve their organizations' management systems. They came to Cleveland to learn about major revisions in the Baldrige criteria before assessing their organizational management systems against the requirements in the updated criteria.

That year's revision had reduced the points earned for satisfying requirements for systematic and effective strategic planning. When a group of army officers in the class heard about this change, they became upset and vocal. They complained that feedback from the previous year's assessment had given high marks for their organization's strategic planning approaches. The army contingent argued that reducing the weight placed on planning was wrong. They insisted that strategic planning was the most important element in any management system and was a central element in their unit's management system.

The assumption that the goodness of a system was the sum of the goodness of its parts surfaces in discussions of Baldrige assessment. The critics ignored my argument that planning was important to the extent that it helped people maximize mission achievement. Also, the "Baldrige Bicycle" explanation was no help in convincing the skeptics. Finally, time came for a break and as the class filed out of the room an air force officer approached and said:

"The army folks aren't going to agree with you about systems. They think of assessment points on each part of a management system as the importance of that part of the system. We in the air force really understand systems, because at 50,000 feet and 1,200 miles per hour, every part of the aircraft is the most important part."

An important strength of a high-performance organizational system is its ability to innovate. It innovates by combining existing elements and capabilities into new and higher-value combinations that attract and satisfy customers more fully than before. The following section illustrates this, and if you read it, you'll like it—it's a piece of cake.

INNOVATION: WHY WAS THE MARSHMALLOW PUT IN THE CUPCAKE?

The mission of a competitive organization is to seek and find product and service innovations that will attract and please more customers than those of the competition. Much of the confusion about organizational innovation results from ignoring the fact that innovations never come from customer surveys. Here's why.

There was a baker whose granddaughter regularly visited her Grandpa in his bakery shop. For each visit, the baker decorated a special cupcake and set it aside for his grandchild's visit. At first, the girl was delighted with her special cupcake. However, in time, the novelty of the cupcake wore off, although she still expected and enjoyed eating it when she visited.

One day, the baker had already set aside his grandchild's special cupcake and was working with a pastry bag full of marshmallow cream. On a whim, he picked up his granddaughter's cupcake, stuck it on the end of his pastry bag, pumped it full of marshmallow cream and put it back on its saucer awaiting her visit as usual. When she arrived, he gave her the cupcake and she bit into it. To her surprise, this time her cupcake was filled with sweet, delicious, creamy marshmallow, which delighted her as never before and was an instant success.

Seeing how happy the marshmallow-filled cupcake had made his granddaughter, the baker made a batch of them and began giving out samples and selling them in his shop. Of course they caught on and eventually others imitated his surprising cupcake innovation. His whimsical idea to charm his granddaughter with a marshmallow-filled cupcake became the model for bakery products that have generated many billions of dollars in revenues over the years.

So, why did the baker innovate with this cupcake? Was he a natural market researcher anticipating Hostess Cupcakes™ and Twinkies™? Not really.

He had noticed that the same old cupcake was losing appeal. He wanted to see his grandchild as happy as when the cupcake was once very special. This desire to offer something special to please his dearest customer triggered the baker's impulse to surprise her with this combination of ingredients that he concocted on a whim.

The baker did not ask the girl how to make her cupcake more special. She had no knowledge of baking and confections anyway. She only knew after her first bite that she preferred the new marshmallow-filled cupcake to her plain old cupcake, as nice as that had tasted. The baker's innovation arose from his knowledge of baking, his desire to please his customer and his imagination. The ingredients he needed were all at hand—but it was his desire to make his granddaughter happy that sparked innovation. His pilot test of a new combination of old ingredients, using a single cupcake, pointed the way to a multibillion dollar baking innovation.

Strategic improvements leap beyond listening to customers. No customer ever asked Edison to develop the electric light; no customer knew that such an improvement could exist. Similarly, no customer ever asked for mass production, television, the telephone, the electronic digital computer, or any other significant improvement over what was tried and true. Customers cannot possibly know to ask for such things. All these innovations initially existed in the imagination of motivated engineers, designers and producers in the same way the cream-filled cupcake existed only in the baker's imagination, until he made one to give his granddaughter a new experience. Seeing is believing—but in the baker's case, one taste was all it took.

Innovators like the baker, strive to deeply understand the hearts of their customers and to produce innovations that address the hopes, dreams, and ideals of customers. To accomplish this, innovators must design and run pilot tests that link critical *strategic planning* issues to *actions,* which require the know-how to make and test what might please the customer more than what is currently offered. The baker's new cupcake shows how innovation works, although some innovations take many small tests whose failures point the way to improvements on the initial inspiration.

You have seen how real innovation arises when an organization's purpose is to find new and better ways to go beyond merely satisfying customers to surprising and delighting them. The next section shows how understanding employee motives and psychological drives helps clarify some unseemly organization-level behavior.

MORAL MAZES, POWER GRABS AND POSITIVE VALUES

Hal, a colleague with forty years of consulting experience in organizational behavior and change casually commented to me one day, "I conclude that organizations are collections of consenting adults committing indecent acts in public." This spur-of-the-moment comment was so startling that I failed to ask him to explain. Later, while reading Robert Jackall's famous sociological study of management behavior in large organizations I thought of Hal's comment.

Jackall's book, *Moral Mazes*, presents results from in-depth sociological studies of management behavior in several large organizations. (Jackall, 1988) *Moral Mazes* paints a disturbing picture of social behaviors in several large hierarchical organizations, which may have been the types of behaviors Hal had in mind. Why do these behaviors occur? Jackall's answer is that such organizations create mazes of moral confusion that replace doing what is moral with doing what makes self-selected management cliques feel comfortable. Not all organizations create confusing moral mazes for managers and other members to navigate.

In an article in a leading organizational science journal, Jeffery Pfeffer and Christina Fong argue that the cause of much amoral organizational behavior is a basic human need to see oneself and one's behaviors, activities and personal qualities in a favorable light and to have others share this favorable view. They call this need for esteem "self-enhancement motivation." Much as a starving person cannot ignore hunger, the drive for self-enhancement in organizations cannot be shut off or ignored. (Pfeffer and Fong, 2005)

When an individual suffers from a gap between desired and actual self-image the resulting frustration generates behaviors such as seeing him- or herself as superior to others, doubling down on past errors; tolerating abuse by powerful, but intimidating superiors; blaming personal failures on others; joining cliques; and attributing other people's actions to character flaws (e.g., "He's a weasel") rather attribute those actions to the situation that person is responding to, and so on. Organizations that avoid moral mazes find ways to enhance self-esteem by recognizing and rewarding those who do the right thing for the right reasons.

Power is the ability to have things the way you want them, and influence is the ability to change the thinking and behavior of those with power. For example, in some organizations low ranking members satisfy their need for self-enhancement by currying favor with powerful and influential people higher in the organizational hierarchy. In such organizations, hunger for approval and favorable recognition from higher-ups drives people to affiliate with powerful individuals to satisfy their need for feelings of self-esteem.

Cliques and in-groups form in some organizations until social and political behaviors determine most peoples' status and rank. Members of in-groups share information, support each other, and use access to power and influence to inform, enhance and defend fellow "gang" members as needed. Members of successful cliques who become powerful and influential tend to degrade outsiders and other cliques. Organizational researchers have found that CEOs keep membership in their inner circle flexible and fuzzy. When information and responsibility are fragmented, people rely on the grapevine to make sense of what is going on—and are thus marginalized or misinformed.

When members of powerful in-groups feel threatened, they tend to set overly risky goals and double down on failed decisions. These behaviors heighten risks and work against the interests of those feeling threatened as well as organizational interests. When powerful managers ignore others, they miss social cues. The result is those managers lack awareness of realities while ignoring people who find those realities obvious. Powerful members of the organization, whose internal messaging controls credit for successes may blame failures on scapegoats unable to defend themselves; the result, blaming, slows learning down.

Embarrassing powerful people into defending their self-images invites retaliation. So problems that embarrass powerful people are not discussed in the sort of organizations that Hal referred to and which Jackall studied. Once everyone in an organization stays silent about a topic that is never discussed, even the silence about that embarrassing topic becomes un-discussable. The late psychologist Chris Argyris named such hush-hush silences about that which cannot be discussed, "self-sealing situations."

Those outside of powerful or connected organizational cliques lack access to power and influence. Many become un-promotable to positions of higher status and rank. Un-promotable individuals are kept ignorant of their un-promotable status by those in power. This social dynamic slows or stops individual and organizational learning and slows down development of both.

When social and political behavior leads to power and influence in an organization, people judge actions by how "comfortable" higher-ranking people feel with those actions. So, instead of fostering honest behavior, members of organizations that use comfort level instead of right or wrong in deciding whether or not to take some action that will foster types of behaviors that Hal referred to (Jackall, 1988).

By contrast, some organizations defuse moral and managerial confusion by valuing constructive ways for people to be viewed favorably. These organizations correlate status and rank with integrity, initiative, productivity, participation, cooperation, profitability and other important "moral goods" that justify that organization's existence and increase member loyalty. Such organizations however take existential risks when they import high-ranking executives from outside the organization into positions of power.

The CEO of a major system engineering organization challenged by shrinking defense budgets once told me that he had spent thirty years climbing the ladder to more and more powerful positions in his company. When he became its CEO and had all the power he had ever wanted, he realized that to keep his power he had to give it away. This example shows confusion over the nature of power. Those in power may use their power to isolate themselves from negative feedback and problems, or they may share their power by informing and empowering those they lead to do the right things in right ways. Organizations in which high-ranking people amplify the power and influence of those in lower ranks may be better able to adapt to drastic environmental change. In high-tech fields, failing to empower those in mid-organization encourages the most ambitious individuals to leave for better prospects.

The next section shows how one man overcame confusion between high rank and job satisfaction by leaving a management job with power and influence to take a lower ranking position in a service organization that emphasized cooperation and trusted its workforce.

WHAT WORK CULTURE IS WORTH A DROP IN RANK?

My expectation is that most people view climbing to higher rank on the organizational ladder as progress. Here is an example of an organizational culture that made a drop in rank feel like a promotion.

When I arrived at the Ritz-Carlton Atlanta to deliver a three-day seminar on Baldrige Assessment, the concierge escorted me to the meeting room where my seminar was to meet the next day. The meeting room was not set up as requested, so the concierge summoned a gentleman from the banquets department, who listened as I described how the room should be arranged. The banquets person said that resetting the room would take a half hour, so the concierge invited me to be his guest in the hotel café until the room was rearranged.

In the café, which obviously was a cocktail lounge, the concierge told the bartender that I was his guest and disappeared. I asked the bartender what I could have and he replied that as a guest of the concierge I could order anything I wanted—which was a decaf cappuccino. Before I could finish my cappuccino the concierge returned and escorted me back to the room, which was now precisely as needed.

Early the next morning, I went to the classroom to grab a quick breakfast from the buffet that a waiter was just then laying out. After the waiter finished setting up, I introduced myself as the instructor in a class on using the

Baldrige Award criteria and asked his permission to grab breakfast before my class arrived. The waiter, a distinguished looking man in his fifties, remained in the room, so I asked if he had worked for the Ritz-Carlton for long. He replied that he had joined this hotel when it opened several years earlier. Previously he worked for over thirty years at another major Atlanta hotel, where he started as a waiter and worked his way up to manager of the banquets department.

Finding a former banquets manager of a major hotel working as a waiter surprised me. So I asked how working at the Ritz-Carlton compared with managing the banquet department at his previous hotel. The gentleman explained that in the banquets business things always went wrong —it is just the nature of the banquets business. As the banquets manager at his previous hotel, when things went wrong he ran around asking friends to help him or called around the hotel asking people to do favors or plead with people for help solving problems and keeping guests happy. His facial expression and tone showed that this was stressful.

Then the waiter began contrasting the previous hotel with the Atlanta Ritz-Carlton. He said the banquets business was no different at Ritz-Carlton—things still went wrong. But, "At the Ritz-Carlton everything works," because everyone is trained to help one another to ensure the guests are happy. At this hotel when he needs help all he has to do is ask someone and if they are not busy serving a guest at that moment, they immediately help him. He said there is rarely any difficulty solving problems and making guests happy. When I asked the waiter how he liked working at the Ritz he told me that he loved working there and that his only regret was not coming to work at Ritz-Carlton sooner.

As an aside, at that time The Ritz-Carlton Hotel Co. relied on an agile work system they called "lateral service." All jobs and work responsibility were designed to put the power to solve problems and make decisions directly in the hands of employees dealing with any unusual guest situation. The Ritz-Carlton lateral work design together with the chain's Gold Standards of Service delivered amazing service experiences for guests and timely and extraordinary recovery from upsets, as I found out on many occasions—but that is a whole different set of stories.

You can learn most of what you need to know about an organization and its performance by listening to front-line service and occupational employees. This former manager, now waiter, gave an example of how an organization can overcome confusion about job responsibilities when things go wrong. The organization created a social system that dealt with the reality that things go wrong in the hotel business. Competition for sophisticated customers who demand luxury compels organizations such as Ritz-Carlton Hotels to set and attain high standards in order to gain top rank in luxury hospitality markets. Luxury hotel guests expect extraordinary attention to their individual wishes and scripted and pre-programmed service cannot fulfill their high expectations. This organization developed a system for removing all barriers to being: "Ladies and Gentlemen serving Ladies and Gentlemen" by giving "genuine care and comfort to our guests."

Service process upsets are inevitable in hospitality because of individual variations in guest requirements. As this story shows, an agile work system that exceeds guests' expectations in situations beyond an individual employee's capability works. Any system's performance arises from how well all its parts work together to achieve the organization-level mission.

NOTE: This story took place a few years before the Marriott Corporation bought the Ritz-Carlton Hotel Company. Mr. Horst Schulze, who led the creation of the Ritz-Carlton service system, retired. One hopes that the Marriott owners retained and continue strengthening the service management system that Mr. Schulze and his team built at the Ritz-Carlton.

In the next section, a reliability engineer tries to educate top management on the need to embrace a new idea—that of pleasing customers by constant improvement and the systematic removal of imperfections and waste.

EVER-RISING RELIABILITY PUT DAVID AHEAD OF GOLIATH

Many organizational executives define their organization's success in terms of profits because businesses must have more income than expenses to sustain themselves. Engineers however often view their organization's success by how proud they feel about its products and services in technical terms, such as product quality and reliability.

Miles was a retired reliability engineer. Just before he retired however, he had promoted systematic improvement to the senior executives of a once-leading consumer products manufacturer. As a reliability engineer, Miles had watched his company's product reliability slip compared to that of their Japanese competitors. One day after looking at automobile reliability ratings in Consumer's Reports, Miles imagined a simple way to sell his top management on the need for a greater emphasis on systematic improvement of product quality and reliability.

Miles knew that Toyota had risen steadily from obscurity to become a market leader over a thirty-year period. During those years the Toyota organization implemented millions of product and process modifications by creating an organization-wide system for continuous product and process improvement. So, Miles decided to show how Toyota competed on continuously improving product quality and reliability.

Each year Consumer's Reports (CR) asks hundreds of thousands of subscribers to rate their satisfaction with important aspects of their automobiles. CR analyzes their subscribers' ratings and graphs a six year history of results for each make and model. These "bubble charts" show a six-column-by-twenty-row gird of lines with circles (bubbles) where each pair of horizontal and vertical grid lines crossed. Each of the twenty rows in the table for a given car names a major system in the car (for example, major engine, minor engine, cooling, transmission and so on, down to the audio system). The six columns stand for each of the past five years plus a sixth column for forecasted reliability of the current year's model of that vehicle.

The portion of each bubble that is shaded shows what proportion of owner/subscribers reported a problem with the corresponding system for that year. The worst rating, a bubble colored in solid black, signals that more than 3 percent of respondents reported trouble with the system (row) and model year (column) that the black bubble represents. At the opposite extreme, the highest reliability is shown by shading the corresponding bubble completely grey, indicating that fewer than one out of a hundred respondents reported any problem.

Miles obtained 25 years of back issues of Consumer's Reports (CR) annual auto issue and created a chart summarizing 25 years of side-by-side consumer ratings on each Toyota model's reliability. In year one, nearly all bubbles were solid black, indicating really poor reliability of Toyota models. In the next year, the rating for one system (for example, body integrity) went from poor to much better than average. Then the row of bubbles for body integrity stayed solid grey (much better than average) for the remaining 24 years of history. In the second year another bubble that had been solid black went from bottom rated to top rated in one year, and then stayed at the better than average rating for the remaining 23 years on the chart. And so on, with one or two major reliability trouble spots being completely and permanently wiped out year after year.

Data from the 25 years on Mile's chart showed clearly how Toyota models systematically went from among the worst cars on the market to some of the most reliable cars on the market. Miles also used a separate graph to show that how Toyota's profitability had paralleled its product and market success.

Miles then presented a similar comparison of his company's historic product quality compared with its competitors. His company's product improvements were random in comparison to Toyota's steady climb to excellence. Miles's comparison convinced his top management to take systematic improvement of product reliability seriously—by looking at it from the customer's point of view.

This story illustrates confusion by top managers about why customers choose their organization's products or services. After years of defining existence in terms of profit to shareholders, an engineer tried to convince the organization's executives of the need to systematically make sure their products were at least as reliable as others that customers could choose. When asked why management did not aspire for their company to lead, Miles said that his top managers viewed product reliability in financial terms—how much warrantee and repair cost could be saved by improvements—rather than in terms of current or prospective customer experiences.

As an engineer, Miles understood in technical terns what his organization's chiefs did not understand strategically. Their Japanese competitors were systematically using a "better, cheaper, faster and more reliable" product-innovation strategy to gain market share. They included estimated customer losses (of time and money) due to product non-performance when evaluating the cost of defects. In contrast, his company's top executives watched price/earnings ratios and earnings per share but became confused about what caused those earnings. Improving qualities such as product reliability attracts customers, keeps them loyal and reduces the costs of waste, defects and rework, not to mention the expense of recovering lost customer goodwill.

Miles was retired when he told this story. Sad to say, but his refocusing on product reliability and customer service came too late. The firm, which had been a pioneer and one of the largest American firms in its industry for decades, went out of business.

Paying enormous bonuses to executives based on annual earnings growth confuses people about what causes earnings to grow. Each year's earnings result from the cumulative impact of many large and small decisions and risks taken in prior years. Paying bonuses that distract management from making the right decisions and taking prudent risks on innovation and improvement for the future confuses management and destroys once great companies. In contrast, a banking executive eliminated that killer confusion by creating a systematic approach to planning and making improvements. This next section shows how.

STARTING UP THE ENDLESS SEARCH FOR SYSTEM-WIDE PRODUCTIVITY

Managing some long-term client relationships feels like playing Whack-A-Mole to a consultant. When you whack one problem and drive it underground, another pops up at random. This reality gives rise to consulting arrangements that commit random acts of improvement in response to problems that pop up. Such consulting confuses first aid with a healthy lifestyle.

Dan, the CFO of Yankee Bank (not the bank's real name), invited me to meet with him. He had organized the bank's senior executives for annual planning. As a group they identified their most critical issue: resolving to face increased competition and the low productivity of their lenders. (Lending is the primary business development and selling process in commercial banks.) The bank's top management set a target to double lending productivity, and to bring it in line with top performing banks of their asset class and type of market.

Dan formed a cross-functional team, which included lenders, credit managers, branch managers, loan administration personnel and information systems analysts. As the team's coach we began mapping their as-is lending process from start to finish. While mapping the current process, the team also ran a month-long time diary study on a cross-section of lenders and markets. Analysis of the activity data showed that lenders worked about 50 hours per week during the month we studied. This implied about 2,500 hours of work per year, including travel time to call on customers. However, the big surprise was that lenders spent an estimated 300 hours of face time per year discussing new business with new customers—but three times more hours doing routine administrative paperwork generated by existing business for existing customers.

The team designed a new lending-sales process incorporating five major changes. Within nine months of deploying the new process bank-wide, lender productivity was up 80 percent; after 18 months lender productivity had more than doubled to 140 percent above the pre-improvement level. The tremendous increase in sales volume began stressing "back office" service delivery processes, which soon bottlenecked further volume increases.

Dan did not go back to business as usual, as most clients would have after such a success. As CFO, Dan had set up and led the bank's strategic planning process. Now that the planning process had successfully linked the critical issue of lender productivity identified during strategic planning to an improvement team, process changes and great results, he repeated that cycle the next year on the next three strategic issues. After planning, Dan linked ownership of the top three issues (and their targets for performance improvement) to individual executives. Each executive sponsor, in turn, formed a team (including members from the previous year's successful team) and repeated three process-improvement projects on the three strategic issues.

After several repetitions of this annual cycle, dozens of the bank's managers and others had become skilled at analyzing and improving processes. A few teams brought in specialized consultants on branch staffing or information systems to help find ways to deliver more and better service at lower cost. Eventually the bank adopted the motto "more value and customer service for less cost and effort" as its definition of service productivity.

During my visits to the bank, people who had participated on improvement teams told me how grateful they were that the bank had instituted process improvement. One branch manager said that she and her branch staff had lived with many of the same problems for twenty-five years. But when she worked on a process-improvement team, the team solved those problems once and for all.

After the first few annual cycles, as the bank's growth sped up, Dan and the executive team set up a bank-wide system to measure expenses, customer satisfaction and other actual results versus improvement targets set during planning. Dan was promoted from CFO to CEO and within five years the bank-wide cycle had lifted Yankee Bank to top-tier profitability among more than 1,000 US banks in its asset class.

Dan's first planning-cycle pilot had tested each step in an organization-wide cycle for identifying the number one bottleneck blocking growth and for achieving a performance breakthrough on that issue. As productivity improved, maintaining staff loyalty became important. To avoid staff reductions as productivity improved, cost savings from strategic improvements were used to cut fees and attract new business volume from higher cost competitors. The combination of lower fees and better service levels attracted enough new business from competitors each year that no staff reductions were needed to boost return on assets and the banks growth soared.

At the end of each annual improvement cycle, Dan promoted "plate breakers" into executive positions that he held open until proven candidates appeared. In fact, Dan gave the plate-breaker nickname to team members who excelled in their day jobs, and who also excelled in sparking process-improvement teams. Dan rapidly promoted successful plate breakers to fill executive positions several levels above their rank. In a status-conscious bank such promotions sent the message that ambitious people who excelled in their jobs and in leading strategic process improvement would be fast-tracked into senior positions.

After five annual cycles, all major processes had improved so that total bank business volume had doubled with no change in head count. The bank's return on assets quadrupled—all in the face of new and intense competition as interstate banking competition arrived from out of state. Yankee Bank had become the lowest-cost producer of banking services in its state, growing several times the rate of market growth even while facing new competitors. The board of directors then merged the bank into a major regional bank where Dan became CEO of a division several times larger than Yankee Bank.

On April 18th, 1989, about five years after the Yankee Bank experience, Dr. W. Edwards Deming visited Boston University. (Dr. Deming is credited with playing a role in stimulating the quality, productivity and competitiveness revolution in postwar Japan.) When Deming was asked what message he gave to Japanese top management during the 1950s to change their thinking about competing on high quality at low cost he answered that he did not think there was any change in thinking. The Japanese combined some of what Deming taught with knowledge they had already and their spirit of cooperation, as well as the use of flow diagrams to see customer driven quality and production as a system, not as isolated events. The Japanese managers began seeing what they needed to learn to produce quality. Deming said he believed their focus was on service—finding and conceiving what might help the customer. The flowchart that Deming referred to showed how managers and workers of an organization replaced random acts of improvement with systematic, purposeful cooperation to make planned improvement for customers.

Deming's flowchart described how Dan and his executive sponsors and their teams had improved Yankee Bank's competitiveness. Members of the bank's improvement teams spent two days each month working on organization-wide improvement. The flowchart Deming referred to was an organization-wide Plan-Do-Check-Act cycle that operated to find new ways to attract and please customers—like the increased customer value for the lowest cost on the market that Yankee had achieved. Appendix G — The Deming-Nishimura Systematic Improvement Flowchart extends and explains why I have renamed Deming's flowchart as the Deming-Nishimura Cycle.

Dan and his executive team had invented their own organization's method for leading systematic improvement. They combined things they already knew, such as their existing organization and limitations and their competitions' strengths and weaknesses with knowledge and skills they learned from outside coaching—cross-functional teams, process mapping, and analysis tools such as root cause analysis and Pareto diagrams—and created an organizational system for linking process-improvement projects in critical areas blocking customer acquisition to offer the lowest cost and highest quality banking products in their marketplace.

Also Yankee Bank's first project created a small pool of experienced improvement-team members who became core members of the next year's improvement teams. Dan and other senior executives had linked activities and responsibilities into a simple and powerful annual strategic improvement cycle.

If you read the Appendix on the Deming-Nishimura cycle, you will better understand that systematic improvement takes deeper capabilities than mere skill using a set of tools and activities. Such a cycle may ignite a profound organizational spirit and commitment to unending improvement—to give more value to customers with less cost and wasted effort.

CONCLUSION: CONTINUOUS IMPROVEMENT MUST OUTPACE CREATIVE DESTRUCTION

This chapter's stories have shown how organizations that provide new and better products to replace what has become outdated avoid Schumpeter's prediction of creative destruction. If organizations wish to avoid the fate described in the book's Introduction, they need management systems that reliably keep some of their human and economic resources employed creating the next wave of innovation in technology, product design and customer delight.

As pointed out in the Introduction, huge, old organizations such as General Electric, State Street Bank, Toyota Motor Co., JPMorgan-Chase, and others have avoided creative destruction. Could their survival have been due to long runs of lucky random improvements? Perhaps, however, the odds are that these organizations and their leaders invented new destinies through systematic organization-wide improvements and innovations.

This chapter's stories have shown how to resolve confusion about random versus systematic improvement. This chapter and Appendix G — The Deming-Nishimura Systematic Improvement Flowchart should give you a head start on understanding why you should seek to participate in systematic improvement linked to your organization's strategic planning and purpose.

A rule of thumb is that most permanent shifts in market share occur during slumps and recessions. Its rationale is that smaller, less risk-averse innovators use market slow-downs to test innovations. In contrast, older organizations trapped in institutional status quos slow down innovation to cut expenses, which leaves them less competitive when economic activity picks up and customers resume buying.

Innovation arises from producer impulses and compulsions to find new and better ways to attract and delight more customers. Some improvement ideas are free for the asking from workforce members who understand the hearts of their customers. Innovation also takes leaders with the courage to envision a better future and the skills to move in the direction of that future.

Whether you accept Schumpeter's theory of creative destruction or not, the odds are that during a long career you may find yourself in an organization that is not improving and innovating rapidly enough to escape Schumpeter's recycling of its people and assets. As an individual, developing a broad and adaptable set of skills and replacing confusion with a systems understanding of organizational performance will help prepare you to recognize and seize opportunities whatever the trends.

Appendix A

Success Motivated Skill Assessment

Thinking back over your last five to ten years of work (including significant academic or volunteer involvements) list your 7 to 10 most satisfying project/job/experiences in Figure 8 below:

	Most Satisfying Work Experiences
1	
2	
3	
4	
5	
6	
7	
8	
9	
10	

Figure 8 — Seven to ten most satisfying work experiences

- Next label the corresponding columns in Figure 9 with a hint word that reminds you of each satisfying experience.

Heavily Used Skills	1	2	3	4	5	6	7	8	9	10	TOTAL
Developing Theories and Concepts											
Learning about and applying the latest theories											
Searching literature to find out what's new											
Understanding business situations											
Framing and reframing business situations											
Developing marketing and business strategies											
Developing performance measurement systems											
Making sense of complicated, confusing data											
Seeing how parts work together as systems											
Architecting and designing high level systems											
Artistic and Creative Production											
Starting up innovative new projects											
Researching new and unconventional subjects											
Producing original art works											
Imagining original solutions to problems											
Inventing unconventional solutions											
Creating new product possibilities											
Seeking improvements beyond good enough											
Conceptualizing out of the box solutions											
Learning new skills or techniques											

Most Satisfying Experiences →

- Select a column for analysis beginning with your first most satisfying experience.
- Read down the list of skills in Figure 9 and make a check next to each skill *you made heavy use of* during that work experience. (Check that you have not checked off more than 7 to 10 skills in each column to ensure you focus on *heavily used skills* associated with each peak experience.)
- When you cover all skills for the first experience, move to the next column and repeat the process of checking off the skills you used heavily. (Remember to check that you have not checked off more than 7 to 10 skills in this column to focus just on *heavily used skills* associated with this peak experience.)
- Continue identifying all skills (rows) used heavily in each satisfying experience (column) until you have considered the full list of heavily used skills for all your highly satisfying experiences.
- When you finish considering every skill row for every column, count the number of check marks across each row and write that total in the last column on the right labeled "TOTAL."
- Circle any skill with a total of 5 or more check marks. (You may wish to plot a bar chart of skills where bar heights show the total check marks by skill from highest to lowest total check marks. This type of chart is called a Pareto diagram and helps focus on the vital few versus the useful many skills)
- Experiences that you found highly satisfying often involved heavy use of these vital few circled skills.

References: Butler and Waldroop (1999) and Haldane (1974).

Most Satisfying Experiences

Heavily Used Skills

	1	2	3	4	5	6	7	8	9	10	TOTAL
Developing Theories and Concepts											
Learning about and applying the latest theories											
Searching literature to find out what's new											
Understanding business situations											
Framing and reframing business situations											
Developing marketing and business strategies											
Developing performance measurement systems											
Making sense of complicated, confusing data											
Seeing how parts work together as systems											
Architecting and designing high level systems											
Artistic and Creative Production											
Starting up innovative new projects											
Researching new and unconventional subjects											
Producing original art works											
Imagining original solutions to problems											
Inventing unconventional solutions											
Creating new product possibilities											
Seeking improvements beyond good enough											
Conceptualizing out of the box solutions											
Learning new skills or techniques											

Figure 9 — Skill Assessment Template

Most Satisfying Experiences / Heavily Used Skills	1	2	3	4	5	6	7	8	9	10	TOTAL
Counseling, Teaching and Mentoring Others											
Responding to others who need help											
Providing feedback and mentoring											
Talking with others, not talking at them											
Developing those who work for you											
Teaching and coaching others											
Training others in new and better skills											
Listening and understanding how others feel											
Contributing to society through work											
Keeping morale up											
Resolving complaints											
Volunteering to help with community services											
Managing people and relationships											
Connecting and coordinating units and groups											
Organizing and working on teams											
Helping teams focus to achieve their goals											
Working with partners or contractors											
Managing people at work											
Working closely with others day to day											
Identifying, anticipating and dissolving barriers											
Supporting peoples: day to day efforts											
Sharing work, responsibility, credit											
Serving as a liaison to others											
Repairing damaged social or work relationships											
Crediting others for their accomplishments											

Figure 9 — Skill Assessment Template (Continued)

Most Satisfying Experiences → Heavily Used Skills ↓	1	2	3	4	5	6	7	8	9	10	TOTAL
Influencing People with Language and Ideas											
Setting Expectations											
Negotiating win-win agreements											
Negotiating budget, schedule, requirements, etc.											
Rehearsing presentations and speeches											
Presenting or speaking in public											
Writing proposals or reports											
Selling projects											
Reframing ideas to make others feel comfortable											
Making complex ideas easy to understand											
Using stories to persuade or influence											
Influencing customers, users or others											
Running Things -- Teams, Departments or Organizations											
Creating opportunities to run things											
Taking charge of overall direction											
Running projects and managing project teams											
Dividing large projects into tasks											
Making things happen											
Taking responsibility for project success											
Identifying, anticipating, resolving barriers											

Figure 9 — Skill Assessment Template (Continued)

	1	2	3	4	5	6	7	8	9	10	TOTAL
Most Satisfying Experiences → Heavily Used Skills											
Designing or Using Technology											
Analyzing and re-engineering processes											
Identifying new and better technology solutions											
Architecting system hardware or software											
Defining requirements a system must fulfill											
Reusing existing hardware or software											
Inventing better systems or processes											
Designing data bases or files											
Defining functionality to meet requirements											
Designing system's modules											
Building prototype hardware or software											
Planning system tests											
Diagnosing failures and malfunctions											
Selecting hardware											
Installing hardware											
Designing and writing software											
Integrating parts into whole systems											
Documenting systems and procedures											
Testing systems against requirements.											
Anticipating and planning system maintenance											
Maintaining systems, sustaining engineering											

Figure 9 — Skill Assessment Template (Continued)

Most Satisfying Experiences / Heavily Used Skills	1	2	3	4	5	6	7	8	9	10	TOTAL
Quantitative and Qualitative analysis											
Developing business case											
Benchmarking systems and processes											
Preparing market or financial forecasts											
Developing spreadsheets or simulation models											
Optimizing profits, costs or benefits											
Gathering and analyzing quantitative data											
Gathering and analyzing verbal data											
Analyzing risks and impacts											
Analyzing and making sense of survey data											
Measuring progress toward goals											
Inspecting quality											
Analyzing hardware capacity											

Figure 9 — Skill Assessment Template (Continued)

Figure 9 — Skill Assessment Template (Continued)

Appendix B

Flowcharting Simplified

When ten or more interrelated activities or steps produce an outcome or accomplish some goal, drawing a flowchart showing what happens from start to finish is a simple way to understand what is going on. Flowcharting as you go is especially helpful if you are new to the set of activities. Others who do know what is going on can provide you with step-by-step information for your flowchart.

This appendix shows a simple example of flowcharting a familiar work process, baking a cake. The appendix introduces just a few flowcharting basics to help you get started making sense of organizational work streams and processes.

Figure 10 below uses the SIPOC model to give an overview of a process of interest. The capital letters, S-I-P-O-C, stand for the first letters in each of the five flowchart blocks shown in Figure 10 below – **S**upplier; **I**nput; **P**rocess; **O**utput; **C**ustomer:

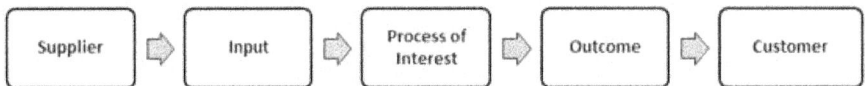

Figure 10 — Simple SIPOC Flowchart

You draw and read an SIPOC flowchart from left to right. Start on the left with suppliers of inputs that feed the process. Then follow the arrows step by step as the process flows toward the right to deliver its outcomes (or outputs) to customers or end users on the far right. Note that the customer of a process may be a second process. A chain of end to end processes is sometimes referred to as a value stream.

When baking cakes, process suppliers might include grocery stores or supermarkets, electric or gas utilities, kitchenware shops, and appliance stores. However for flowcharting the process of baking just one cake in your kitchen, the supplier might be the kitchen cabinet. The other inputs—stove, cooking utensils, gas or electricity for heating, etc.—are assumed to exist as infrastructure ready to support the process of baking one cake.

Process outputs are usually customer-desired outcomes, products or services. If a process also produces undesired results, they may be noted in a callout so the information is not lost. Desired process outcomes or outputs are any combination of products, services, and information that attract customer demand and satisfy that customer demand. For example the output of a cake-baking process is a cake, while the output of a new-product-development process is a new product ready for test marketing with customers.

Customers of a process may be other processes, individuals, work units, or whole organizations that depend on the process output or outcomes. Process customers are defined by the fact that they depend on the outputs and outcomes of that process. In this cake-baking example, the customers would be family members, guests and others who eat the cake.

You choose a level of detail at which to flowchart any process based on your purpose and the types of questions you want to answer. In most cases, this choice is between flowcharting a process at the "what it is or what it does" descriptive level versus the "how to do it step by step" procedural level of detail. The purpose of this example is to illustrate flowcharting. So we will flowchart the process of baking one birthday cake at the descriptive, "what each step is," level. This descriptive flowchart does not document *how* to perform each step. The what-versus-how distinction differentiates a flowchart, which just describes the work, from a procedure or job aid, which explicitly says how to do that work properly.

Any process, such as baking a cake, begins with an initiating event—something that triggers that process (cake-baking)—rather than some other process, such as cooking a roast. The initiating event in this case is a birthday party tomorrow.

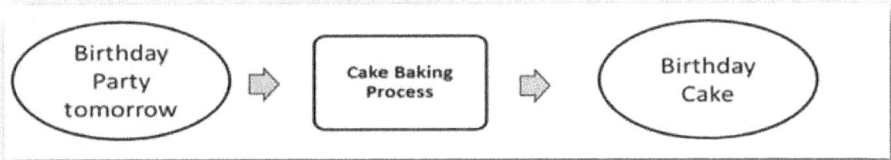

Figure 11 — Flowcharting Initiating Event

For this birthday cake, suppose all needed supplies are on hand, so suppliers will be omitted. The documentation of our cake-baking process is the written recipe. The recipe states the type of cake (some recipes show a picture of the finished cake), and lists the tasks to make the finished cake step by step.

A cake recipe is an example of "process documentation". (Note that process documentation assumes the process operator has all skills needed to perform the process.) Process documentation may also outline special quality requirements of process inputs. For example, the recipe may call for cake flour rather than all-purpose flour, or unsalted rather than salted butter. Finally, most cake recipes begin by initiating a parallel sub-process: "Preheat oven to 350 °F." This parallel sub-process of preheating the oven, shown in Figure 12, ensures that the oven will already be at baking temperature when the moist cake batter is ready for baking later in the process. The sub-process is placed on the left hand side of the flowchart to leave room for subsequent process steps.

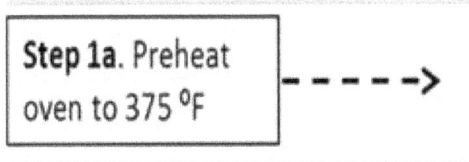

Figure 12 — Flowcharting: Initial Process Step

Next the recipe calls for buttering a ten-inch cake pan and measuring all dry ingredients. These two activities take place about the same time, so in Figure 13, the flowchart represents them vertically on the left side of the flowchart (to show that they happen at roughly the same time as the process moves from left to right). The two horizontal arrows running toward the right indicate the need to connect the activities, preheating the oven and buttering the cake pan, to activities that follow later.

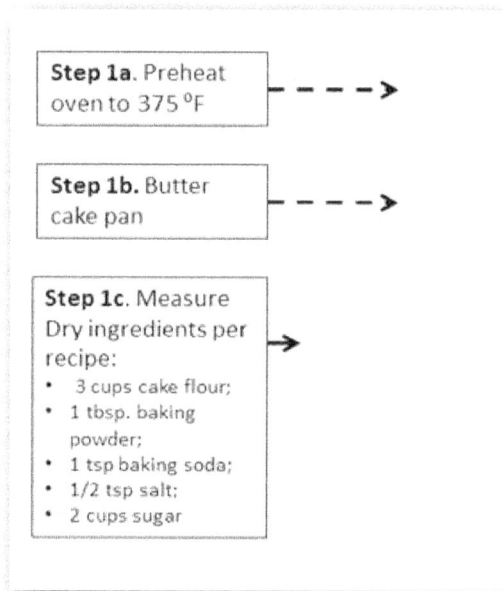

Figure 13 — Process Inputs and Initiation

With dry inputs measured, the process next indicates sifting them together as shown in Figure 14. Add process steps in sequence when possible to simplify and shorten the arrows connecting each step with the next. Usually time flows from left to right. If space or aesthetics make a left-to-right arrangement of the boxes of a flowchart difficult, arrow heads on connectors always run from the earlier activity and end by pointing to the next activity or step that follow. So we add Step 1d to the right as shown in

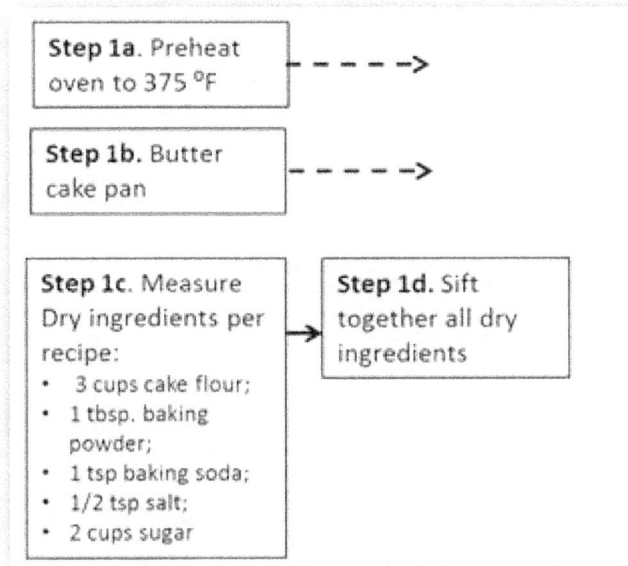

Figure 14 — One Step Follows Another in Time Sequence

Next, as shown in Figure 15 the recipe launches a second process for wet ingredients in parallel with the process for the dry ingredients.

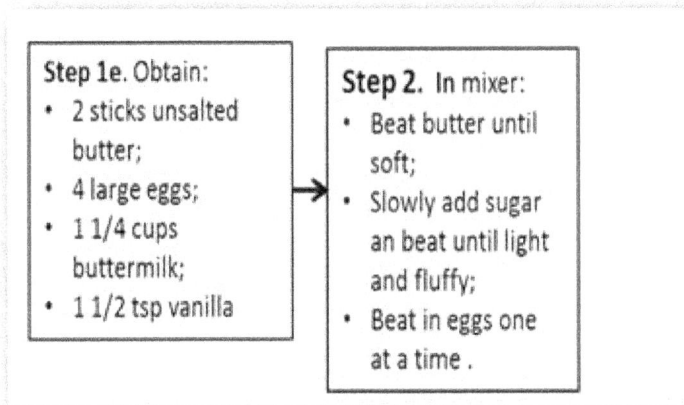

Figure 15 — The Start of a Parallel Process for Wet Ingredients

Figure 16 below adds the parallel sub-process for the wet ingredients (which begins with Step 1e.) to the earlier activities already flowcharted (activities 1a and 1b not shown for brevity). The dotted line has been added to connect the output of a previous step 1d, the sifted dry ingredients, to the activity of mixing them into the wet ingredients shown in Step 3. Placing the wet ingredient sub process below parallel sub-processes shows that this thread (as a path through a process is called) may parallel the earlier threads.

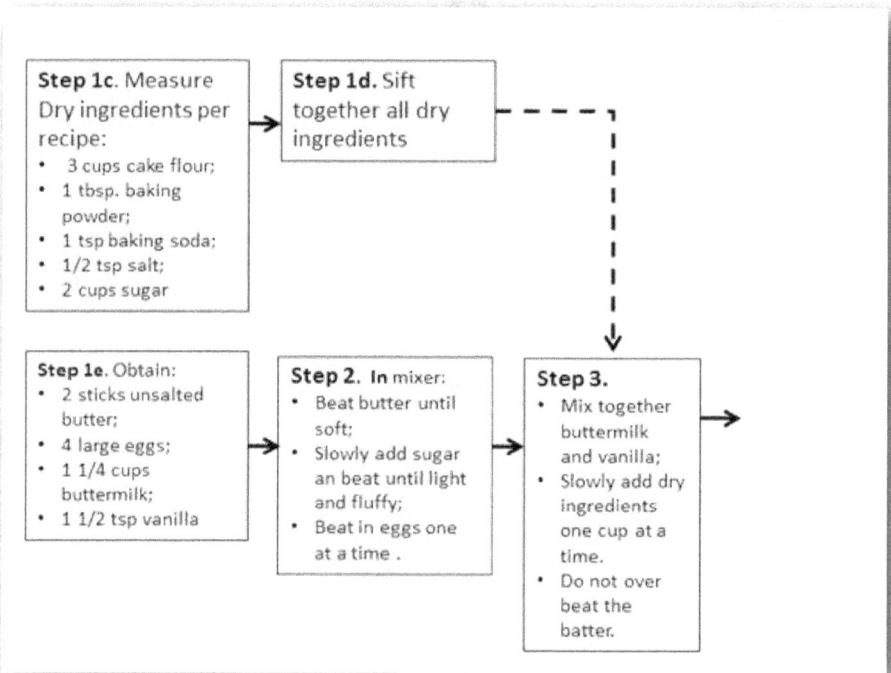

Figure 16 — Linking a Parallel Sub-process to the Main Process Flow

Next, the previously buttered cake pan step becomes necessary so that the batter can be poured into its baking pan for baking. Figure 17 shows that the completed assembly of pan and batter go into the preheated oven, shown by a third set of dotted lines connecting the preheat-oven (Step 1a) from the start of the process at the top left corner to Step 4b in which the final cake is baked which terminates the process.

Even a simple flowchart condenses a surprising amount of descriptive information. First, the flowchart contains mainly descriptive information, with minimal procedural information. It *describes what* to sift, mix beat, measure and so on, but does not detail *how to do it.* Know-how (such as how to measure, beat or sift) is procedural knowledge that a recipe's author assumes a cook following the recipe would already have. The lines and arrows of the flowchart convey sequence information and show how different activities relate to each other in parallel or one after another.

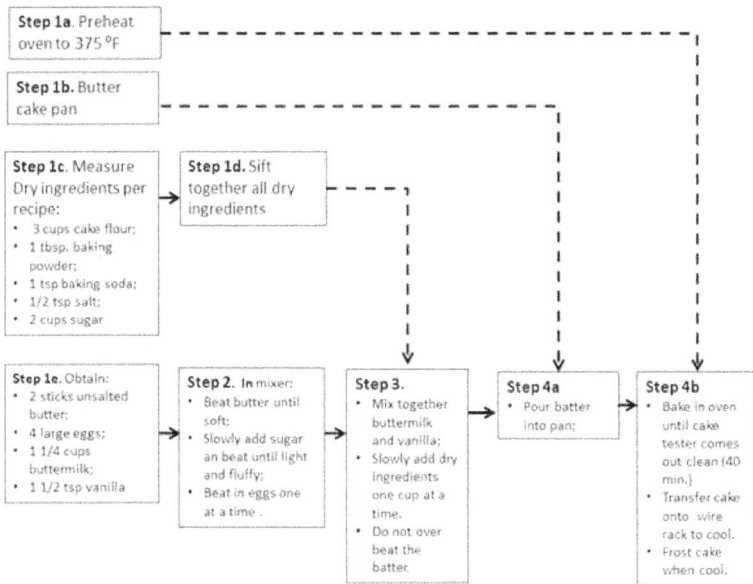

Figure 17 — Completed flowchart of cake baking process

Appendix C

Flowchart for Resolving Confusion

This appendix explains a flowchart of a process for gaining clarity when confused about an important decision. This flowchart describes what happens but does not state how to do it. This example shows how a flowchart can suggest a sequence of activities that repeat in cycles until an end result is achieved. In this example, the cycles are inquiries that reduce confusion by reframing your confusion every so often, in ways that let you continue finding and filling gaps in understanding and replacing your assumptions with reliable information (facts if possible). Appendix G on the Deming-Nishimura Cycle shows a more compact way to flowchart a cycling process by connecting its final output back to its beginning input step.

Figure 18 flowcharts a process that begins with confusion about something important to you and those you care about. The process of resolving your confusion begins in the upper left corner of the figure and moves through layers of inquiry to arrive at clarity in the lower right hand corner. Between confusion and clarity, the flowchart shows two inquiry processes moving from left to right though more than two inquiry cycles may be needed in complex situations.

In Figure 18, steps 1 through 4 in the top line of the flowchart ask you to describe your confusing situation or issue. The description should recap problems, decisions you face, their risks, gains and other concerns about failure. Following the top line of the flowchart from left to right, by Step 4 you will have summarized your confusing situation in a short story (sometimes referred to as a framing). Next talk you situation over with a few experienced mentors who have faced similar circumstances. These conversations will help you clarify your purpose and their questions may help you spot hidden assumptions. If the situation has more than a dozen elements at this early stage you may benefit from creating an interrelationship (spider-web) analysis of those elements to find the few elements that impact your situation most heavily.

Assumptions may be partially or wholly untrue; so each assumption in your story must be tested against facts. For example the story told by a new poultry farmer went as follows: "First I bought a hen. The hen laid an egg. Next there was a poultry farm." Hidden logical gaps, omissions and contradictions rely on assumptions. Analyzing what you know can help you surface previously hidden assumptions that explain some or most of your confusion.

For example a marketing executive was confused by difficulties launching a new and innovative product. He identified over 40 interrelated problems and used a spider-web analysis to discover that four problems drove the whole mess. By asking the Five Whys for each of these problems he discovered that the design and manufacturing teams had assumed that product innovations would attract more customers. However, they had not user-tested their new product prototypes, but directly launched the product. Their assumption that the innovations would attract buyers turned out to be false. The lack of market research or user testing of assumptions about the product prototypes had led to the problems in sales and distribution. Those assumptions turned out to be wrong.

So, Step 5 says that your current framing of the situation, however credible on its surface, includes only parts of the situation that you know about or can foresee.

Step 6.1 asks you to identify the assumptions this story about your situation makes and tests them against reality. Box 6.1A asks you to figure out how to reframe your situation to test the truth of assumptions in your story. For example discussing your story with an experienced mentor or colleague can provide a new point of view on assumptions that surface issues and problems your previous story had overlooked. Adopting a new point of view on the situation (some call it a reframing) lets you check your assumptions importance and validity. In the case of the poultry farmer, how did the farmer go

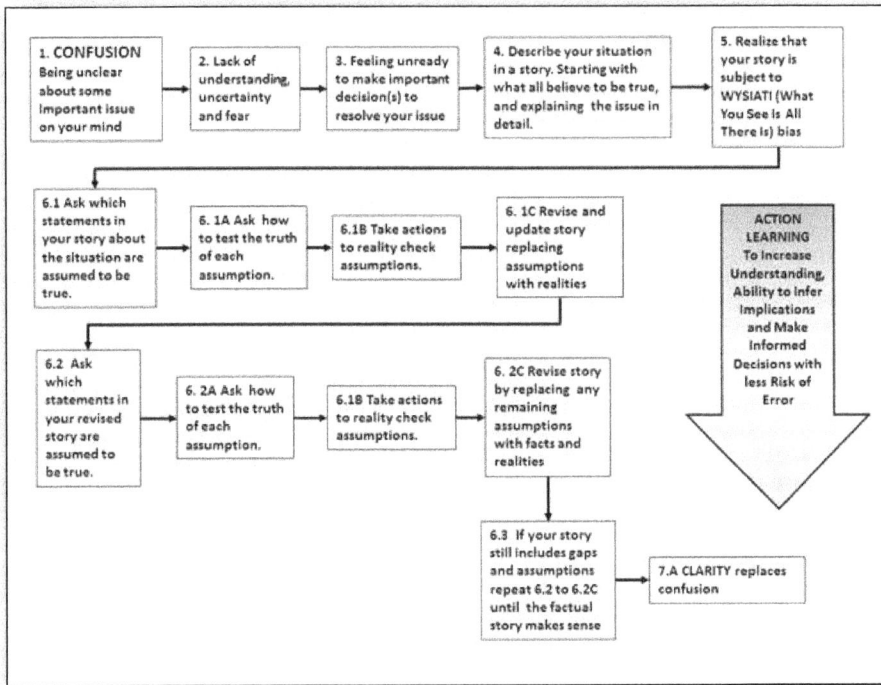

Figure 18 — Flowchart of Process for Resolving a Confusing Situation

from the first hen and its egg to a poultry farm? Filling the gap between an egg and a whole farm with facts in place of ignorance or assumptions leads to a more complete and valid story, shown in step 6.1C. The same is true for the product marketer in the earlier example, who was asked to sell a product before anyone had checked whether customers actually preferred its new features to what they already used.

In the flowchart, statements 6.2 through 6.2C represent a second round of inquiries that expand understanding beyond the obvious by replacing assumptions with facts. The product marketing example shows how a narrow inquiry into marketing confusion revealed previously unrecognized shortcomings in new product development, which increased confusion and led to a re-evaluation of the new product design process, and eventually greater involvement of customers and dealers in new product development. So, Step 6.3 at the bottom of the flowchart asks if gaps and unchecked assumptions remain in your story. As long as serious confusion blocks decision making, further repetitions of Steps 6.2 to 6.2C may be needed (for brevity, not shown in Figure 18). Inquiry stops when clarity replaces confusion, as shown in statement 7.A.

Flowcharts often use visual size, placement and arrangement of elements on the diagram to provide a higher-level perspective on a process. For example, the first five statements at the top of Figure 18 run from left to right at the same level across the page. The subsequent inquiry process (from statement 6.1 on the left to 6.1C on the right) seeks missing facts to resolve confusion that has been discovered. If serious confusion remains, statements 6.2 to 6.2C repeat the inquiry process from a new or different point of view (called a reframing). The downward pointing arrow on the right side of the figure suggests graphically that taking action and learning from what happens gradually increases clarity of understanding, improves decisions and reduces the risk of error. Resolving confusion in this way accumulates experience and eventually mastery of situations that once confused you.

Appendix D

Data-Gathering Interviews

This appendix outlines an approach you can use to plan and conduct interviews that let you understand subjects you want to learn about. What you learn by listening depends on your questioning skills as well as your interviewee's knowledge. Your mastery of the following interviewing skills and approach will grow with experience, practice and coaching.

Qualitative data often comes in the form of stories that approximate the truth you are asking about. So, interviewing is a process of gathering, comparing and making sense out of what you have heard. Although interviewing people can become one of your most powerful learning tools, the process of interviewing many people in new and unfamiliar situations tends to cause confusion at the start. So you must tame growing confusion by using tools such as affinity diagrams, spider-web diagrams and root cause analysis outlined elsewhere in this book to gain clarity.

To maximize what you learn from face-to-face interviews you need to prepare and practice. The following are specific pointers on the five essentials of data-gathering interviews.

Define the objective and scope of your data gathering effort in terms of what is included in your scope as well as what is not included. Starting with your objective, invite those you work for to brainstorm examples of dimensions that are or are not in scope. For example, suppose your objective is to evaluate and recommend improvements in your organization's corporate HR strategy. Is Alaska included or not included in your scope? How about Hawaii?

Which human resource practices are in or out of scope by function and organizational level? And so on.

Create a short list of major topics or questions you wish to cover with your subjects. Before you begin interviewing, confirm the need for each question by asking and answering: How will knowing the answer to this question make a difference in achieving my objectives? If answers to a question add little to accomplishing your objective, either drop that question or put it at the bottom of your list.

Toward the start of your interview, read or show your list of short topics to give your interviewee an idea of the topics you want to cover. Use short simple sentences. For example: "Please tell me how you stay in touch with your markets." Avoid long-winded, overly specific explanations of your need to understand how the interviewee uses market research methods, for example. Toward the end of your interview, or if time is running out before you have covered all your questions, you can use your opening list to check if you need to schedule additional time with this interviewee.

Create an initial list of "must-see" people to interview and what to ask them about based on your scope and objective. Usually those who know or are studying the situation you are gathering data on, will give names of must-see individuals. Beyond must-see subjects and those to whom they refer you, use three basic strategies for selecting interview within an organization. The first interviewing strategy, horizontal-slice, follows a process or flow from A to Z through all functions. The second strategy, vertical-slice, checks for vertical alignment of strategic initiatives down through lower-ranking delegation chains to verify alignment of high level strategy with action planning, execution and deployment at the operating level. The third strategy, referral-driven and opportunistic (conducted by "walk-around" intercept interviews), obtains perspectives on and confirmation of cultural norms, values, and knowledge of future directions.

Horizontal-slice interviews, from external or internal suppliers passing through the sequence of functions through which the process flows to its outcomes for both internal and external customers, let you see a process from end to end (SIPOC). This interviewing strategy usually produces verbatim problem statements of potential improvement opportunities and helps you understand functional work and self-identities.

Vertical-slice interviews start with a CEO or a top functional executive who led or participated in strategic planning. With the interviewee's input, you select a strategic initiative to follow through each level from the top executive down the chain of delegation and involvement to the lowest organizational levels involved in implementing that initiative. Vertical-slice interviews are useful for spotting gaps and disconnects in strategic deployment.

Referrals and opportunistic interviews arise while interviewing your initial must-see list of people. Each such interview ends with a request for suggestions of others to contact on specific subjects. You then add these referral names and topics to your interviewee list. Referral interviews help spot-check cultural values and institutions, assess power centers (where power means controlling sufficient resources to have things their own way), and patterns of influence, (where influence is the ability to change the behavior of those with power). Opportunistic interviews end when they produce no new information, or you have interviewed everyone on your list.

Schedule and conduct interviews. Try to schedule interviews at times and places your interviewees find convenient. For short interviews, ask for fifteen minutes, on the half hour. Schedule interviews lasting thirty to forty minutes to begin on the hour. For important, longer interviews, for example with senior executives, plan on ninety minutes every two hours. Few interviews run longer than that. You may wish to break long interviews into two shorter sessions. Taking a short break between interviews lets you and your interviewee prolong the interview if needed; it gives you time to check and expand your notes while details are still fresh in your memory; and it gives you time to get to your next interviewee. Be sure to add details to your notes from an interview within an hour or two of that interview. Facts that were clear during the interview are quickly forgotten. A week or two later you may be left with only sketchy notes that no longer make sense the way they did during the actual interview.

If you are new to interviewing, begin interviewing the people on your list with whom you feel most comfortable. When you must interview people at different organizational ranks, if you begin with lower-ranking interviewees and work your way up you may feel more relaxed as you go. It may also be wise to go on your initial interviews with an experienced interviewer as your coach. As you gain confidence, arrange with your coach to ask more and more questions on your own, while the coach observes. If you flub an important question, the coach can step in and recover the situation. After each interview, your coach should review what you did well and what you need to improve.

Open each interview by thanking the person you are interviewing for taking the time to speak with you. Briefly introduce yourself and state the purpose of the interview simply. Confirm the length of time the person has available to speak with you. Also preview the short list of the topics you want to cover so your interviewee has an idea of what you want to know about. (Keep the preview short, not more than a few seconds each on five or six broad topics).

Ask your interviewee to, "Please take a few minutes to tell me about yourself, your current position, and briefly about your previous experience." (Let the interviewee talk, while you listen, for about 5 minutes or so.) People are comfortable talking about themselves. So this opening usually creates a comfort level and rapport with your interviewee. Also you may learn that this person, who you had planned to ask about subject X, has experiences that qualify her or him to provide insights on subjects Y and Z, if they are relevant to your objective.

Use interviewing tools such as open probing—e.g., Please tell me about subject X; concrete questioning—e.g., Please give me a specific example of "what" and "how;" and listening, with special attention to "ABC" —A for affect, B for behavior, and C for cognition.

Listening for affect means that you are attentive to how your subject feels about what he or she is saying. To do this you must learn to put yourself in your interviewee's shoes and empathize with his or her feelings. You can also confirm what you hear by restating it in your own words periodically and testing your inferences about your interviewee's feelings about what he or she is telling you.

Listening for behavior seeks understanding of how people (for example, customers, managers, employees and suppliers) behave and why they behave in those ways. What choices do they face, what is their response to those situations and why do they respond in those ways?

Listening for cognition consists of understanding the logic that people use to explain or make sense of a situation. What assumptions are they making, what conclusions do they consider proven? What assumptions connect their facts to their conclusions?

Finally, separate gripes from problem statements. If an interviewee states a problem and gives an example, ask when that problem happened. After that, ask for a second example of the same problem and when the second example occurred. If the first problem instance was a week ago, and the second was three weeks ago, the frequency suggests that the problem is real. However, if the most recent problem instance was two years ago, and the second instance years before that, the "problem" is probably a gripe—a remembered complaint that is not recurrent and serious.

At the end of each interview, thank your subject and ask for suggestions of other knowledgeable people you should interview and about what topics. Then add those names to your interviewee list with notes on the topics to cover with them. End by sincerely thanking your interviewee for helping— even if he or she was tough on you—and ask for a business card or phone number in case you need to call back to ask follow-up questions later.

Appendix E

Interrelationship (Spider-web) Diagram

An Interrelationship (spider-web) diagram helps you, or your team, make sense of a situation in which dozens of problems or missed opportunities exist in the organization. Interrelationship diagrams are often nicknamed "spider-web diagrams" because a finished diagram for a complex organizational problem often looks like a spider web, as shown in Figure 19.

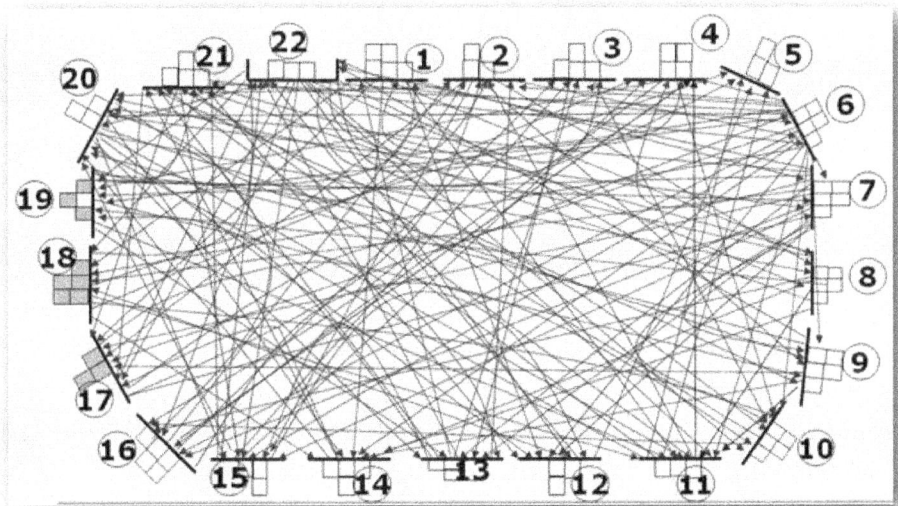

Figure 19 — Example Spider-web Diagram (aka Interrelationship diagram)

The number of arrows from any one problem in a finished spider-web diagram shows how many other problems in a process or organization the initial problem makes worse. So the more arrows pointing from problem X to other problems (out-arrows), the greater the benefits of eliminating problem X.

To make sense out of a confusing mess (defined as a system of interacting problems so tightly linked that solving any one or two problems has little effect on resolving the whole mess) a spider-web diagram is the tool of choice. During a process-improvement project, team members state each problem in the current situation on a sticky note, one problem to each note. Each problem should be stated in specific, concrete terms. If there are more than a dozen problems, team members may group several problems of the same type together into what are called affinity groups. Grouping like problems with like should be completed before arranging problem groups on a wall chart for analysis.

Avoid general descriptions such as "communications problems" because such a statement is easily misinterpreted, and because different communication errors and breakdowns with little else in common would fit under that label. To be useful, each affinity group of problems should include only those problem statements with similar causes and effects. Often one of the problems in an affinity group may be selected as the name of the group; otherwise use a clear, concrete statement describing all problems in the group as the group's title. (Figure 20 does not show a group title or label.).

As a check on problem affinity groupings, test if each individual problem in a group is an example of the group title, the whole group title and only that group's title. Any problem statement that fails this test does not belong in the group and should be placed into a group it does belong in or it should stand by itself (which sometimes is necessary). Figure 20 depicts an affinity group in which each rectangle (which represents a sticky note) states a problem. So, problem statements A, B, C, D and E are all instances of the label for the whole affinity group (not shown). If any problem fails this test, the team may find a better group in which it fits, or put it in its own group.

Several dozen individual problem statements usually contract into one-third to one-fifth as many problem affinity groups, each resembling Figure 20.

The next step is to construct the framework of the spider-web, by arranging all problem affinity groups around the edge of a large wall chart, as shown in Figure 21. The affinity group in Figure 21 appears as group 6 on the upper right hand corner of the chart framework.

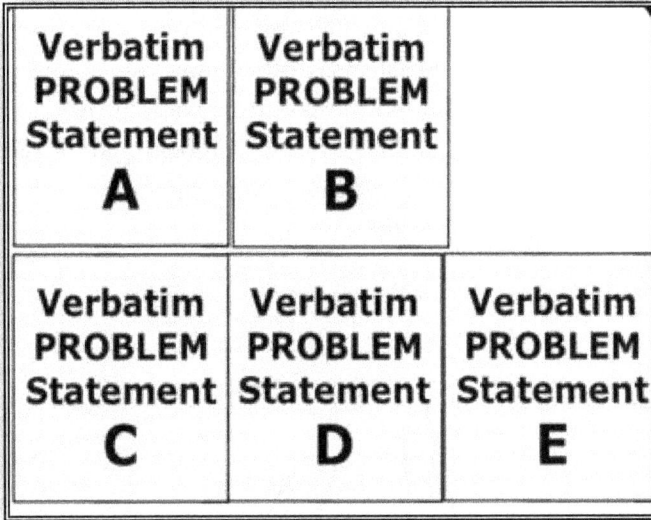

Figure 20 — Example Affinity Group of Problems Written on Sticky Notes

You may place the affinity groups in any order around the outer edge of the chart. (Tip: Make sure the corners of your chart are round, as shown in Figure 21, so arrows between any two problems will not have to cut across a third problem.) When several problems appear within the same organizational unit, grouping each unit's problems together around the edge of the chart

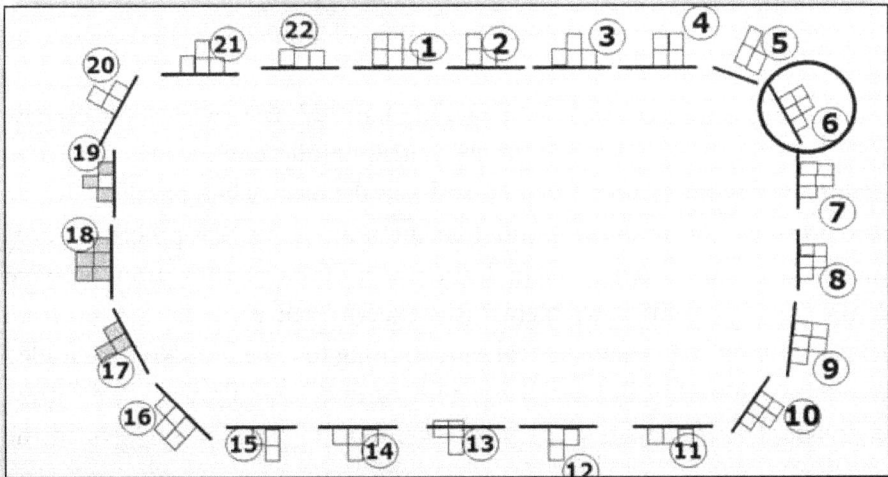

Figure 21 — Arrange Problem Affinity Groups Around The Edge of The Chart

provides useful information about which organizational units are most heavily involved in, or impacted by problems in other units.

Even if you gathered data on the problems yourself, work with a small team of experienced people to analyze which problems are linked and why. When you meet with your team colleagues, the diagram should be positioned so that all can read the problem titles.

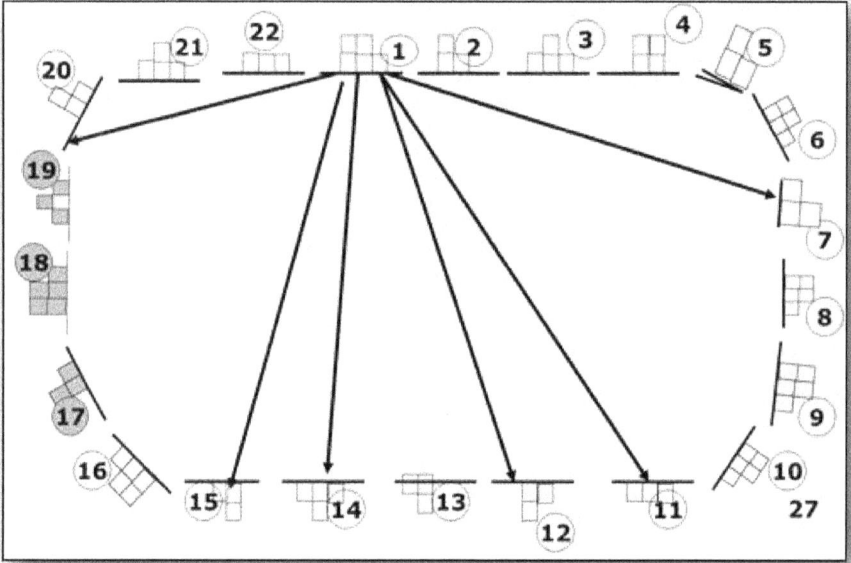

Figure 22 — Cause and Effect Arrows Show How Problems Interrelate

Starting with problem 1, as shown in Figure 22, the leader of the exercise points to the current problem group (initially group one), reads one or two examples of problems in that group and asks the team: Does problem 1 cause or tend to worsen problem group 2? If the team agrees that problem 1 does cause or tend to worsen Problem 2, the leader draws an arrow from problem 1 (the cause) pointing to problem 2 (the effect). Each arrow always runs from its tail, starting at the cause, to its head, pointing to the effect. No two-headed arrows are allowed. If Problem 1 has nothing to do with Problem 2, no arrow is drawn. The leader shifts the team's attention to the next problem in the clockwise direction, and repeats the question sequence for Problem 1 against Problem 3. If Problem 1 sometimes causes problem 2 and problem 2 at other times causes problem 1, use two one-way arrows to show that reality.

The six out-arrows from Problem 1 in figure 22 show that Problem 1 tends to strengthen or cause Problems 7, 11, 12, 14, 15 and 20. Discussing and agreeing on all 21 pairs of interrelationships may take ten or fifteen minutes just for problem 1. Next the team repeats the cause and effect analysis for Problem group 2 against every other problem, and subsequently problems 3, 4, and so on until every possible pair of problems involving 2 as the cause has been analyzed. Twenty-two trips around the whole diagram asking if the "from-problem" worsens the "to-problem" will take time. When the process is thoughtful and thorough however, the results will be worth the time invested.

As a double check the total number of in- and out-arrows for all problems in the diagram must be equal because every arrow has one tail and one head. If in- and out-arrow counts are not equal, for example 15 out arrows in the diagram, but only 14 in-arrows, you probably started an out arrow from one problem, but were interrupted before you connected that arrow to the problem it impacts. So to ensure accuracy, check that every arrow begins in a problem and ends in a problem (Problem A à Problem B).

A final acid test of a spider-web diagram is to substitute the wordings of pairs of individual problem statements (A and B) from the tail and the head of the same arrow into the sentence: (wording of Problem A) tends to worsen (wording of Problem B). If that constructed statement does not make sense, either problem statement A or problem statement B is in the wrong problem affinity group.

Once the diagram is finished, count the number of in- and out-arrows for each problem and write the totals next to each affinity group (#1in, #1out). Figure 23 is an example of a spider web, with many causal connections from just a few critical problems. This pattern of cause and effect can be dealt with using problem-solving approaches, without resorting to a complete redesign, which would be needed to clear up a mess as shown in Figure 19 earlier.

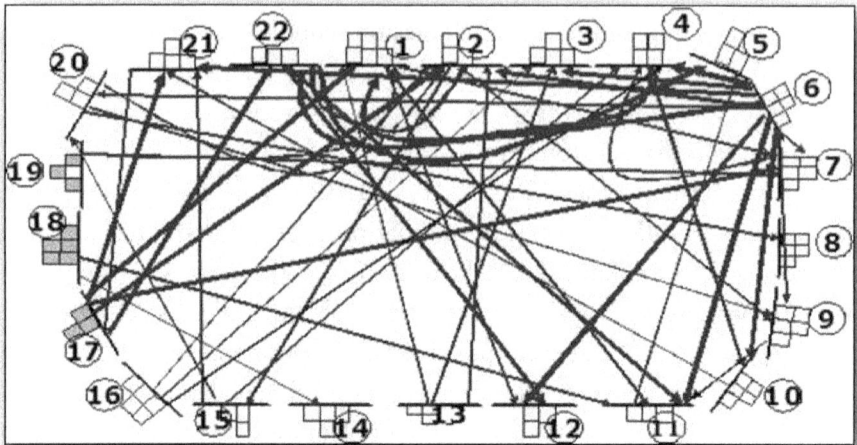

Figure 23 — Spider-Web Analysis Highlighting the Impact of Problems 6 and 17

Figure 23 shows a spider-web Analysis with darkened arrows for Problems 6 and 22 to show how these two problems impact all others in the situation. The two or three problems in such a diagram that impact the most problems in the situation, (such as 6 and 7) are usually designated the vital few high leverage problems. They are high leverage because solving each weakens many other problems.

The count of total in-arrows by problem is also useful. Problems with the most in-arrows suggest where to measure overall improvement. Solving or removing problems with the highest count of out-arrows diminishes their effects on other problems. So reducing those problems with the most in-arrows pointing to them, is a gauge of improvement.

While creating an interrelationship diagram can take a few hours of tedious asking, thinking and arrow drawing, getting people to pool their knowledge of how things really work in an interrelationship diagram can make profound sense of complex and confusing situations and clarify what problems are driving the whole situation. Once a team identifies the vital few (high out arrow) problems, it should use the five whys of root cause analysis to discover the cause of each.

Appendix F

Leading from the Middle of Your Organization (LftM)

This appendix gives you an overview of an ideal leadership from the middle approach. First it defines relevant types of legitimacy needed to lead from mid-organization without formal authority. Next it charts a generic LftM process flow, and presents a template for communications outward from an LftM initiative to stakeholders up, down and sideways in the organization.

The following working definitions are useful in defining a current understanding of leadership from the middle of an organization.

- **Leading from the Middle (of your organization)**—taking responsibility without having formal authority for actions that make you the leader you have been looking for in an uncertain and risky environment.
- **Power** (over) —sufficient control over resources to have things the way you want them.
- **Influence**—the ability to change the behavior of those with power.
- **Legitimacy**—a social determination by members of an organization that some action or behavior is desirable, proper, or appropriate by the organization's cultural standards and norms.
  - **Structural (or regulatory) Legitimacy** —exercise of power by traditional authority (management). "We are doing X because the boss told us to."

- **Moral Legitimacy**—a social judgment that the action being taken is "the right thing to do."
- **Cognitive Legitimacy**—a logical and credible explanation of how the proposed action makes sense and will make all stakeholders better off than they are likely to be in the status quo.
- **Pragmatic Legitimacy**—a consensus view that the outcomes of the action taken did indeed make everyone better off than before the change.

All organization members who are aware of an LftM initiative may be thought of as a jury deciding if the LftM initiative is the right or wrong thing for their organization. The jury's social deliberation results in a consensus, similar to a verdict, except it is based on conversations about whether the initiative is or is not legitimate from points of view such as moral, pragmatic, logical or organizational responsibility.

Get Ready	Get Set	Get Going	Keep Change Going
Project AS-IS Trends and Outcome if No Change	Who is affected by this delta/change?	How do we engage those willing to participate?	What do we need to do to:
• Feeling pain with the Status Quo	• What is their stake?	• How do we divide up the work?	• Keep the success alive and expanding.
And	• Which of them are willing to participate?	• How do we keep the effort legitimate -- pragmatically, morally and cognitively?	and
Recognize and describe the needed change	• On what basis?	• Ask how is it going?	• Broadcast the good news about who and what
• A sense of opportunity	• What are the key roles?	• How do we recognize and react to problems quickly as we execute?	• Share the credit and lessons learned.
	• Who will do what and when?	• How will we keep everyone informed?	

Adapted from Class 6 Consensus Session December 3, 2011
DYNM634-11c -- Penn Center for Organizational Dynamics

Figure 24 — Overview of Ideal Leading-from-the-Middle Flow

A Basic LftM Cycle shown in Figure 24 includes a selection of the following activities as needed:

- **Get Ready** • Agree on what is now going on; • Project current adverse trends into the future assuming that no change occurs (the base-case scenario); • Discuss and envision a feasible, sustainable and agile future scenario that makes all stakeholders better off (or no worse off) than they will be if the base case becomes reality; • Identify stakeholders and analyze their stakes and their probable responses to change
- **Get Set** • Discuss critical gaps between the base case (no change) and ideal future scenario; • Seek out allies; • Work out how to keep everyone in the loop as your initiative progresses; • Discuss the pathway forward—which critical gaps to close first, which can wait; • Do a pre-mortem on ways to fail and revise a pathway to reduce foreseeable risks; • Evaluate the difficulty of each step on the pathway forward and break all difficult steps into several smaller, easier steps
- **Get Going** • Decide who will do what based on skills; • Align the initiative with priorities of higher ups and adapt it as needed; • Establish that the effort will benefit all concerned when implemented (pragmatic legitimacy); • Establish that the effort makes sense to all who will be impacted (cognitive legitimacy); • Establish that the initiative is the right thing to do given the organizational norms and culture (moral legitimacy); • Volunteers run small scale pilot tests of steps on the pathway and assess impacts
- **Keep Change Going** • Learn from pilots; • Embrace new issues: • Share credit and lessons learned; • Expand legitimacy; • Build confidence; • Sustain progress

A team and its leader in mid-organization must communicate with all stakeholders who may be impacted by the planned initiative or who have power or influence over the success of the initiative. When operating without formal authority, people leading from mid-organization must hear, understand and respond respectfully to any stakeholder who may oppose their initiative.

The LftM effort should strive to win opponents over, or at least convince them to abstain from opposing pilot efforts to test initiatives. Figure 25 shows negotiations and conversations needed for a typical LftM initiative.

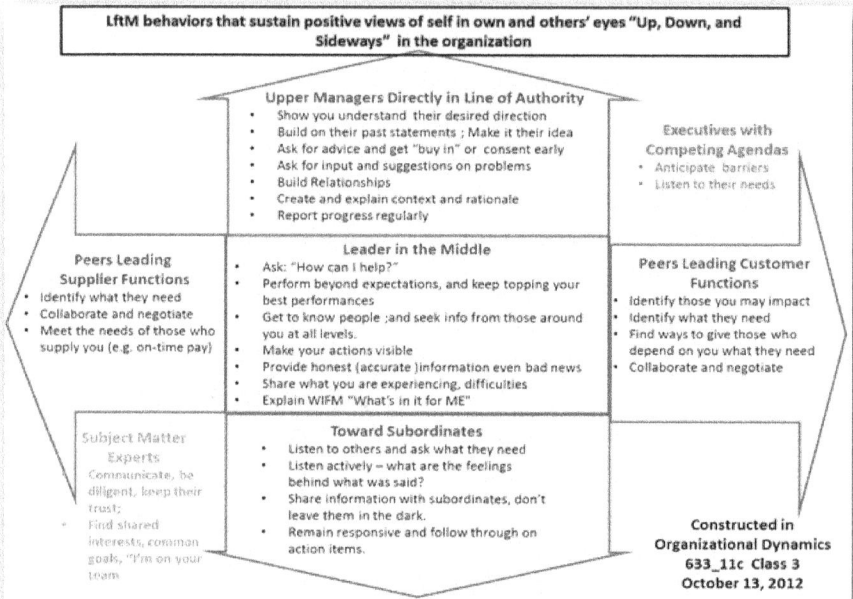

Figure 25 — Communications with LftM Stakeholder Groups

Appendix G

The Deming-Nishimura Systematic Improvement Flowchart

(Excerpted and adapted by permission from Stankard, 2011)

In the 1950s Dr. W. Edwards Deming used a flowchart to explain how an entire organization could be organized into a system whose purpose was to discover what might attract and please customers. This flowchart shows how listening to and observing customers can be fed back to improve product designs and production processes delivering products and services to customers. The feedback from customers links processes and suppliers into a continuous improvement (*Plan, Do, Check, Act*) cycle that discovers and delivers outputs that attract and satisfy more customers at a profit.

Several decades later, Dr. Koichi Nishimura, a champion of the Baldrige process in the United States, advised that a continuous *Plan, Do, Check, Act* cycle should be organization-wide in scope. Adding Dr. Nishimura's name to an organization-wide version of Deming's flowchart links all organization levels, suppliers, processes and customers together into a system of collaborations and changes that continuously improve the organization's ability to excel for customers and other stakeholders. The term Deming-Nishimura Cycle will be unfamiliar to folks; it means viewing how all levels and functions of an organization fit into an organizational system for continuous learning and improvement.

Figure 26—Deming Nishimura Cycle depicts how the following elements are linked into a system by conversations, collaborations and cooperation among all levels and members of an organization.

Visionary Leadership—Visionaries coach their organization in defining and agreeing on their shared purpose or mission. This purpose explains why the organization exists within its containing contexts: markets, society, industry and so on.

Suppliers—individuals or organizations that provide inputs that meet the organization's requirements for products and services.

Production and Delivery Processes—the series of work tasks that transform suppliers inputs into products and services that satisfy customers.

Supporting Processes—processes such as accounting, supply chain management and training, which do not produce products for customers, but which are needed to operate production and delivery processes.

Customers—individuals, organizations and others who depend on the products and services the organization produces.

Customer Listening—seeking to understand customer choices by listening to customer and non-customer focus groups, conducting market surveys, social media analysis and direct customer contact by service personnel.

Improvement Planning—using factual data to identify bottlenecks blocking better performance in pursuit of the organization's mission and identifying actions to remove each bottleneck in the coming period (usually a year). Bottlenecks may exist inside the organization (for example process limitations) or outside the organization due to inadequate customer demand.

Supply Chain Improvement—creating win-win partnerships with suppliers, which strengthen the combined competitiveness of the organization and its supplier partners.

Process Improvement—projects in which employees and others work to remove bottlenecks and improve the flow of value through work processes.

Product Improvement—designing products and services that are closer to customers' ideal choices compared with competitive products and substitutes.

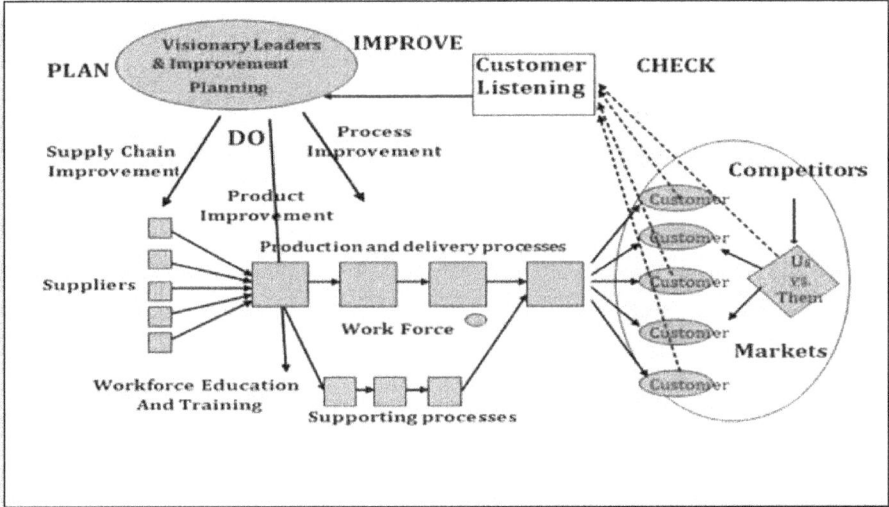

Figure 26 — Deming Nishimura Cycle

As shown in Figure 26, an annual sequence of events in a *plan, do, check, act* cycle begins in the upper right corner with listening to customers and non-customers in the marketplace. "Voice of the customer" data are gathered from current and competitor customers by listening posts, such as focus groups, direct customer contacts for service and sales, as well as market surveys of customers and potential customers to understand what they like, dislike and hope for in choosing between "us" (your offerings) and "them" (your competitors 'offerings).

The organization's managers study voice-of-the-customer information to understand how customers choose between your or competitors' products and services. The organization's top managers then set strategic improvement targets for cost and service or product qualities necessary to attract customers away from less attractive competitive products. The managers also deploy their strategically targeted improvements by setting detailed improvement goals for all products, processes or suppliers that currently limit the organization's capacity to attract and satisfy customer demand away from competitors.

Next managers of products, processes, or suppliers translate these detailed improvement targets into targeted improvement projects they must lead in the coming year to fulfill strategic goals. Each improvement project is planned and carried out by a cross-functional team, with periodic reviews of progress and problems by top executives during the year. Customer input is sought after planned improvements are pilot tested, to check whether changes successfully increased customer preference for the organization's products and services over competitive offerings.

After analyzing the outcomes of each completed organization-wide improvement cycle at the end of each year, the sequence of events repeats, building on lessons learned from checking with customers and participants in the previous year's cycle. The cycle repeats again in each coming year and yields improvement at a rate that is sometimes measured in improvements per full-time employee per year (I/FTE/YR). It is estimated that a small US business averages between one and ten Improvements/FTE/YR. The most competitive Baldrige Award winning firms range between 20 and to 40 Improvements /FTE/YR. Some top-performing Asian companies run as high as 70 Improvements /FTE/YR.

Appendix H

Navigating Career Confusion

During your career in the arts, business, management, sciences and other professions such as healthcare or consulting, you are likely to face confusing career decisions. This appendix describes an inquiry-based approach to help you tame such confusion. Here is a preview of the steps to take in navigating career confusion. This appendix will tell you how to organize your own career navigation system as you read. Here is an executive summary of steps for navigating career confusion.

1: Complete a Motivated Skill Assessment in Appendix A to identify an A-list of skills and traits that powered your most satisfying work experiences and energize you. These top five or more motivating skills and traits give you an edge in performing work which demands those skills.

2: Clarify your purpose by stage of your career. Early career opportunities explore diverse types of work and organizations to find activities that engage and energize you the most. Midcareer challenges and opportunities build expertise and mastery. Late career opportunities use mastery in work that you find most meaningful. Once you discover your most highly motivating skills, use them in pursuing causes you care about and never give up.

3: Brainstorm concrete actions or challenges in your next career decision that let you deepen and broaden your most engaging and motivating "A-list" skills. If your recent work experience has not been highly satisfying or motivating, ask if it is time to seek a new career direction.

4: Envision work scenarios that maximize the use of highly motivating skills on your A-list and list elements in each scenario that give you butterfly feelings. Having a short list of scenarios in the back of your mind will keep you alert to information and contacts that may lead to a better future.

5: Listen to and take note of personal and career rules of thumb that people share with you. Select rules of thumb that fit your current situation to use as guides in resolving your confusion. When one of your top career scenarios satisfies Rule A or Rule B but not both, reframe the scenario so it satisfies both.

6: Use the rules of thumb that seem most applicable to frame your most powerful questions (MPQs). The answers to these questions should resolve anxious feelings, concerns and confusion about your pathways forward. Seek experienced people as informal coaches and mentors, describe your scenarios and confusion and ask your most powerful questions.

7: Reality check your top scenarios by asking helpful, friendly contacts who have already navigated the same type of confusion to answer to your MPQs. Listen to what they say, and be alert to new unknowns they tell you about. Ask them to help you identify assumptions underlying your scenarios and how to check them.

8: Decide if it is time for a change every few years—because you cannot recover lost time. Staying on the up escalator for too long, if your organization is riding a down escalator, may cost you the chance to step onto the up escalator in some other organization that's on an uptrend.

9: Continue reducing confusion until two scenarios, A and B, remain. First give Scenario A your best effort. If scenario A becomes a dead end, then pursue Scenario B without regrets.

Early in your career, your paid or volunteer work experiences let you use a range of skills; the broader the range the better. Among all the skills you have used, some will make you feel great, highly satisfied and energized, while others, in which you may be highly proficient, will feel less energizing. If you have not already, please assess your highly motivating skills with the assessment tool in Appendix A before reading further.

Skills and capabilities grow with experience. So seek opportunities early in your career to widen and diversify your portfolio of highly motivating skills. As you gain experience, periodically assess the skills and traits you used heavily during your most satisfying experiences. Seek increasingly challenging (and therefore risky) assignments that demand those skills as well as new ones, to keep the butterfly feelings. Success may not be guaranteed, but learning from experience is.

Your future depends on past sequences of challenges that led to the present. For example, a college student who chose hard work to gain admission to medical school became a surgeon, but his friend, whose top priority as a student was his social life, later regretted that he could no longer switch to a biomedical career. Eventually, unexpected roadblocks, upsets, problems and crises will challenge you to combine your most motivating skills and traits in unique ways which other people cannot appreciate as you do, nor replicate your response.

Build and maintain a broad network of friendly professional and social contacts. Previous colleagues, customers and members of alumni and professional associations you have met, attendees at professional development courses and conferences you participated in, and personal or social networks of professionals on the Internet are often willing to share advice and insights about career opportunities.

Organize your own virtual system for navigating career confusion. Pasteur once said, "Chance favors the prepared mind." Here's how to prepare to navigate career confusion toward career goals that you find most meaningful. As you read keep a pad of sticky notes at hand and write each idea, action, rule of thumb, or bit of guidance on a sticky note. Each note should express a complete, clear thought so that in future years, you will still understand what you wrote earlier. Next park your sticky notes on a large sheet of paper (or on pages of a notebook) so you won't lose them. The end of this appendix suggests how to organize your sticky notes systematically. To start on your career navigation system, complete your assessment of your most engaging and energizing skills in Appendix A.

Clarify your purpose. Purpose is like a compass needle pointing toward true north. No matter which way your present career points, your purpose lets you check whether your goals and your path toward them will produce deep satisfaction and meaning in the life you truly seek. Defining your purpose helps you adapt your behaviors to benefit yourself and your family, employers, communities and society. Your most powerful question to answer is, What use of my time and talents do I find most meaningful? Your next most powerful question is, Which skills must I develop and which opportunities should I seek to pursue my purpose?

Rate the development of your most engaging and motivating skills. Are they undeveloped, moderately developed, or highly developed? For any motivating skill you rated less than highly developed, list ways you can develop and improve that skill. Accepting tougher challenges and responsibilities in order to expand and strengthen your motivating skills may cause butterfly feelings. But escalating your aim and stretching your skills expands the scope of your accomplishments and builds confidence to face greater challenges as you fulfill your purpose. Don't panic, and don't give up.

Generate a range of career scenarios to explore. A scenario is not a decision, but is a story depicting a possible, might-be or could-be near- or long-term future. Scenarios do not express wishes and hopes. Career scenarios should be qualitative stories about possible futures, opportunities and pitfalls. Each scenario should maximize the use of your most motivating skills from your skill self-assessment. Scenarios help orient your thinking and alert you to information that may be useful in the future. In effect your scenarios create memory compartments that retain, organize and let you access remembered information for future use.

Your scenarios should both fulfill your purpose and match your most engaging skills, work ethic and level of ambition. Seek inputs from friends, social and professional contacts and others with a range of careers. Ask people who know you what type of work they think you would be good at and why. Avoid either-or thinking by using both-and thinking to combine old ideas into new scenarios. You should plan on three different career scenarios between your first full time job and eventual retirement. These three scenarios are akin to your career's youth, maturity, and old age.

In the youth of your career your total experience doubles in one, then two, then four years. Repeating one year of experience for four years reruns one year of experience four times. Varying work experiences over those same four years provides much wider and more challenging experiences. So three rules of thumb for a young career scenario are: tackle a wide variety of different types of work to discover which activities consistently energize and excite you in satisfying ways; make changes when your work becomes repetitive or the organization does not offer learning opportunities; and build a personal network of social and professional contacts who have unconventional wisdom and knowledge that complement yours.

When beginning a career, early-stage scenarios in growing sectors or industries tend to provide future opportunities. So, begin by defining your career navigation challenge by researching and discussing macro trends in industry growth and decline. Seek assessments of how likely these trends are to continue into the future. Industry-level trends matter more than specific organizational prospects because industries often grow even as individual firms come and go. Anticipating unsustainable trends also may help you avoid future career disruptions. Here are a few common career scenarios.

Early in your career, seek advice and insights from a range of senior, experienced mentors and advisors in industries in which you envision alternative career scenarios. Engineers and technologists often foresee future trends based on the implications of early research. Listen to them. If you know people already working in attractive industries, you may wish to consider "follow the leader scenarios," in which you network with someone who is several years ahead of you in an industry that attracts you. Tap such people's experiences and insights into career scenarios that fit you well and could brighten your future.

People who begin careers in rapidly growing industries may adopt a go-with-the-flow scenario. Employers in growing industries create opportunities to promote experienced people into more senior responsibilities. For example the minicomputer industry grew from nothing to large scale at the expense of mainframe computers. When growth in minicomputers slowed, thousands of experienced engineers and managers either founded or joined networking firms, which were expanding as the Internet grew. During periods of rapid industry growth, studies have shown that job migration from rising firms to new entrants helps stimulate industry growth.

For some people declining trends for a whole industry make an "industry switching" scenario necessary. For example, declining domestic manufacturing left many skilled quality and process-improvement trainers and coaches underemployed at the same time the healthcare sector began seeking ways to reduce cost and error rates and improve outcomes. The result was that many process-improvement and organizational-change professionals were able to switch from manufacturing into healthcare improvement careers.

As you grow older and more mature, the time scale for making changes stretches out. By midcareer, your earlier career experiences let you assess your most engaging and winning talents and skills. So in midcareer, the rule of thumb should be to seek opportunities that escalate the scope and scale of challenges that demand your most energizing skills, talents and interests.

Some middle career scenarios envision a stepping-stone pathway in which each position progresses step by step toward fulfilling your ultimate purpose and ambition. Stepping-stone approaches are especially important if tasks listed under the "running things—teams, projects and organizations" show up often in your most satisfying experiences. If running things is a vital part of your personality, your navigation rule might be to seek a more challenging position every time your butterfly feelings quiet down in your current position.

Eventually, in career "old age" you may seek to revalidate and redouble your focus on fulfilling your purpose. For some, sharing what they have learned and experienced by helping others achieve their own purposes creates meaning and satisfaction. Many individuals run into life situations, such as changes in health or family obligations, which steer them toward scenarios far from earlier career directions. For example a practicing physician who became hearing impaired pursued his appreciation of art by becoming a highly successful art dealer. Another experienced financial executive quit a high paying job and became a priest. When asked years later if the change had made him happy, he replied that the change made him feel content, which he had not felt in his finance career.

At least one scenario should envision a future that puts your entire base of peak experiences to use in a high risk, high return scenario. Including such an extreme scenario among your range of possible futures may actually help prepare you psychologically to recognize an unexpected opportunity and take a calculated and informed risk that less alert individuals overlook. Even if you decide after careful reflection not to pursue your extreme scenario, including that scenario in your thinking may reduce future regrets. At least you considered and decided against it and need not regret the road not taken.

Collect rules of thumb for guiding career decisions. Listen for rules of thumb that may help translate confusion about occupations, work ethic and ambition into reality-based career choices consistent with your purpose. When you obtain guidance from colleagues, social and professional contacts and mentors, write down any career rules of thumb they share with you. Later, when evaluating career scenarios, you will be able to refer to them. For example, if you are young and single, a navigation rule of thumb might be: Set goals, work hard, have fun, and never act in panic. Or if you have a young, growing family, slim savings, a big mortgage and the usual job insecurity, you may choose a risk-averse rule such as: Never move except on a sure thing, or, Always look before you leap; case the joint first.

Suppose after a string of professional successes, you envision starting your own business. You may choose to rely on the rule of thumb that most scientists, technical experts and computer scientists with ten or more years of experience in their fields, who start businesses, are still in business five years later. Or, this rule for business startups: Don't start your own business until you learn how to sell while working for someone else.

In occupations where customers or clients expect experience, the adage, Show that you can lance a boil before you offer to perform brain surgery suggests that past successes in earlier tasks prepare and qualify you to tackle larger challenges.

When planning to change jobs, some people follow the rule of thumb: Change jobs if your responsibilities and skills have not grown significantly in the last X years. Young, fast-track individuals set X at two or three years. Others decided when to job hop based on how much experience, knowledge, networking and satisfaction their current job provides.

When diminishing returns have set in on your current course consider the rule: look for new opportunities when your job stops being fun. This rule does not define fun, but you would be aware if your job is not fun. And one rule you should always include in your personal navigation system is, Seek new challenges when your butterfly feelings disappear.

Prepare your most powerful questions. If your choice of A-list scenarios is confusing, you must gather information to answer your most powerful questions (MPQ) so you can make sound decisions. Time is your most irreplaceable resource. So, consider your personal answer to the powerful question: What is the best and most meaningful use of my time to achieve my purpose?

To generate powerful questions, consider your purpose and convert career rules of thumb that fit your situation into questions to answer. Write down your two or three top questions, the answers to which should resolve most of your career confusion. To answer your MPQs seek out willing and knowledgeable mentor-coaches. Begin your coaching conversations with a few facts, then how you feel. Just explaining the facts and your feelings will clarify and narrow areas of confusion. Then move on to your MPQs. Continue gathering input until you stop learning anything new or clarity replaces confusion.

As you narrow your focus, revise your powerful questions to find out how the people advising you got established when they were new members of their current organization. How did they fit in? What have been their toughest challenges and greatest satisfactions? What opportunities and experiences gave them the professional and personal skills of greatest value? How actively did their organization assess, support and advance their development after they joined? Also seek examples from others who were in positions similar to yours about how they moved on to more complex and significant challenges. They may have found paths that you find appealing.

Reality-check your top scenarios Use conversations with experienced, forward-looking professionals and entrepreneurs to reality-check your scenarios. Ask those with whom you discuss scenarios to point out assumptions your scenarios rest on. Use what you learn from these conversations to reevaluate and revise your scenarios or add new ones. As long as a scenario's assumptions are realistic put scenarios that make heavy use of your most engaging and motivating skills on your "A-List."

Use a "pre-mortem" to surface the risks and assumptions of each scenario. Imagine that you are now five or ten years into the future and that pursuing your top scenario has led to failure. Brainstorm reasons why that failure could occur and then revise the scenario to prevent or reduce those causes of failure.

Early in your career, classmates and professional or social contacts who are a few years ahead of you in working for diverse employers may share inside information on what working in their industry and organizations is really like. Such input provides reality checks, and may also provide pathways into organizations or industries. Also people who have already experienced one of your top scenarios may share their experiences and help you check your assumptions. Demote scenarios that depend on shaky assumptions to your B list of lower priority futures or make them more realistic.

Finally, convert your scenarios and powerful questions into actions (or thought experiments if action still feels too risky). Here is an example.

Suppose your current job requires that you travel away from home several nights each week, which stresses your family. To stop your overnight absences you search for a similar local job that does not require travel. Your search turns up no openings. Your B-list scenario was to start up your own business in a field in which you have fifteen years of experience. So you contact people who made similar moves, share your start-up scenario and listen as they tell you about starting their own businesses. Learning from these conversations focuses on your most powerful question: can you attract enough business within a day trip of home to succeed?

Over lunch with an acquaintance who had launched her solo market research business several years earlier, you ask your question. Your luncheon guest mentions that before she quit her job she spoke with other independent marketing consultants. She found that the successful new consultants had at least three hundred contacts when they started their businesses. You then go through your card file of people you already know within a day trip of home and find 155 potential clients for your services.

Your most powerful question now becomes: what are the odds of success if you start up 145 names short of the 300 contacts that correlated with your acquaintance's success? Next consider the odds that you will obtain enough work by contacting and offering your services to 155 people who have already met you. If you have sales experience, success seems within reach if you call two or three contacts each day, chat about what is going on and follow up with a cordial and thoughtful letter. A few exploratory phone calls to feel out the reaction of some prospects could help increase confidence your likelihood of success.

Decide if it is time for a change. Some changes are forced by personal matters, such as business failures, illnesses or the like. But most changes are either opportunistic or deliberate. Consider whether to stay or leave your current path under these four future scenarios:

Bright organizational future, slow personal advancement—what causes your slow advancement and what can you do about it?

Bright organizational future, fast personal advancement—would change produce enough added benefits to offset the risks of leaving a winner?

Dark organizational future, slow personal advancement—would an organization with brighter future trends offer richer growth opportunities to you, given your skills and experience?

Dark organizational future, fast personal advancement—do you really want to continue going up on a down escalator? Are you riding the down escalator so far down that your chances to climb back up elsewhere will be compromised?

Organize your personal career navigation system. As you read this appendix, if you wrote statements you found helpful on sticky notes you can now organize them into your career navigation system. Even if you do not use this system now, organizing your thoughts will help prepare you to recognize opportunities that fit you.

To start, tape together several large sheets of newsprint or flip chart pages at eye level along an empty wall in a private space. Put the long edge of the paper parallel to the floor; the more sticky notes you have, the wider the space you will need. Leave room on the right side for expansion. To help you group sticky notes where they belong, make new sticky notes with headings (Top Motivating Skills, Possible Scenarios, MPQs to ask, Who to Contact, Actions to Take, and other titles you need,) Arrange the sticky note titles across the top of your chart. Finally place your sticky notes under the title on the chart, or arrange them from left to right in time sequence with first things first.

If you have too many sticky notes to fit on the chart, you may either enlarge the chart or group closely related ideas together and park them for safe keeping on a separate sheet (called a parking lot) for future reference. Then write a title on a new sticky note describing each group of closely related ideas, and put just that one note on your flip chart page, with a number that refers to the parking lot group which it substitutes for. If there is enough room at the bottom of your wall chart, park the groups of sticky notes you have removed at the bottom of the chart for easy reference.

Periodically revise your navigation system by moving irrelevant notes to the parking lot. Rotate each parked note forty-five degrees so it looks like a diamond, to indicate that that particular sticky note is no longer relevant to your situation.

However your chart looks, the discipline of organizing your issues, concerns, rules, scenarios and key questions will help you explore your options fully and systematically. Organizing your personal system is better than trying hard and hoping for good luck. Be sure to start by assessing the skills you used heavily in your most satisfying experiences (Appendix A). When you have finished using your navigation system, fold it carefully and keep it safe so you can refer to it later. You may be surprised at how well you navigated periods of career confusion because; The winds and tides favor the ablest navigator. Don't panic, and keep trying.

Selected References

BOOKS

Ackoff, Russell L. (1962) *Scientific Method: Optimizing Applied Research Decisions,* John Wiley & Sons, Inc, New York, NY

——————, (1994) *The Democratic Corporation*, Oxford University Press, New York, NY

——————, (1999) *On Re-Creating the Corporation*, Oxford University Press, New York, NY

——————, and Emery, Fred E., (2006a) On Purposeful Systems: An Interdisciplinary Analysis of Individual and Social Behavior as a System of Purposeful Events, Transaction Publishers, New Brunswick, NJ.,

——————, Magidson, Jason and Addison, Herbert J. (2006b) *Idealized Design: Creating an Organization's Future,* Wharton School Publishing, Upper Saddle River, NJ

Argyris, Chris (2000) Flawed *Advice and The Management Trap*, Oxford University Press, New York, NY

Arrow, Kenneth J. (1974) *The Limits of Organization,* W. W. Norton & Co. Inc., New York, NY

Block, Peter, (1981), *Flawless Consulting – A Guide To Getting Your Expertise Used.* Pfeiffer and Company, San Diego, CA

Brassard, Michael and Ritter, Diane (1994), *The Memory Jogger II:* A Pocket Guide of Tools for Continuous Improvement and Effective Planning. GOAL/QPC Methuen MA.

Buber, Martin, *Ich und Du*; translated as *I and Thou*, by Walter Kaufmann,(1970) First Touchstone Edition (1996) Charles Scribner's Sons, Simon and Schuster, Inc., New York, NY.

Churchman, C. West (1971) *The Design of Inquiring Systems – Basic Concepts of Systems and Organizations*, Basic Books, Inc., New York, NY

Cummings Thomas. G. & Worley, Christopher G.; (2005) *Organizational Development and Change*, Eighth Ed., Thomson South-Western, 2005

Deming, W. Edwards (1986), *Out of the Crisis*. Massachusetts Institute of Technology, Center for Advanced Engineering Studies, Cambridge, MA

——————— (1993) *The New Economics for Industry, Government, and Education,* Massachusetts Institute of Technology, Center for Advanced Engineering Studies, Cambridge, MA

Diamond, Stuart (2010), Getting More: How to Negotiate to Achieve Your Goals in the Real World, Crown Business (Random House), New York

Gawande, Atul (2007) *Better: A Surgeon's Notes on Performance,* Picador—Metropolitan Books, Henry Holt and Company, New York, NY

Grant, Adam, (2013) "Givers Take All: The hidden dimension of corporate culture," McKinsey Quarterly 2013, No.2, pp 52-65

Haldane, Bernard (1974) *Career Satisfaction and Success,* AMACOM, New York, NY.

Hammer, Michael, and Champy, James (1993) *Reengineering the Corporation: A Manifesto for Business Revolution.* HarperBusiness, HarperCollins Publishers, Inc. New York, NY, 233 pages

Heath, Chip and Heath, Dan (2010) *SWITCH – How to Change Things When Change is Hard,* Broadway Books an imprint of Crown Business (Random House), New York , NY

Jackall, Robert (1988) *Moral Mazes: The World of Corporate Managers,* Oxford University Press, New York, NY

Katzenback, Jon R. (1997) Teams at the Top –Unleashing the Potential of Both Teams and Individual Leaders, Harvard Business School Press, Boston, MA

——————, Smith, Douglas K. (1994) The Wisdom of Teams – Creating the High-Performance Organization, Harper Collins Books,

Mitroff, Ian I. and Linstone, Harold A. (1993) *The Unbounded Mind— Breaking the Chains of Traditional Business Thinking,* Oxford University Press, New York, NY

Morgan, Gareth (1998) *Images of Organization: The Executive Edition,* Berrett-Koehler Publishers, San Francisco.

Ohno, Taiichi (1978) *Toyota Production System, Beyond Large Scale Production.* Productivity Press, New York, NY

Pfeffer, Jeffrey, (1992) *Managing With Power; Politics and Influence in Organizations,* Harvard Business School Press, Boston, MA

Rummler, Geary A. and Brache, Alan P. (1995) Improving Performance – How to Manage the White Space on the Organization Char, Second Edition, Jossey Bass, A Wiley Imprint, San Francisco, CA

Schaefer, Christine (Lead Author) and Bailey, Dawn (Lead editor) et. al., (2011) *Baldrige 20/20 --An Executive's Guide to the Criteria for Performance*

Excellence. Baldrige Performance Excellence Program, National Institute of Standards and Technology, U.S. Department of Commerce, Gaithersburg, MD.

Shön, Donald A. (1983) *The Reflective Practitioner: How Professionals Think in Action,* Basic Books, Member of the Perseus Book Group, New York, NY.

Shewhart, Walter A (1931) *Economic Control of Quality of Manufactured Product.* D. Van Nostrand Co., Inc. New York, NY

Stankard, Martin F. (1981) Successful Management of Large Clerical Operations: A Guide to Service Transaction Systems. McGraw-Hill Book Co., New York, NY

——————— (1986) *Productivity By Choice: The 20-to-1 Principle,* John Wiley and Sons, New York, NY

——————— (2002) Management Systems and Organizational Performance: The Search For Excellence Beyond ISO9000, Quorum Books, Westport, CT

——————— (2006a) *Basic Tools for Facilitating Group Processes,* Productivity Development Group, Inc., Westford, MA

——————— (2006b) *Tools for Lean Sigma Projects, 9th edition*), Productivity Development Group, Inc. Westford, MA

——————— (2011) *Art and Science of Process Improvement,* Self-Published by Martin F. Stankard, Westford, MA, Spring 2011 Edition

Whyte, David (2009), *The Three Marriages, Re-imagining Work, Self and Relationship,* Riverhead Books, published by the Penguin Group, New York, NY

——————— (2001) *Crossing the Unknown Sea – Work as a Pilgrimage of Identity,* Riverhead Books, a division of Penguin, Putnam, Inc. New York, NY

——————— (1994, 1996) *The Heart Aroused, Poetry and the Preservation of the Soul in Corporate America,* A Currency Paperback, published by Doubleday, a division of Bantam, Doubleday, Dell Publishing Group, Inc. New York, NY.

Womack, James P. and Jones, Daniel T. (2003) *Lean Thinking: Banish Waste and Create Wealth in Your Corporation,* Free Press Division, Simon & Schuster, Inc. New York, NY

Wren, Daniel A. and Greenwood, Ronald (1998) *Management Innovators, The People and Ideas That Have Shaped Modern Business.* Oxford University Press, New York, NY

ARTICLES AND OTHER SOURCES

Ackoff, Russell L. (1990) "The Management of Change, and the Changes it Requires of Management" *Systems Practice,* (Plenum Publishing Corporation(Volume 3. No. 3, 1990 pp 427-440

Adler, Nancy J. (2006) "The Arts and Leadership; Now That We Can Do Anything, What Will We Do?" *Academy of Management Learning and Education,* Vol 5, Nol 4, 2006 pp 486-499

Altman, Lawrence K. (2008) "W.H.O. Issues a Checklist to Make Operations Safer," New York Times, June 25, 2008

Anderson, John C., Rungtusanatham, Manus, and Schroeder, Roger G., (1994) "A Theory of Quality Management Underlying the Deming Management Method, *Academy of Management Review,* 1994, Vol. 19, No. 3., pp472-509

Baldrige Performance Excellence Program (2013-2014), "Criteria for Performance Excellence, " Baldrige Performance Excellence Program, National Institute of Standards and Technology, Gaithersburg, MD

Barnett, William P. and Pontikes, Elizabeth G. (2004) "The Red Queen: History-Dependent Competition among Organizations," Stanford Graduate School of Business, forthcoming publication in Research *in Organizational Behavior.* November, 2004

Barsh, Joanna. (2008) "Innovative Management: A Conversation with Gary Hamel and Lowell Bryan," *McKinsey Quarterly*, 2008, No. 1, pp. 25 - 35

Birkinshaw. J., Hamel, G., and Mol, M., (2008). Management Innovation. *Academy of Management* Review, No. 33: pp. 825 - 845

Bergeron, Diane M. (2007) "The Potential Paradox of Organizational Citizenship Behavior: Good Citizens at What Cost?" *Academy of Management Review,* vol. 32, No. 4 pp. 1078-1095

Bryan, Lowell L. and Joyce, Claudia I. (2007) "Better Strategy through Organizational Design" *McKinsey Quarterly,* 2007, No 2, pp. 20-29

Butler, Timothy and Waldroop, James. (1999) "Job Sculpting: The Art of Retaining Your Best People," *Harvard Business Review*, September – October, 1999 pages 144-152. HBR Reprint 99502

Cappelli, Peter; and Hamori, Monika, (2005), "The New Road to the Top." *Harvard Business Review*, January 2005 pages 25-32. HBR Reprint R0501B

Coutu, Diane, (2009) "Why Teams Don't Work –Interview of J. Robert Hackman," *Harvard Business Review,*Vol. 87. No. 5, pp 99-105

De Smet, Aaron, Loch, Mark and Schaninger Bill "The Link between Profits and Organizational Performance" *McKinsey Quarterly*, 2007 Number 3

Davenport, Thomas H. (2009) "How to Design Smart Business Experiments," *Harvard Business Review*, Vol. 87. No. 2, pp 68-76

Deming, W. Edwards, (1989), Personal interview of Dr. W. Edwards Deming by the author (Martin Stankard) during Deming's visit to Boston University, April 19th, 1989, Boston, MA

Denrell, Jerker. (2004) "Random Walks and Sustained Competitive Advantage," *Management Science*, Vol. 50 No. 7. pp 922-934

——————, (2005) "Selection Bias and the Perils of Benchmarking," *Harvard Business Review*, April, 2005 pp 114 – 119

Devan, Janamitra, Klusas, Matthew B. and Ruefli, Timothy W. (2007) "The Elusive Goal of Corporate Outperformance," The McKinsey Quarterly, Premium Edition, 30 April 2007

Domrose, Cathryn (2010) "The Time is Now: 'Culture of Safety' Key to Preventing Errors," New.Nurse.com, an on-line publication, August 23, 2010, p.1

Fisher, Caroline, M. Barfield, Jesse, Li, Jing and Mehta, Rajiv (2005) "Retesting a Model of the Deming Management Method" *Total Quality Management* Vol. 16, No. 3, 401–412, May 2005

Ford, Jeffrey D; Ford, Laurie W.; and K'Amelio, Angelo: (2008) "Resistance to Change: The Rest of the Story" *Academy of Management Review*, 2008, vol. 33, No. 2. pp 362-377

Ford, Jeffrey D; and Ford, Laurie W. (2009) "Decoding Resistance to Change" *Harvard Business Review,* Vol. 87 No. 4, pp 99- 103

Garvin, David A. and Roberto, Michael A. (2005) "Change Through Persuasion," *Harvard Business Review,* 83 no.2, pp 104-112.

Gawande, Atul, (2007) "The Checklist – If something so simple can transform intensive care, what else can it do?" *The New Yorker,* December 10, 2007 (Available online).

Gottschalg, Oliver and Zollo, Maruizio (2007) "Interest Alignment and Competitive Advantage," *Academy of Management Review,* Vol. 32, No 2. pp 428-437

Green, Jr. Sandy, Edward; Li, Yuan; and Nohria, Nitin, (2009) "Suspended in Self-Spun Webs of Significance," *Academy of Management Journal,* Volume 52, No. 1 pp 11- 36

Hall, Joseph M. and Johnson, Eric M. (2009) "When Should a Process Be Art, Not Science?" *Harvard Business Review,* Vol 87. No. 3 March, 2009 pp. 59-65

Hammer, Michael (2007) "The Process Audit," *Harvard Business Review,* 85 no.4, pp 111-123.

Hargrave, Timothy J. and Van De Ven, Andrew H., (2006) "A Collective Action Model of Institutional Innovation," *Academy of Management Review,* Volume 31 No. 4, 864 -888

Harvey, Paul, Madison, Kristen, Martinko, Mark, and Crook, Tamara. S. (2014) "Attribution Theory in the Organizational Sciences: The Road Travelled and The Path Ahead", *Academy of Management Perspectives,* Vol.28, No. 2, p 128-146

Hirst, Giles, Fan Knippenberg, Daan, and Zhou, Jing. (2009) "A Cross-Level Perspective on Employee Creativity: Goal Orientation, Team Learning Behavior, and Individual Creativity", *Academy of Management Journal*, Vol. 52, No. 2, p 280-293

Huyett, William I. and Viguerie , S. Patrick (2005) "Extreme Competition: The Forces of Globalization, Technology, and Economic Liberalization Are Combining to Make Life Harder Than Ever for Established Companies" *McKinsey Quarterly*, 2005 No. 1 pp 46-57

Kegan, Robert and Lahey, Lisa Laskow. (2001)"The Real Reason People Won't Change," *Harvard Business Review*, November 2001 pages 85-92, HBR Reprint R0110E

Kellogg, Katherine C. (2011) "Hot Lights and Cold Steel: Cultural and Political Toolkits for Practice Change in Surgery" Organization Science Vol 22, No. 2, Mar-Apr 2011, pp. 482-502

Knott, Anne Marie, (2001) "The Dynamic Value of Hierarchy," *Management Science,* Vol. 47, No. 3, March 2001, pp. 430-448

Kotter, John, P, (2007) "Leading Change: Why Transformation Efforts Fail" Originally 1995, reprinted in Harvard Business Review, January 2007, pp 96-102.

Lawson, Emily and Price, Colin (2003) "The Psychology of Change Management" *McKinsey Quarterly*, 2003 Special Edition, pp 31 – 41

Leavitt, Harold J. (2007) Big Organizations Are Unhealthy Environments for Human Beings, *Academy of Management Learning & Education*, Vol. 62, No. 2, 253–263.

—————,. March, 2003 "Why Hierarchies Thrive" *Harvard Business Review*, 81, no. 3, pp 96-102

Lüscher, Lotte S. and Lewis, Marianne W (2008) "Organizational Change and Managerial Sensemaking: Working Through Paradox" *Academy of Management Journal*, Vol. 51, No. 2, pp. 221-240

Martin, Roger (2007) "How Successful Leaders Think" *Harvard Business Review*, 85, no. 6, pp 60-67

Mintzberg, Henry and Van Der Heyden, Ludo (1999) "Organigraphs; Drawing How Companies Really Work," *Harvard Business Review*, September – October, 1999 pages 87-94. HBR Reprint 99506

Pfeffer, Jeffrey,, and Fong, Christina T. (2005) "Building Organization Theory from First Principles: The Self Enhancement Motive and Understanding Power and Influence." *Organization Science,* Volume 16, No. 4 July – August, 2005, pp. 372-388

Porter, Michael and Siggelkow, Nicolaj (2008) "Contextuality within Activity Systems and Sustainability of Competitive Advantage," *Academy of Management Perspectives*, Vol. 22, No 2, May 2008

Reay, Trish, Golden-Biddle, Karen and German, Kathy (2006),"Legitimizing A New Role: Small Wins and Microprocesses of Change," Academy *of Management Journal*, Vol. 49 No. 5, 977 – 998

Rouesseau, Denise M. and McCarthy, Sharon (2007) "Educating Managers From an Evidence Based Perspective," *Academy of Management Learning and Education*, Vol 6 No1. pp 84-101

Schaffer, Robert H. and Thomson Harvey A. (!992) "Successful Change Programs Begin with Results," Harvard Business Review, January-February, 1992 pp 80-89

Spear, Stephen, "Fixing Healthcare from the Inside, Today," *Harvard Business Review*, September 2005, pages 78-91. HBR Reprint R0509D

———————— and Bowen, H. Kent. "Decoding the DNA of the Toyota Production System," *Harvard Business Review*, September – October 1999 pages 97-106. HBR Reprint 99509

————————, "Learning to Lead at Toyota," *Harvard Business Review*, May 2004 pages 79-86. HBR Reprint R0405E

Stanfield, R. Brian, editor, (2000) "The Art of Focused Conversation," *New Society Publishers,* New Gabriola Island, British Columbia, Canada.

Stankard, Martin F., (2005) "The Dark Side of Process Measurement" *Quality Progress*, Vol. 38 No. 7, July, 2005, pages 53-58.

————————, (2004) "Rethinking How We Assess and Improve Management Systems," Article presented at the *International Conference on Systems Thinking in Management -- 2004,*

————————, (1989) "Feelings and On-The-Job Behavior – Beyond Self Interest, an Interview of Cornell's Ronald Frank," *Productivity Views,* Productivity Development Group, Inc., Westford, MA

————————, and Snell, Todd M. (2007), "Designing a Baldrige-based Service to Improve Business Health" *Total Quality Management and Business Excellence,* Routledge – Taylor and Francis Group, Vol. 18, No. 9-10

Stuart, John W. (1973), Presentation by Mr. Stuart to Arthur D. Little's Management Science Staff on his work with Dr. Eiji Toyoda. Arthur D. Little, Inc. Cambridge, MA

Suchman, Mark C. (1995) "Managing Legitimacy: Strategic and Institutional Approaches" Academy of Management Review, Vol 20 No 3, pp. 571-610

Takeuchi, Hirotaka, Osono, Emi, and Simizu, Horihiko. (2008) "The Contradictions that Drive Toyota's Success," *Harvard Business Review*, vol 86, No. 6 pp 96- 104

Tsutsui, William M. (1996) "W. Edwards Deming and the Origins of Quality Control in Japan," *Journal of Japanese Studies*, Vol. 22, No. 2. (Summer, 1996), pp. 295-325

Tucker, Anita L., Nembhard, Ingrid M. and Edmonson, Amy C. (2007) "Implementing New Practices: An Empirical Study of Organizational Learning in Hospital Intensive Care Units" *Management Science,* Vol. 53, No. 6, June 2007, pp. 894-907

VanDeusen Lukas, Carol; Holmes, Sally K.; Cohen, Alan B.; Restuccia, Joseph; Cramer, Irene E.; Schwartz, Michael, Charns, Martin P. (2007) "Transformational Change in Healthcare Systems: An Organizational Model, *Healthcare Management Review,* Wolters-Kluwer Health, Vol. 32, No. 4, October-Decmeber, 2007 pp.309-320

Zaleznick, Abraham (1977) "The Manager's Job: Folklore and Fact," *Harvard Business Review*, May – June, 1977; Reprinted 2010; *Leadership Insights: A Special Article Collection of the Harvard Business Review*, pp. 15-24

About the Author

Martin F. Stankard, Ph.D.,** Martin F. Stankard is a well-known author, speaker and consultant on process improvement and performance excellence. Since 2005 Dr. Stankard has been a member of the Affiliated Faculty of the University of Pennsylvania's Organizational Dynamics Program and a Lecturer in Penn's Graduate School of Arts and Sciences. At Penn he teaches graduate courses in Process Improvement, Leadership from Mid Organization, and the Power of Confusion.

Previously, he developed and delivered Boston University's Presidential Briefing on White-Collar Productivity. He developed and was the lead instructor for The American Society for Quality's (ASQ) National Seminar on Baldrige Assessment for Business Improvement and he served for over 10 years as a member of the examiner-training faculty for the Massachusetts Quality Award. His book, The Art and Science of Process Improvement is the first comprehensive graduate-level textbook written on the subject of Process Improvement. He has authored three other books on organizational performance and management systems. In over 40 years of management consulting and coaching he has helped over 300 clients, including many leading banking, consumer credit, insurance, manufacturing, military, retailing, research and development organizations in the U.S. and internationally.

Until 2008, Dr. Stankard served as President of Productivity Development Group, Inc. where he developed and delivered courses on Lean Sigma Process Improvement, Process Re-engineering, Software Engineering Process Improvement, Baldrige Assessment, Group Facilitation Tools and Skills,

Creating a Culture of Continuous Improvement, Value Added Auditing and Process Improvement Sponsorship for Executives. Motorola University certified him as an instructor for its Six Steps to Six-Sigma program. He has led training programs for over 7,000 management attendees, including courses given in The Netherlands, Sweden, and The People's Republic of China.

Before entering consulting, training and publishing, Dr. Stankard was a Lecturer in Statistics and Operations Research at the Wharton Business School of the University of Pennsylvania, and on the staff of Wharton's Management Science Center. While at Penn, he earned a Ph.D. in Statistics and Operations Research, as well as an MBA in Industrial Management, and a B.S. in Mechanical Engineering. He was a member of the 16th cohort of the Harvard School of Public Health professional education program on Healthcare Outcomes Measurement in 2011.

Dr. Stankard has served on the Malcolm Baldrige National Quality Award Board of Examiners for 1991 to 1993, 1999 and 2000 Boards of Examiners. He chaired ASQ's Banking Industry Committee in 1990- 1991. He helped organize the Massachusetts Quality Award, patterned on the Baldrige. He also served for over 10 years on the Board of Directors of MassExcellence, Inc. a non-profit corporation dedicated to raising awareness and understanding of Performance Excellence in his home state of Massachusetts, and a member of the Board of Directors of the Business Ethics Foundation. He is a member of several academic and professional societies.

www.ingramcontent.com/pod-product-compliance
Lightning Source LLC
Chambersburg PA
CBHW060544200326
41521CB00007B/483